EMOTIONAL DISORDERS
AND METACOGNITION

EMOTIONAL DISORDERS AND METACOGNITION

Innovative Cognitive Therapy

Adrian Wells
University of Manchester, UK

JOHN WILEY & SONS, LTD
Chichester · New York · Weinheim · Brisbane · Singapore · Toronto

Other Wiley Editorial Offices

John Wiley & Sons, Inc., 605 Third Avenue,
New York, NY 10158-0012, USA

WILEY-VCH GmbH, Pappelallee 3,
D-69469 Weinheim, Germany

Jacaranda Wiley Ltd, 33 Park Road, Milton,
Queensland 4064, Australia

John Wiley & Sons (Asia) Pte Ltd, 2 Clementi Loop #02-01,
Jin Xing Distripark, Singapore 129809

John Wiley & Sons (Canada) Ltd, 22 Worcester Road,
Rexdale, Ontario M9W 1L1, Canada

Library of Congress Cataloging-in-Publication Data

Wells, Adrian.
    Emotional disorders and metacognition : innovative cognitive therapy / Adrian
Wells.
        p. cm
    Includes bibliographical references and index.
    ISBN 0-471-49168-3 (cased : alk. paper)
    1. Cognitive therapy.   2. Metacognition.   I. Title.

    RC489.C63 W46 2000
    616.89'142—dc21

                                                                00–043469

British Library Cataloguing in Publication Data

A catalogue record for this book is available from the British Library

ISBN 0-471-49168-3

Typeset in 10/12pt Palatino by Dorwyn Ltd, Rowlands Castle, Hants.
Printed and bound in Great Britain by Bookcraft (Bath) Ltd, Midsomer Norton, Somerset.
This book is printed on acid-free paper responsibly manufactured from sustainable
forestry, in which at least two trees are planted for each one used for paper production.

CONTENTS

LIST OF FIGURES

LIST OF TABLES

ABOUT THE AUTHOR

Adrian Wells is appointed as Reader in Clinical Psychology at the University of Manchester. He is an international leading authority on cognitive theory and therapy, and has contributed significantly to the understanding and treatment of psychological disorders. His contributions include the development of new models and treatments of anxiety disorders, and, in collaboration with Gerald Matthews, the development of an influential theory of cognitive vulnerability to emotional disorder. He has published widely in academic journals, and has authored and edited several books in the areas of cognitive therapy. His book *Attention and Emotion: A Clinical Perspective* (Wells & Matthews, 1994) was recognised with an award by the British Psychological Society (1998) for significant contributions to psychology. This book was followed by his highly acclaimed work, *Cognitive Therapy of Anxiety Disorders: A Practice Manual and Conceptual Guide* (Wells, 1997), in which he presented an unrivalled state-of-the-art description of how to conceptualise and treat anxiety disorders. Dr Wells's pioneering ideas and contributions to understanding and treating emotional disorders continue with the publication of this volume, which marks the culmination of 15 years' work on metacognition, attention and emotional disorders.

PREFACE

In 1994 I published a book with one of my distinguished colleagues, Gerald Matthews, entitled *Attention and Emotion: A Clinical Perspective*. That award-winning work aimed to integrate cognitive therapy and information processing in a framework that provided a basis for explaining performance data on attention, and a basis for understanding the mechanisms of the regulation of attention, beliefs and thinking in emotional disorder. We advanced a theoretical explanation of disorder maintenance and of personal vulnerability, in which self-attentional processes, metacognition and worry strategies play a central role. Moreover, we argued that maintenance of disorder could be understood in terms of dynamic disturbances in processing and self-regulation located within a multi-level cognitive system. Our approach was the first to place strategic processes and metacognition at the centre of a general model of psychopathology.

This book develops the model presented in *Attention and Emotion*. It presents this in a more detailed way and expands on the metacognitive aspect. This elaborated model offers implications for the design of new treatment strategies, and for the application of cognitive-behavioural therapy. New clinical strategies are described in detail and the clinician is guided towards developing a metacognitive-focused approach to treatment. Armed with a basic understanding of how the mind becomes locked into negative and distorted patterns of processing, and how internal metacognitive processes can be used to bring about changes in negative thoughts, distorted beliefs and distressing emotions, we may push back the frontiers of cognitive therapy.

Adrian Wells
Manchester, January 2000

ACKNOWLEDGEMENTS

I am very grateful for the assistance of Joyce Russell and offer sincere thanks for the many hours she has spent typing this manuscript. Many thanks also to Karin Carter for helpful comments on draft copies of the chapters and helping to collate references.

Finally, I would like to express great thanks to Michael D. Coombs, Senior Publishing Editor at Wiley, for all of his support. Have a happy retirement Mike.

PART I

THEORETICAL PERSPECTIVES

Chapter 1

SETTING THE STAGE: METACOGNITION AND COGNITIVE THERAPY

Cognitive theories of emotional disorder, such as schema theory (Beck, 1976), are based on the principle that psychological disorder is linked with a disturbance in thinking. In particular, anxiety and depression are characterised by negative automatic thoughts and distortions in inter- pretations. Negative thoughts or interpretations are thought to emerge from the activation of negative beliefs stored in long-term memory. The aim of cognitive therapy is to modify negative thoughts, beliefs, and associated behaviours that maintain psychological disturbance. Central components of the generic schema theory of emotional disorders are depicted in Figure 1.0.

According to this approach, emotional disorder is linked to the activation of dysfunctional schemas. Schemas are memory structures that contain two types of information: *beliefs* and *assumptions*. Beliefs are "core" con- structs that are unconditional in nature (e.g. "I'm vulnerable"; "the world is a dangerous place") and are accepted as truths about the self and the world. Assumptions are conditional and represent contingencies between events and self-appraisals (e.g. "If I have unexplained physical symp- toms, it means I must be seriously ill"). The dysfunctional schemas that characterise emotional disorder are thought to be more rigid, inflexible and concrete than the schemas of normal individuals (Beck, 1967), and schema content is supposed to be specific to a disorder. Anxiety schemas

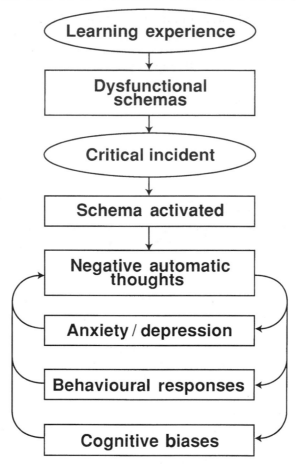

Figure 1.0 Generic schema theory of emotional disorder

are comprised of beliefs and assumptions about danger (Beck, Emery & Greenberg, 1985) and an inability to cope. In depression, schemas centre on themes of the "negative cognitive triad", in which early experiences provide the basis for forming negative concepts about the self, the future, and the external world (Beck, Rush, Shaw & Emery, 1979).

Once activated, dysfunctional schemas introduce biases in the processing and interpretation of information. These biases are manifested at a surface level as negative automatic thoughts (NATs) in the stream of consciousness. Negative appraisals of this kind are a manifestation of underlying cognitive mechanisms that maintain emotional disturbances.

Beck's theorising and description of emotional disorder phenomena within the schema framework still provides a rich and clinically useful account of psychological disturbance. However, problems with the schema theory and cognitive therapy have been highlighted by several recent theorists. For instance, Teasdale and Barnard (1993) summarise four difficulties, including evidence that negative thinking may be a consequence rather than an antecedent of depression, and that dysfunctional attitudes only appear elevated during depressive episodes and they return to normal with recovery. A further criticism is that the model only deals with one level of cognition and cannot deal with the distinction between "hot" and "cold" (i.e. emotional and intellectual) belief. Teasdale and Barnard go on to propose their own more comprehensive information-processing framework (interacting cognitive subsystems; ICS) for representing all aspects of cognition in depression maintenance, and for resolving the difficulties set out above.

However, it is premature to reject all of the basic principles of schema theory, and ICS, like most theories, generates its own set of difficulties, as discussed in Chapter 4. A useful principle of schema theory is that knowledge stored in long-term memory influences the content and nature of processing. By developing a theoretical framework that links the top-down influence of self-knowledge to important concepts such as self-regulation, and by viewing self-knowledge (beliefs) in a dynamic rather than a static way, the criticisms raised at schema theory begin to disappear. As Wells and Matthews (1994) point out, it is not helpful to view schemas as disconnected information that the therapist can erase and replace with more realistic propositions. People seem to construct and revise beliefs actively on the basis of internal rules. Thus, it is important to formulate the internal cognitive processes, rules and mechanisms that lead patients to arrive at maladaptive interpretations and beliefs. What is required is a comprehensive cognitive framework for representing interactions between self-knowledge and emotional disturbances.

There are other more fundamental theoretical limitations of schema theory, but these can also be resolved in a relatively straightforward fashion by reformulating the way knowledge is represented in information processing. Schema theory has focused almost exclusively on the content of appraisals and beliefs in emotional disorder, in which beliefs are represented in the human information processing system as declarative statements such as, "I am a failure"; "I am bad"; "I am vulnerable"; "I am physically ill". However, it is unlikely that knowledge is represented in this way. One of the arguments throughout this book is that we should begin to explore ways of representing beliefs and the effects of appraisals in psychological disorder that are more consistent both with developments in cognitive psychology and with a view of the mind as a dynamic self-regulating system. In Chapter 2, we will see how one such model, the Self-regulatory Executive Function model (S-REF, Wells & Matthews 1994, 1996), views processing in dynamic and multi-level terms. Equipped with frameworks of this kind, we may begin to elucidate key processes involved in vulnerability to and maintenance of psychological disturbance. Moreover, this model not only provides details of what we should aim to do in cognitive therapy but also gives information on how cognitive change may be effectively achieved. Schema theory lacks the psychological sophistication to provide specific theory-based predictions on how best to modify beliefs, appraisals and emotions.

A crucial level of psychological explanation that is needed if we are to help individuals change their minds is the level that enables us to conceptualise the factors that control, correct, appraise and regulate thinking itself. This is the domain of metacognition. Furthermore, whilst the content of thought is undoubtedly important in determining the nature of psychological disturbance, *how* people think is an important dimension that has implications for psychological disorder and recovery. As we will see in Chapter 2, the model of emotional disorder presented by Wells and Matthews has directly linked metacognition and the form of thinking to emotional vulnerability and the maintenance of emotional disorder. Before describing and developing that model in Chapter 2, for the remainder of this chapter, we will be concerned with defining and understanding the general concept of metacognition and begin to establish links between metacognition and emotional disorder.

METACOGNITION

Metacognition is defined as any knowledge or cognitive process that is involved in the appraisal, monitoring or control of cognition (e.g. Flavell, 1979; Moses & Baird, in press). On one level, it can be thought of as a general aspect of cognition that is involved in all cognitive enterprises and some specific aspects of metacognition have been linked to psychological disturbances (Wells & Matthews, 1994; Wells, 1995; Nelson, Stuart, Howard & Crawley, 1999). Theory and research in metacognition has emerged predominantly through work in cognitive developmental psychology (Flavell, 1979) and interest in the area has spread to fields of neuropsychology, memory performance and ageing (Metcalfe & Shimamura, 1994).

Metacognition is a multi-faceted concept. It comprises knowledge (beliefs), processes and strategies that appraise, monitor or control cognition (e.g. Moses & Baird, in press). Most cognitive activities are dependent on metacognitive factors that monitor and control them. Moreover, the information that emerges from metacognitive monitoring is often experienced as subjective feelings, which can influence behaviour. For example, the "feeling of knowing" experience, a subjective sense that information has been encoded in memory, motivates efforts to retrieve information. An example of a strong and common metacognitive experience involving memory is represented by the "tip-of-the-tongue" effect, in which individuals experience a strong subjective sense that an item of information is stored in memory but is currently unretrievable. This effect has been explored experimentally and it is generally experienced as a mildly aversive state which leads individuals to continue retrieval efforts. Research on the accuracy of feeling of knowing shows that it is well above chance, but is far from perfect (Leonesio & Nelson, 1990)

A basic distinction has been made by most theorists between two aspects of metacognition: metacognitive knowledge and metacognitive regulation. Metacognitive knowledge is the information that individuals have about their own cognition and about task factors or learning strategies that affect it. Metacognitive regulation refers to a range of executive functions, such as the allocation of attention, monitoring, checking, planning, and detection of errors in performance (Brown, Bransford, Campione & Ferrara, 1983). The idea that metacognition controls and monitors general cognition implies a distinction between two cognitive levels.

Nelson and Narens (1990), have proposed that cognitive processes operate on two or more inter-related levels. These levels are known as the meta-level and the object level. Two processes are identified in their model that correspond to the direction of information flowing between the two levels, as depicted in Figure 1.1.

Information flowing from the object level to the meta-level is called *monitoring*, and this informs the meta-level of the state of the object level. Information flowing from the meta-level to the object level is called *control*. Control informs the object level what to do next. The meta-level contains a dynamic model (e.g. a mental simulation emphasising changes over time) of the object level. It is likely that this simulation will contain a goal and knowledge concerning ways the object level can be used to achieve this goal. However, a difficulty with proposing two levels is that

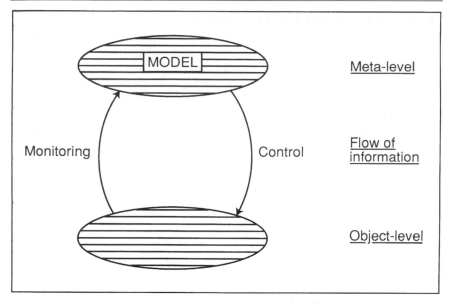

Figure 1.1   Nelson and Naren's (1990) Meta-level/object-level mechanism (adapted from Nelson and Narens, 1990)

it raises the question of what it is that controls the meta-level. One possibility is that the meta-level is controlled and modified by feedback from on-line processing, in which the individual appraises the effectiveness of particular cognitive and behavioural strategies in relation to activated goals, as in the S-REF model (Wells & Matthews, 1994).

The relationship between a meta-level and object level can be applied to understanding cognition in psychological disorder. As monitoring is the input process for an individual's self-regulation and control system, any inaccuracies or distortions in monitoring could contribute to psychological dysfunction. Similarly, control processes can change the object level by, for example initiating a new action, continuing or modifying a previous action, or terminating an activity. Thus, disturbances or biases in control, for example selection of certain (inappropriate) coping strategies, may contribute to psychological disturbance. The distinction between meta-level and object-level cognition and their dominance relation is a feature of the Wells and Matthews (1994) model of emotional disorder presented in the next chapter. In this model, choice and execution of coping strategies is a central determinant of the continuation or termination of psychological distress.

VARIETIES OF METACOGNITION

In earlier work (Wells, 1995), I have distinguished between three basic varieties of metacognition in understanding worry processes in Generalized Anxiety Disorder: (1) metacognitive knowledge; (2) metacognitive experiences; (3) metacognitive control strategies. In this section, each of these categories will be described and elaborated since they have particular conceptual relevance to exploring metacognition in emotional disorders.

Knowledge

Metacognitive knowledge refers to the beliefs and theories that individuals have about their own cognitions, such as beliefs about the meaning of particular types of thoughts, and beliefs concerning the efficiency of memory and cognitive control. It is useful to consider two types of metacognitive knowledge, explicit and implicit, particularly in the context of emotional disorder. *Explicit metacognitive knowledge* is that which is conscious and can be verbally expressed, for example individuals with generalized anxiety disorder believe that worrying is uncontrollable and dangerous, and more generally people appear to hold the belief that worrying can be advantageous (Wells, 1995; Cartwright-Hatton & Wells, 1997). Patients with obsessive-compulsive disorder believe that having certain types of thought will cause negative events or unwanted actions (Rachman, Thordarson, Shafran & Woody, 1995; Emmelkamp & Aardema, 1999; Purdon & Clark, 1999), and people with depression appear to have positive beliefs about rumination (Papageorgiou & Wells, in press (a)).

Implicit metacognitive knowledge is not normally amenable to consciousness and cannot be expressed in verbal form. These are the rules or plans that guide processing, such as attention allocation, memory search and use of heuristics and biases in forming judgements. As we will see in the next chapter, it may be useful to think of this knowledge as a procedure or plan for processing, and such metacognitive plans may be at least as important as declarative knowledge in emotional disorder.

Experiences

Metacognitive experiences include appraisals of the meaning of specific mental events (e.g. thoughts), metacognitive feelings themselves and judgements of the status of cognition. Metacognitive appraisals and judgements can be defined as the conscious interpretations and labellings of cognitive experiences. They are the on-line manifestation of the use of metacognitive knowledge to appraise cognition.

Metacognitive experiences can be linked to emotional disorder in several ways. First, a range of disorders are associated with negative metacognitive appraisals and judgements. For instance, obsessive-compulsive patients appraise thoughts and memory phenomena in a negative way, and several disorders are associated with catastrophic appraisals of negative thought intrusions [e.g. generalized anxiety, post-traumatic stress disorder (PTSD), depression, panic, obsessional disorder]. Nelson, Kruglanski and Jost (1998) identify two different types of information that provide the basis for metacognitive judgements: momentary feelings or impressions, and lay or implicit theories that are more enduring. We saw above how one type of theory represented as beliefs about thoughts may be linked with psychopathology. Schwarz and Clore (1983, 1988) suggest that people use feelings as information for appraisals and judgements. Wells and Matthews (1994) have applied the notion that feeling provide metacognitive information in psychological disorder. In particular, on an implicit level, emotion may bias selection of plans for processing: more explicitly, emotionally disordered patients tend to use feeling-based information as a guide to appraising threat and for regulating the execution of coping strategies. For example, obsessive-compulsive patients may repeat a ritual until they "feel certain" that it has been completed correctly. Subjective feelings can be subject to different interpretations, and therefore the meaning of feelings and their influence on processing operations are likely to be mediated by self-knowledge. In a demonstration of the effects of interpretations of feelings on cognition, Clore and Parrott (1994) induced feelings of uncertainty by hypnosis; some subjects were led to believe that hypnosis had caused the feelings, other subjects were given no attribution. Subjects were then asked to read and rate the extent to which they understood a poem. Feelings of uncertainty influenced poem comprehension but only in the absence of the external attribution.

Metacognitive control strategies

Metacognitive control strategies are the responses individuals make in controlling the activities of their cognitive system. These strategies may intensify or suppress thinking strategies and may be directed at enhancing monitoring processes. In everyday life, people use strategies ranging from the use of memory aids for encoding, such as the use of mnemonics or rehearsal of to-be-remembered material, and strategies of recall, such as cueing. In clinical disorders, control strategies often consist of attempts to control the stream of consciousness. In anxiety disorders where mental events are often interpreted as a sign of mental breakdown [e.g. panic disorder, generalised anxiety disorder (GAD)], individuals may attempt to suppress particular thoughts or attempt to think in special ways that prevent catastrophe. For example, a patient suffering from obsessions was blighted by intrusive images of the Devil. His metacognitive beliefs were such that he believed that these images were dangerous and could lead to the evocation of evil. In order to protect himself and his family, he tried hard to control his mind during prayer. This strategy consisted of concentrating fully on every word in the prayer and keeping in mind a perfect image of Christ. Here we have examples of running a particular coping strategy (metacognitive control process) and also of intensified monitoring in the form of checking for uncontaminated images of Christ. Any failure in the strategy was associated with a compulsion to return to the beginning of his prayers and repeat the process until they were perfect. The strategy could eliminate threat and reduce anxiety when the personal goal was met. However, the demands of the strategy and the nature of the goal were such that they were difficult to achieve without repeated attempts and sustained effort.

Metacognitive strategies may involve responses aimed at intensifying the flow of information from the object level (i.e. monitoring), or may involve strategies aimed at terminating or modifying object-level processing. Wells and Matthews (1994) have linked emotional disorder to a threat-monitoring strategy, which is characterised by sustained attention on internal or external sources of threat. With respect to strategies aimed at modifying processing in emotional disorder, individuals have at their disposal a range of strategies that can be used to control unwanted and/ or distressing thoughts. In a factor-analytic study, Wells and Davies (1994) identified five control strategies measured by the Thought Control Questionnaire (TCQ): reappraisal, punishment, social control, worry and distraction. Empirical studies with the TCQ suggest that worry and punishment coping strategies are associated with a range of indices of negative psychological health. Studies have also shown that the use of particular control strategies may be associated with poorer outcomes in individuals with PTSD and depression following treatment (Reynolds & Wells, 1999). These data indicate that metacognitive strategies are positively associated with vulnerability to emotional disturbance and recovery.

EMOTION, METACOGNITIVE MONITORING AND CONTROL

Emotions represent internal data that influence motivations and behaviour. Indeed, emotion may be more primitive than cognition and empirical data suggests that it is controlled by subcortical brain structures. It is well established that emotions can affect a range of cognitive processes, including attention bias, memory bias (Wells & Matthews, 1994; Williams, Watts, MacLeod and Mathews, 1988), judgements and decision-making (Clore and Parrott, 1994).

Several theoretical approaches have emphasised the effects of emotion on cognition and information processing. A popular idea is that emotion is associated with an interrupt function. Simon (1967) argues that adaptation requires monitoring for significant stimuli and replacement of concurrent goals with new goals following interruption. Here emotion is produced as part of the interruption process. In a similar way, Oatley and Johnson-Laird (1987) suggest that emotions are generated by changes in the perceived success or failure of a planned action. Once generated, emotions act as a primitive but rapid means of biasing the current plan to be implemented. For example, anxiety is generated by threat to a self-preservation goal and activates plans associated with vigilant attention to the environment and/or escape. Other approaches to emotion have emphasised the social significance of such responses. In Bower's (1981) original network model, emotions are represented by discreet nodes or units. Emotion nodes may be activated either by external inputs or through activation of network nodes associatively linked with emotion, such as nodes representing the memory of an unhappy event. Once activated, emotion nodes influence the course of future processing through the spreading of activation to associated nodes. The general effect is that emotional states prime processing that is congruent with the emotion. Effects of mood on cognition, such as mood state-dependent retrieval, have been accounted for by the network model. When retrieval takes place in the same emotional state, the emotion node partly activates or primes the nodes for the material remembered, rendering it more or less accessible. More recently, Bower (1992) proposed that emotions may activate not just isolated semantic concepts but rule-based actions, which have proved useful in similar previous situations.

Williams, Watts, MacLeod and Mathews (1988) distinguish different biases in cognition associated with trait and state depression and anxiety, and locate them at different stages of processing in a model of attention and memory. Here, anxiety effects are pre-attentive, and state anxiety increases the threat value assigned to a stimulus, whilst trait anxiety and clinical anxiety bias subsequent resource allocation. Depression influences processing only after stimulus identification, when attended stimuli are elaboratively processed. State depression biases negative evaluations of stimuli, whereas trait/clinical depression facilitates elaboration of negative material. A feature of these theoretical approaches is the idea that emotions can impact on metacognitive control and monitoring functions. As we will see in the next chapter, emotions may signal discrepancies in self-regulatory processes and provide the impetus for sustained self-processing.

CONCLUSIONS

All thinking requires a meta-level input involving combinations of control and monitoring processes. This input specifies the initiation, discontinuation or change in ongoing thought. Contemporary cognitive approaches to clinical problems have not addressed the multiple range of components constituting thinking. We have seen how metacognition consists of conscious knowledge about one's cognitive states, metacognitive experiences and control strategies. However, it also consists of nonconscious implicit knowledge that guides the central executive in cognitive activity. For example, much of the activity contributing to appraisal and behaviour is not verbally expressible.

We have seen how feelings can be a source of information influencing judgements, and how emotions may bias cognition. In human information processing, cognition is influenced by emotional and metacognitive factors. Thus, manipulation of feeling states may promote changes in appraisals and cognition. However, it follows that if metacognition controls and regulates cognition, and disturbances in thinking characteristic of emotional disorder are located at the belief level, it is important to consider the influence of metacognitive knowledge. An important possibility is that if metacognition can be integrated in a general cognitive model of self-regulation and emotion, it will begin to provide a basis for conceptualising and developing cognitive modification processes in cognitive-behavioural therapy.

Chapter 2

THE SELF-REGULATORY EXECUTIVE FUNCTION (S-REF) MODEL

An assumption of cognitive-behavioural therapies is that the cognitive system of disordered individuals can be modified through conscious verbal and behavioural manipulations, so that emotional readjustment can be accomplished. Curiously, however, there have been few attempts to conceptualise the internal cognitive self-regulatory mechanisms that are involved in translating these manipulations into actual cognitive change or recalibration processes. One of the difficulties has been a paucity of detailed information-processing frameworks in clinical psychology for modelling self-regulation and cognition. More specifically, theoretical accounts of psychological disorder must address the role of beliefs in guiding information processing, and how beliefs or self-knowledge are modified over time as processing unfolds. Cognitive-based clinical theories of disorder tend to be descriptive of clinical phenomena, rather than offering a deeper explanation of the mechanisms of interaction between beliefs and the functioning of the information-processing system of emotionally disordered individuals. In order to progress in this area, theory must consider a wider range of cognitive components than have been considered by clinical theories such as schema theory.

Schema theory and cognitive therapy have focused predominantly on the content of cognition at the knowledge (belief) and appraisal levels.

Broader aspects of cognition, such as metacognition, attention, the regulation of processing and dynamic aspects of processing, have been overlooked. In proposing that negative thoughts in anxiety and depression result from the activation of dysfunctional beliefs, cognitive theory has focused on the origin of the content of thought and has ignored the form that negative thinking takes, and the mechanisms that give dysfunctional thoughts their salience. Schema theory provides an explanation of the content of people's thoughts, but not an explanation of the reasons for their style of thinking. We may consider these basic issues as "missing links" in cognitive theory and therapy, since, as we shall see, the style that thinking takes may be a key factor in psychological disorder. In exploring thinking styles, we will need to focus on beliefs about thinking and the individual's strategies for controlling attention and thinking that arise from metacognitive beliefs. The clinical consequence of a lack of theoretical detail of this kind has been the development of a conceptual framework in which therapists know what should be done in treatment—modification of the knowledge base—but it is difficult to specify in detail how this can be accomplished. Therapists rely on their personal experience of treatment strategies that have been effective with particular clients, but this does not take us any closer to an understanding of the general principles of cognitive modification.

Mysteries and missing links in cognitive-behavioural theory continue to emerge if we begin to question exactly what is meant by the terms "belief" or "schema". The schema concept has been criticised on various grounds (e.g. Segal, 1988), and for our present purposes it is unclear how beliefs should be represented in information processing. Schema theory has tended to view beliefs as specific propositions, such as the belief "I'm inadequate". However, as we shall see, Wells and Matthews (1994) suggest that it may be helpful to view declarative beliefs in emotional disorder as the output of situationally activated processing routines. In an attempt to overcome these issues and link schema theory with information processing and self-regulation, Wells and Matthews (1994, 1996) advanced the Self-regulatory Executive Function (S-REF) model of psychological disorder. The model expresses the reciprocal causal interplay between multiple components of cognition, including beliefs, metacognitions, attentional control, on-line processing and self-regulation. The model also aims to account for experimental data on attentional bias in laboratory paradigms, such as the emotional Stroop task. However, this latter area is not the focus of this particular book (see Wells & Matthews, 1994).

COGNITIVE-EMOTIONAL REGULATION: THE S-REF MODEL

Outline of the S-REF model

The S-REF model is based on an architecture of three interacting levels of cognition. A schematic representation of these levels and the links between components of the processing system is given in Figure 2.0.

The three levels consist of: (1) a stimulus-driven lower-level network of processing units which function outside of conscious awareness, the products of which may intrude into consciousness. Processing at this level is not highly dependent on cognitive resources and is largely reflexive; (2) a level of on-line controlled processing which is involved in the conscious appraisal of events and the control of action and thought; (3) a store of self-knowledge (beliefs) in long-term memory. These beliefs have a metacognitive component and consist at least partly of plans for processing.

The lower level and the "on-line" level differ in their resource requirements. The lower level is predominantly automatic, in the sense that attentional demands are minimal and processing occurs predominantly outside of conscious awareness. The on-line level is dependent on attentional resources for the execution of processing and its activities are amenable to varying degrees of conscious awareness. The processing executed at this level is voluntary, and the individual is normally aware of voluntary control, although in some clinical disorders this awareness may be diminished. On-line processing is dependent on the accessing of self-knowledge (beliefs) for its execution. It cannot function independently and relies on self-knowledge from memory to guide it.

This three-level architecture supports the total range of processing operations available to the individual, but different *modes* and processing *configurations* can be executed. The term "mode" in the present context refers to the perspective the individual has with respect to his/her thoughts and beliefs. Two modes are distinguished, the *object mode* and the *metacognitive mode*. When in object mode, thoughts (i.e. appraisals) and perceptions are taken as unevaluated and accurate representations of events; this is the default mode of cognitive operation that usually runs in daily circumstances. When in metacognitive mode, the individual is distanced from thought, and thoughts and perceptions can be evaluated and not necessarily accepted as direct representations of reality.

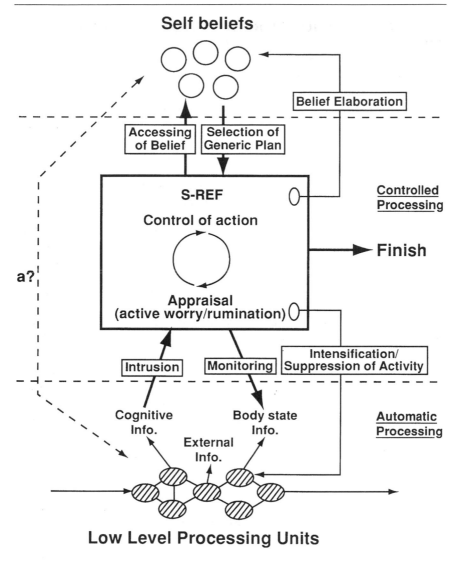

Figure 2.0   The Wells and Matthews (1994) Self-Regulatory Executive Function (S-REF) Model (adapted from Wells and Matthews, 1994)

The term "configuration" refers to the pattern of cognitive processes that are activated at a particular time. The configuration most relevant to psychological disorder is the S-REF configuration, which is intimately linked to self-relevant processing. It serves a goal-directed executive function of reducing self-discrepancies between a representation of the current status of the self and a desired or "normative" representation. Under normal circumstances, periods of S-REF activity are short. For instance, when internal responses signalling hunger intrude into awareness, the S-REF accesses self-knowledge that guides appraisal of such responses and execution of strategies to return the individual to a "normative" state of satiety. This aspect of self-regulatory functioning is consistent with cybernetic approaches to self-regulation and self-representation (Carver & Scheier, 1981; Higgins, 1990). The S-REF configuration focuses attention on the self, and appraises the personal significance of external stimuli, body state stimuli and cognitions, usually in object mode, so that such appraisals are accepted as accurate.

Under typical conditions, episodes of on-line S-REF activity are of short duration, in that a person is able to select a strategy that deals successfully with the discrepancy, either by task-focused coping or through modification of beliefs. However, in psychological disorder the person is unable to achieve the self-regulatory goal and the S-REF configuration becomes perseverative. Failure to achieve goals can be linked to selection of inappropriate coping strategies, repeated negative appraisal of one's current state based on negative self-knowledge, the existence of unrealistic goals for self-regulation, or external constraints that compromise discrepancy reduction. However, even in cases where external demands prevent goal attainment, such as when an individual is terminally ill and the goal of survival is not possible, S-REF activation can be moderated by abandoning the primary goal, and developing alternative sub-goals (e.g. reducing pain, putting one's life in order, etc.) that are achievable. Such a strategy is likely to moderate emotional effects. However, when goals are rigid and inflexibly held, even this type of strategy of self-regulation may not be available.

SELF-REFERENT KNOWLEDGE (BELIEFS)

The model emphasises the involvement of self-beliefs in psychopathology. On-line S-REF processing is dependent on the accessing of self-knowledge. This knowledge shapes appraisals of the personal significance of stimuli and provides a general blueprint for coping responses. Wells and Matthews (1994) have argued that beliefs may be stored as general plans for processing and coping and not only as the declarative knowledge emphasised in schema theory. Beliefs such as "I'm vulnerable", "I'm worthless", are viewed as products of running particular processing routines. The self-knowledge that gives rise to such recurrent cognitions is a plan for processing that guides attention, information search, memory retrieval, appraisal and behaviour. Thus, the S-REF emphasises the contribution to disorder of a specific type of self-knowledge—*metacognitive knowledge* that guides processing and inter-pretations. Metacognitive knowledge consists of implicit plans that guide processing and operate largely outside of conscious awareness. For example, heuristics and cognitive biases that influence the content of consciousness. However, it also manifests as more explicit (declarative) beliefs about thinking. Examples of such beliefs are: "Worrying helps me cope"; "I must be hypervigilant and then I won't be taken by surprise"; "If I'm pessimistic I can avoid disappointment"; "I have no control over my thinking"; "Thinking bad thoughts can make bad things happen"; "Some thoughts always need to be controlled". These explicit metacogni-tions are linked to plans for processing (e.g. directives for the control of attention) and also act as data influencing interpretations.

Plans and goals

When accessing self-knowledge, individuals are accessing general-purpose self-relevant information about the social and physical world, and also two types of metacognitive knowledge: (1) about the meaning of thoughts; (2) plans that generally guide and shape the form that cognition takes. It may be that all knowledge is represented as a metacognitive plan that guides the processing of the cognitive system and leads to the gener-ation of other types of self-knowledge. Thus, beliefs such as "I'm a failure" may not be stored in their own right, but are outputs of running particular S-REF operations. The declarative belief is therefore a marker for the existence of a plan that guides attention, memory search and coping strategies which repeatedly generate this item of self-knowledge. A plan consists of implicit and explicit metacognitive information that guides and shapes processing activities. These plans have self-regulatory goals embedded in them. At the metacognitive level, these goals may specify the assimilation of new data to existing beliefs or accommodation of beliefs to fit new data.

The conceptualisation of self-knowledge as a set of metacognitive plans that direct attention and appraisal, and assimilate internal information to produce meaning, is appealing because it helps to explain variability in belief ratings observed in patients. A belief is strong when the plan is activated. For example, a spider phobic believes he/she is in danger when confronted with a large spider, but concedes that this is irrational when removed from the situation. The replacement of a maladaptive belief in cognitive therapy can be conceptualised as facilitating the acquisition of a new plan to guide appraisal and processing when exposed to idiosyncratic threat.

SYSTEM-OPERATING CHARACTERISTICS

S-REF processing is initiated by intrusions from automatic processing which may have been generated by an external threat stimulus, or by internal cycles of processing that generate negative threat-related thoughts. Once activated, the S-REF accesses the store of self-knowledge in long-term memory (LTM) in order to generate an appraisal of the threat, and to select a coping strategy. The knowledge base includes general plans for appraisal and coping, which are worked upon by on-line processing to tailor them to the particular situation. The plan has a metacognitive component that guides processing and guides the reciprocal effects of processing on beliefs in LTM. This means the plan itself is amenable to modification, depending on feedback concerning the success or failure of the appraisal and coping strategy adopted (plans may also be modified through repeated practice of behaviours leading to proceduralisation of responses). The involvement of S-REF controlled processing in dealing with threat means that flexibility of response is maintained, so that individuals are able to adapt to a changing environment and to changes in their knowledge (under normal healthy circumstances). S-REF activity can modify the knowledge base (beliefs), as illustrated by the feedback cycle shown in Figure 2.0. Whether or not on-line processing modifies or strengthens beliefs depends on the metacognitive plan and goals activated and on the effects of coping strategies that are specified by the current plan. Some coping strategies impede belief change. For example, avoidance of feared situations can prevent exposure to data that can disconfirm fears; and processing strategies, such as depressive rumination that focus on negative experiences, may strengthen negative self-beliefs. If the plan specifies a mode of processing in which thoughts are taken as facts (object mode) and the goal is to escape threat, then dysfunctional knowledge is less likely to be modified. However, if the plan specifies a metacognitive mode of functioning, in which thoughts are taken as events that should be evaluated, and the goal is to examine and revise knowledge, cognitive change is potentiated.

Aside from the potential to affect upper-level knowledge (beliefs), S-REF activity impacts on lower-level processing. The S-REF implements strategies by biasing lower-level activity. Some strategies, such as monitoring for events in consciousness, may be voluntarily initiated and will prime the lower level for target events, such as the perception of particular external or internal stimuli. Some coping strategies may be directed at reducing the activity of low-level processors, as in examples of relaxation or meditation that are intended to reduce bodily arousal, or mental readiness or anticipation strategies that are aimed at reducing a startle response.

CAUSES AND EFFECTS OF EMOTION

Emotional state is determined by the status of the system with respect to achieving its goals. In general, anxiety is associated with anticipated failure to meet goals, whilst depression is associated with an existing failure. Emotional information itself contributes to the maintenance of S-REF activity by biasing the retrieval of knowledge for processing. Thus, emotion has an informational function and influences processing priorities. In psychological disorder emotional responses often themselves become the focus of S-REF activity, thereby maintaining the configuration. For instance, they may be misinterpreted negatively, as in cases of panic disorder, or used inappropriately as goal-related signals for continuing or discontinuing self-regulatory processing. Internal feelings or metacognitive information is used as a signal to terminate self-regulatory coping strategies, such as worry or rumination. Some patients appear to have limited tolerance of negative emotions and are in a state of chronic S-REF readiness as they attempt to monitor for emotional triggers and suppress emotional responses.

One of the questions that schema and allied cognitive models of emotional disorder have not directly tackled is the question of what it is that stops attacks of strong emotion. For instance, what leads patients to stop being anxious? In other words, why isn't panic or anxiety continuous? The S-REF model asserts that anxiety will only occur when the S-REF is active. Anxiety will cease when alternative goals and plans for processing are called, or processing meets its short-term or long-term goals. In a panic attack the immediate goal is self-preservation through the application of various coping behaviours. The S-REF will be deactivated when the individual assesses that he/she has successfully achieved the goal of preventing physical or mental catastrophe. The data used to form this conclusion may be internal, such as the successful amelioration of particular bodily symptoms, or external, such as the provision of reassuring health information at a local hospital emergency department. The extent to which this data reduces the occurrence of future panic attacks is critically dependent on whether or not it modifies self-knowledge, that is to say, the extent to which it modifies faulty information and the plan for appraisal and coping with subsequent panicogenic stimuli.

INTERNAL EVENTS AND FEELINGS AS METACOGNITIVE DATA

The S-REF model assumes that much of the data that individuals with psychological disorder use to construct appraisals and use as self-regulatory referent guides is internal in origin, and is derived from memory, feeling states, and an impression of the self. This internal data, which is a component of self-focused attention, influences both the appraisal of the meaning of events and appraisal of self-knowledge, and provides a benchmark for the cessation or continuation of coping efforts. The idea that patients use internal data overlaps with concepts of emotional reasoning (Beck et al., 1979) (e.g. "I feel like a failure, therefore I am a failure"), or *ex-consequentia* reasoning (Arntz, Rauner & van den Hout, 1995), in which feeling states are taken as evidence of threat (e.g. "I feel anxious, therefore there must be something to be anxious about—I am in danger"). However, it goes beyond viewing this phenomenon as an occasional bias in thinking and implies that internal data is used not only to signal the presence of threat but also provides a signal for the regulation of coping strategies. On one level, and probably the most basic, emotional and other feeling states serve as an internal signal that biases the activation of beliefs and cognitive processes and provides information that influences the interpretation of self-knowledge. For instance, during the course of cognitive therapy, patients often report a dissociation between an intellectual and an emotional belief. Here the person may state that he/she logically knows that a belief is false but that it still "feels" as if it is correct. In this example, internal feelings are interpreted as evidence that the belief is accurate. A feeling state of this kind may be metacognitive in nature. Feeling states that can be important, other than discrete emotions, include subjective energy levels, agitation and metacognitive events similar to "feeling of knowing", and confidence in judgements. Thus, appraisal is influenced by a range of emotion and feeling states, as well as by more stable information stored in long-term memory.

On another level, typically involving voluntary mediation, internal streams of information are used to guide coping strategies and are part of the maladaption inherent in emotional disorder coping. For instance, obsessive-compulsive ritualisers perform rituals such as checking or repeating actions until it "feels right" to stop or until an internal rule has been satisfied. In generalized anxiety disorder, individuals worry until they feel that they will be able to cope or until they "know" they have worried about most possibilities and thus feel prepared. A problem with the use of internal criteria is that some of these criteria require high (and often unobtainable) levels of cognitive control to achieve them. Moreover, internal felt-senses are prone to disruption by a variety of factors, such as other emotional reactions, hormonal responses and physiological variables. As a consequence, signals for terminating overt and covert coping behaviours are unstable in a way that contributes to instability and perseveration of negative thoughts, emotion and coping strategies. The exact nature of internal information used across disorders requires further exploration in the formulation and treatment of clinical disorders. One clinical implication is that therapists should encourage patients to develop strategies of searching for alternative sources of data as a basis of self-regulatory processing. In this way, new plans for guiding attention allocation when appraising and coping with threat can be established.

THE MAINTENANCE OF PSYCHOLOGICAL DISORDER

The S-REF model proposes that psychological disturbance is closely linked to a syndrome of cognitive-attentional responses characterised by self-focused attention, on-line processing of negative self-beliefs, worry/rumination, threat monitoring, and implementation of particular types of coping that interfere with the development of more adaptive knowledge. The processing and coping activities operating in distressed states interfere with cognitive adjustments necessary to return the individual with psychological disorder back to normal functioning. In particular, processing activities associated with active worry or rumination tend to interfere with both the internal operations of the executive system, such as shifting processing priorities or modifying beliefs, and interfere with implementing coping strategies that are attentionally demanding. In addition, distressed individuals often engage attentional coping strategies of monitoring for threats that are congruent with personal concerns. These characteristics keep individuals "locked into" self-processing activities that perpetuate psychological disturbance.

In these instances, the S-REF model asserts that the distressed patient's scope for cognition and action is constrained by a loss of available processing resources and/or is constrained by the individual's goals, so that the person is ill-equipped to deal with dysfunction and has difficulty in restructuring cognition. This loss of resources is clearly exemplified in cases of intense anxiety, such as panic attacks or social anxiety. During a panic attack the panic patient believes that a heart attack is imminent and resources are channelled towards processing cardiac responses and trying to prevent a seizure. The social phobic who feels embarrassed diverts resources to processing and trying to prevent a facial blush. In each case, responses are limited by the resources available, and patients report difficulty in thinking "rationally" or concentrating on task demands during acute anxiety. The deleterious effects of such loss of resources are especially evident in test anxiety, where an individual's performance on tests may actually be compromised.

For most of us, periods of stress and intense emotion are short-lived, since appraisal and coping strategies are implemented that lead to goal attainment and exit from S-REF processing. The activation of competing goals for processing and the diversion of attention through distraction are also capable of interrupting S-REF activity. However, if discrepancies remain, the S-REF is prone to be reactivated. If coping and processing strategies lead to discrepancy reduction, either by changing beliefs and/or removing the nature of threat, then the S-REF is less likely to be activated by exposure to subsequent threat stimuli.

The S-REF remains active or in a state of readiness for reactivation until self-discrepancies are resolved. A variety of factors contribute to prolonged or repeated episodes of S-REF activity. Threats that are difficult to bring under personal control represent one factor. Cognitive-emotional self-control problems may be a feature of the environment or stressor itself, but in psychological disorder self-control difficulties usually arise from the individual. Individual factors typically include the following. (1) faulty appraisals concerning control (i.e. the individual is unaware of the control he/she actually has). Appraisals of control will be influenced by metacognitive beliefs such as those concerning a lack of mental control and problem-solving abilities. (2) use of unhelpful coping strategies that impede control (e.g. attempts to suppress thoughts or reliance on worry). (3) use of coping strategies that fail to modify maladaptive self-knowledge, so that discrepancies persist (e.g. avoidance of stressful situations reduces exposure to information that can correct inaccurate negative beliefs); (4) dysfunctional self-knowledge in the form of unrealistic goals for self-regulation. Unrealistic goals are prone to activate repeated instances of S-REF processing, as failure to meet goals repeatedly activates S-REF processing aimed at discrepancy reduction. For example, a hypochondriacal patient who believes that unexplained symptoms must be a sign of serious illness is likely to have a self-regulatory goal of attempting to account for all bodily responses in order to reduce anxiety and threat. Such a strategy will lead to repeated instances of failure to explain symptoms and thus activate negative beliefs about illness.

An important factor contributing to the maintenance of S-REF activity is metacognitive beliefs, such as the belief that worry or rumination is an effective and desirable coping strategy. In such cases individuals use catastrophising sequences of thoughts to generate some internal sense that they will be able to deal effectively with threat. A similar process appears to be present in some types of compulsive behaviour, in which the individual feels compelled to perform an overt or covert ritual until some internal "felt" goal state is accomplished. The internal state serves as a signal that rituals or neutralising can be stopped. However, the use of worry/rumination strategies are problematic for self-regulation. They do not provide information that disconfirms negative beliefs or appraisals, they use up valuable processing resources, prolong bouts of self-focused processing, and may bias or disrupt other operations, such as emotional processing (see Chapter 4).

Other influences contributing to perseverative self-focused (S-REF) processing consist of personality traits, such as dispositional self-focus of attention (Fenigstein, Scheier & Buss, 1975), which appears to relate to unhelpful coping characterised by avoidance, especially when the situation is potentially controllable (Wells & Matthews, 1994; Matthews, Mohamed & Lochrie, 1998), and factors such as neuroticism, which may relate to the accessibility of negative self-knowledge (Mayo, 1989) and preference for emotion-focused coping strategies.

Choice of coping strategies directly involving attention, such as sustained monitoring for threat, can also perpetuate S-REF processing if they are not accompanied by strategies that provide evidence of effective coping and lead to the revision of negative self-knowledge. For instance, an individual traumatised in a robbery may subsequently maintain a strategy of scanning for signs of threat, such as looking out for "suspicious" people. A problem with this type of strategy is that it repeatedly refreshes the concept of personal vulnerability and danger, thereby contributing to exaggerated appraisals of threat. Attentional strategies of this type may be closely associated with worry and rumination as the individual plans coping strategies. It should be noted, however, that attention allocation is also affected by lower-level processing, such as an exaggerated startle reflex following trauma that repeatedly captures attention and initiates S-REF activity.

In summary, the S-REF model emphasises the interplay that exists between various components of cognition in the development and maintenance of disorder. It is therefore a model of dynamic disturbances in processing in which beliefs or self-knowledge drive processing of threat stimuli, and are themselves modified by processing. An important issue concerns the conditions under which maladaptive self-knowledge is strengthened or maintained. Clinical disorder is generally associated with dynamic disturbances, such as perseverative cycles of rumination or active worry, and attentional priorities that fail to modify maladaptive beliefs. Since beliefs direct processing activities such as the choice of ideational strategy (e.g. rumination or problem solving) and the direction of attention (e.g. monitoring for threatening bodily sensations), they serve a metacognitive function. Similarly, on-line processing of threat and the execution of coping responses have metacognitive consequences of modifying or maintaining beliefs.

In this short section I have introduced and expanded on basic concepts embedded in the S-REF model. These concepts refer to the general nature of processing in psychological disturbances. A basic tenet is that psychological disturbance is causally linked to a cognitive-attentional syndrome of self-focused attention, on-line processing of negative self-knowledge, choice of worry/rumination-based strategies, monitoring for threat, resource limitations and maladaptive coping. On-line coping strategies are typically goal-directed, voluntarily initiated, and exert an effect on self-knowledge. Strategies are tailored and executed on line to meet the demands of particular situations and exert an effect on processing and behaviour indirectly, by biasing the activities of lower-level automatic cognitive processes that operate predominantly outside of conscious awareness.

It follows from the S-REF analysis that attempts to construct specific models of disorder should examine the content and nature of self-focused processing, threat-monitoring strategies and active worry in detail, and the dynamic relationship between these factors and belief change. We will now examine the relationship between beliefs, coping and belief change in more detail.

BELIEF CHANGE: MENTAL MODES AND COPING

On-line S-REF processing serves a metacognitive self-regulatory function. S-REF activity can feed back into self-knowledge by the assimilation of data to existing beliefs (thereby maintaining or strengthening existing beliefs) or modifying beliefs (disconfirmatory processing) and developing new plans for processing. The occurrence of disconfirmatory processing is dependent on the availability of unambiguous disconfirmatory data, and on internal cognitive factors. Internal factors of particular importance are: (1) the *mode* of processing; (2) attentional capacity; and (3) the flexibility of control over processing. These three factors will now be considered in more detail.

As we have seen, two general modes of S-REF processing can be identified. These modes have different consequences for belief change. Typically, the plan for processing in emotional disorder specifies that cognitions offer true reflections of threat; thus, the individual is operating in "object mode", in which the implicit assumption is that appraisals and beliefs are accurate. However, an alternative S-REF mode, "metacognitive mode", can facilitate belief change. Here the individual is able to examine his/her thoughts, appraisals and beliefs in a detached way and treat them as events that should be evaluated and not merely accepted as depictions of reality. Typically, each mode has a specific primary goal embedded within it. In object mode the distressed individual's goal is to escape or avoid threat, whilst in metacognitive mode the goal is to examine and modify thinking and beliefs. Figure 2.1 illustrates basic components of these modes and likely outcomes for restructuring of self-knowledge. Note that some of the techniques of cognitive therapy can be construed as shifting the individual from a predominant object mode to a metacognitive mode. The object mode is one in which attentional resources and coping efforts are directed towards monitoring, evaluating and preventing threats to the self, whilst the metacognitive mode is one in which attentional resources are withdrawn from threat appraisals and attempts to prevent threat and are invested in appraising and modifying cognition itself. The impact of each mode on self-regulation is moderated by the nature of threat. When appraisals are unrealistic and threat does not exist, object-mode processing is counter-productive for cognitive-emotional change. This is the usual case in psychological disorders. However, object-mode processing is adaptive and desirable when danger and threats to the self are real. Both object and metacognitive mode can be active simultaneously but as resource demands of one mode increase the other mode may be disrupted by lack of resources or due to mutually incompatible goals. It is more likely that normal functioning is associated with a flexible shifting between modes when this is necessary.

In most instances of psychological disorder patients are in a predominant object mode, and may lack either the resources, cognitive flexibility and/ or the general plan (metacognitive knowledge) for implementing metacognitive processing. One of the aims of therapy is to facilitate the acquisition of this latter mode.

Object mode	Metacognitive mode
Metacognitions:	**Metacognitions:**
Thoughts depict reality (threat is objective)	Thoughts are events, not realities (threat is subjective)
Thoughts must be acted on	Thoughts must be evaluated
Goals:	**Goals:**
Eliminate threat	Modify thinking
Strategies:	**Strategies:**
Evaluate threat	Evaluate thoughts
Execute threat-reducing behaviours (e.g. worry, threat monitoring)	Execute metacognitive control behaviours (e.g. suspend worry, redirect attention)
Probable outcome:	**Probable outcome:**
Maladaptive knowledge strengthened	Knowledge restructured
	New plans developed

Figure 2.1   Characteristics of object-mode and metacognitive S-REF mode

Problems of overload of attention are another important influence on belief change. The initiation, execution and monitoring of coping strategies and appraisals and the modification of self-knowledge (beliefs) require controlled processing and attentional resources. Depending on the attentional demands of coping and appraisal, the individual is vulnerable to attentional overload and central self-regulatory operations may be disrupted. For example, Wells and Matthews (1994) present data showing that attentionally demanding forms of coping, such as task-focused coping and the more active forms of emotion-focused coping, which may be effective in some circumstances, may be particularly vulnerable in individuals prone to high self-focused attention. Aside from impairments in coping, lack of resources is also likely to interfere with the restructuring of self-knowledge, such that maladaptive beliefs fail to be replaced with more adaptive routines for dealing with threat. The use of worry or ruminative coping strategies is particularly prone to drain the resources needed for restructuring of self-knowledge. Moreover, rumination is likely to regenerate patterns of data that strengthen negative beliefs and unhelpful processing configurations. For example, depressed patients are prone to ruminate on negative feelings, think about the self as inadequate, and construct an impression of the personal future as hopeless. This activity will strengthen plans for rumination that are called to guide processing on subsequent encounters with depressive stimuli. Rumination uses up resources that could otherwise be devoted to active problem solving and developing alternative and more adaptive routines for handling depression triggers.

Finally, impairment in the flexibility of control of processing may impede belief change. The use of deliberate controlled processing or over-reliance on particular coping strategies may impair the development of metacognitive control plans. The use of deliberate self-monitoring strategies may block the passing of control to more reflexive lower processors, when this would improve performance efficiency. For instance, a socially anxious individual may attempt to articulate his/her words in a careful and controlled way and this may interfere with verbal fluency (at least subjectively). Such effects, resulting from failure to pass control to a lower level when this is more appropriate, could be appraised as evidence of social incompetence, thus strengthening negative self-beliefs. Persistence in effortful strategies when more reflexive strategies would be more efficient represents a failure in executing flexible control over processing.

In summary, several factors impact on processing in a manner that facilitates or impedes belief change. These include the mode of S-REF processing, choice of coping strategy, availability of processing resources, and metacognitions that influence flexibility of control over processing. In general, the clinical implication is that therapy should manipulate an individual's processing mode and coping responses, and manage processing capacity in a way that enhances restructuring of maladaptive knowledge. We will return to a discussion of these principles and practical applications in Part II of this book.

FUNCTIONS OF THOUGHT: A SPECIAL ROLE FOR IMAGERY

Elsewhere I have argued that it should be useful to distinguish between different varieties of thoughts, since particular types may be linked to information processing and self-regulation in different ways (Wells, 1994a; Wells & Matthews, 1994). Such a distinction should aim to examine the *functional* significance of thought types within a self-regulation framework. Clinical cognitive theories have tended to view thoughts as monolithic constructs, implicating "negative automatic thoughts" in particular. However, as we have seen, thinking styles may not only act as appraisals of events but also represent coping strategies. For instance, worrying may be used by some individuals to cope with threat (Wells, 1994a; Wells & Matthews, 1994).

The S-REF model suggests an important role for thinking styles in the metacognitive self-regulation of cognition. A basic goal of self-regulation is the acquisition and compilation of knowledge for guiding appraisals, and guiding coping with threat and self-discrepancies. It is reasonable to assume that humans are normally equipped with multiple pathways for the acquisition of procedural knowledge (plans) for regulating cognition and action. I propose that imagery provides an important vehicle for the development of procedural knowledge that contains within it metacognitive directives for the control of processing. In adaptational or evolutionary terms, the presence of a cognitive mechanism for facilitating the acquisition of plans for dealing with threat, without the need to repeatedly encounter threat, would bestow on the individual a survival advantage. Imagery provides a "virtual world" for programming procedural knowledge that avoids the dangers of on-line behavioural practice during exposure to actual danger.

Why should imagery be a particularly useful candidate for knowledge compilation or modification? In my opinion, two characteristics of imagery point to its candidature in this respect. First, imagery is capable of conveying the dynamic nature of events over a time course, and provides data on cause–effect and other temporal relationships that are necessary for developing a mental model or simulation of real world events. On the basis of such simulations, individuals are able to predict outcomes and thereby prime suitable responses. Second, imagery combines information with behaviour. By keeping both types of data together, knowledge can be compiled that has directives embedded within it that control cognition and behavioural responses. For instance, when I imagine being in a particular situation, I am assuming a cognitive-behavioural relationship with the imaginal object or situation. More specifically, I will be experiencing some combination of paying attention, remembering, appraising and behaving in relation to the imagined situation. Moreover, these activities can be manipulated so that I can not only change the stage or object of the imaginal scenario, I can also manipulate my cognitive and behavioural responses in the situation. In this way, information and behaviour can be combined so that I may acquire general-purpose knowledge that acts as a library of information about events and my behaviour, and also provides a plan for cognition and action in situations. As we will see in Chapter 4, chronic stress symptoms associated with post-traumatic stress disorder following trauma may be conceptualised as resulting from failure to develop a satisfactory plan for coping and cognition because the work of normal imagery processes is thwarted.

It follows from the above analysis that future research efforts should explore the multifaceted nature of imagery in conjunction with its functional significance in emotional disorder and stress. The present hypothesis provides us with a framework for linking imagery techniques in cognitive therapy with the individual's knowledge and beliefs. All too often, imagery has been used in treatment without a clear model of its effects. The present analysis suggests that running mental simulations of events in which cognition and behaviour are manipulated should provide a means of modifying abnormal stress reactions and provide a vehicle for the strengthening of new procedural knowledge. Discussion of these possibilities will be revisited in Chapters 4 and 8.

CONCLUSIONS

The S-REF model presents a three-level cognitive structure for representing processing in emotional disorder. Psychological disorder is associated with dynamic disturbances in processing which manifest as a cognitive attentional syndrome. On-line controlled processing of self-knowledge is a central feature of disturbance, and is required to restructure or strengthen beliefs. Several factors contribute to a perseveration of S-REF activity, which blocks the adaptive restructuring of beliefs. Choice of coping strategy is especially important for self-regulation. Some strategies maintain the focus of attention on threat, whilst others give rise to ruminative or worry-based processing, which maintains activation of negative self-beliefs and drains the resources necessary for developing alternative processing routines and more adaptive self-knowledge. Within the S-REF, two modes of processing can be distinguished, the object mode and the metacognitive mode, which have implications for the restructuring of knowledge.

It is not only beliefs in the non-metacognitive domain that are important in emotional disorder, but metacognitive beliefs are always involved in guiding the content and nature of cognition that modulates emotional disturbance. Beliefs are conceptualised not only as declarative propositions but as plans that have a metacognitive purpose of guiding processing. Maladaptive plans are emphasised as a source of pathology. Plans are dysfunctional to the extent that they promote counterproductive processing operations and behaviours that maintain emotional disorder through various cyclical relationships. For example, metacognitive beliefs and plans in emotional disorder tend to specify the use of threat-monitoring and worry/rumination-based strategies. Strategies such as monitoring for threat, can sensitise the system to threats and self-perpetuating cycles that strengthen maladaptive beliefs. The inappropriate use of internal data such as "feeling states" is a feature of the metacognitive maladaption in coping and goal-directed behaviours of individuals with emotional disorder.

In conclusion, the S-REF model predicts that metacognitive knowledge, appraisals and strategies are a key influence on the vulnerability to and maintenance of emotional disorder. In the next chapter, specific theoretical predictions are evaluated in the context of research evidence on metacognition and emotional dysfunction.

Chapter 3

STUDIES OF METACOGNITION AND EMOTIONAL DISORDER: EVIDENCE FOR THE S-REF MODEL

It is only recently that studies have explicitly examined metacognitive dimensions associated with emotional vulnerability and psychological disorder. Much of the recent interest in this area has been stimulated by the S-REF model and associated work on metacognitions in anxiety. Although metacognition has been implicated in depression and obsessive-compulsive disorder, previous work has not used an explicit and detailed metacognitive model.

In this chapter I will review the empirical literature on metacognition to determine the extent to which it is consistent with S-REF predictions concerning metacognition and emotional disorder. I will not review data on S-REF predictions concerning attentional processes. Attentional data are consistent with the model, for instance emotional disorder is associated with heightened self-focus (Ingram, 1990; Wells & Matthews, 1994), and data supports a role of strategic processes in attentional bias (Wells & Matthews, 1994; Matthews & Harley, 1996).

To evaluate the metacognitive component of the S-REF model, it will be helpful to consider some basic predictions concerning metacognition and disorder. Five inter-related S-REF-based predictions will be examined in the context of empirical data:

1.   Metacognitive beliefs concerned with the regulation and interpreta-
     tion of one's own cognition should be positively associated with emo-
     tional disorder vulnerability, in particular: (a) positive beliefs about
     worry and negative beliefs about cognition (uncontrollability and
     negative consequences of thoughts) should be associated with trait
     emotional disorder measures; (b) manipulating dysfunctional meta-
     cognitive beliefs should affect negative emotional responses.
2.   Metacognitive beliefs should be positively associated with maladap-
     tive forms of coping in emotional disorder.
3.   Emotional disorder is associated with the use of maladaptive meta-
     cognitive thought control strategies. These are typified by persevera-
     tive self-referent negative thinking, such as worry. Thus, individual
     differences in the use of worry and other negative self-focused strat-
     egies should be positively associated with emotional vulnerability/
     disorder.
4.   Use of negative perseveration as a coping strategy (worry and
     rumination) has deleterious effects on cognition and self-regulation.
5.   Emotional disturbance is associated with states of "locked in" nega-
     tive self-processing. Therefore, afflicted individuals should show re-
     duced metacognitive judgements of cognitive efficiency.

PREDICTION 1(a): METACOGNITIVE BELIEFS AND TRAIT EMOTION

Direct support for an association between dimensions of metacognitive
belief and emotional disturbance emerges from studies that have used the
Meta-Cognitions Questionnaire (MCQ; Cartwright-Hatton & Wells,
1997). This instrument was developed to measure dimensions of metacognitive beliefs, cognitive confidence judgements and selective attention
to mental events (cognitive self-consciousness). As described in Chapter
7, the MCQ has five replicable subscales derived through factor analysis,
each of which has acceptable internal consistency, and these have been
established as true constructs in predictive analyses. A copy of the MCQ
is reproduced in Appendix I. In an initial study with the MCQ,
Cartwright-Hatton and Wells (1997) tested the prediction, based on the
S-REF model and Wells's (1995) model of GAD, that metacognitive dimensions of positive and negative beliefs about worry should correlate
positively with measures of proneness to worry and obsessive-
compulsive symptoms. It was predicted that metacognitive beliefs should
also be positively correlated with anxiety proneness, as measured by the
Speilberger Trait Anxiety Subscale (Speilberger et al., 1983). The Anxious

Thoughts Inventory (a dispositional measure of worry: Wells, 1994b; see Appendix III), the Padua Inventory (a measure of obsessive-compulsive symptoms: Sanavio, 1988) and the Speilberger Trait Anxiety Inventory were administered to a sample of 104 undergraduate and graduate students (age range 18–55; mean = 26; 57 females). Pearson correlations between these measures are presented in Table 3.0, which shows that positive beliefs about worry, e.g. "Worrying helps me to get things sorted out in my mind", and the two negative beliefs subscales, (a) uncontrollability and danger, e.g. "When I start worrying I cannot stop; worrying is dangerous for me"; and (b) superstition, punishment and responsibility, e.g. "If I did not control a worrying thought, and then it happened, it would be my fault", were positively correlated with trait anxiety, obsessions, compulsive checking, vulnerability to health worries,

Table 3.0 Correlations between emotional vulnerability measures and MCQ subscales (data from Cartwright-Hatton & Wells, 1997)

MCQ	Pos. bel	Neg. bel (control/ danger)	Cog. confidence	Neg. bel (SPR)	Cog. consciousness
Trait anxiety	0.26*	0.73*	0.50*	0.47*	0.36*
Padua obsessions	0.40*	0.74*	0.58*	0.50*	0.40*
Padua checking	0.42*	0.40*	0.47*	0.28*	0.29*
Social worry	0.35*	0.69*	0.49*	0.46*	0.69*
Health worry	0.26+	0.37*	0.37*	0.30*	0.20*

Note: * $p < 0.01$; + $p < 0.05$.
Pos. bel = positive beliefs about worry.
Neg. bel (control/danger) = negative beliefs about worry concerning uncontrollability and its dangerous consequences.
Cog. confidence = lack of confidence in memory and attentional capabilities.
Neg. bel (SPR) = negative beliefs about thoughts concerning need for control, and superstition/responsibility.
Cog. consciousness = cognitive self-consciousness, i.e. tendency to focus on own thought processes.

and social worries. Overall, negative beliefs concerning uncontrollability and danger showed the strongest pattern of positive associations with the vulnerability measures assessed in this study. Further analyses of MCQ predictors of impaired control of mental activities (Padua obsessions), and obsessional checking were conducted whilst controlling for the statistical interdependency of MCQ subscales and general anxiety proneness (trait anxiety). Here, impaired control of mental activity (obsessions) was independently predicted by trait anxiety, positive beliefs about worry, negative beliefs concerning uncontrollability and danger, and cognitive confidence. Obsessional checking was uniquely associated with positive beliefs about worry, and cognitive confidence. There was a marginal contribution of negative beliefs concerning uncontrollability, which just failed to reach significance ($p = 0.06$). In both equations, the inclusion of the MCQ subscales led to significant increments in the amount of variance explained above that was accounted for by trait anxiety alone. For impaired control of mental activities (obsessions), the MCQ subscales accounted for an additional 12% of the variance, whilst for Padua checking they accounted for an additional 27%.

Wells and Papageorgiou (1998a) tested relationships between trait measures of worry, obsessive-compulsive symptoms and metacognitive beliefs. Because of problems of overlap in measures of obsessive-compulsive symptoms and pathological worry, it is necessary to control for this overlap when testing for specific metacognitive predictors of pathological worry on the one hand and obsessive-compulsive symptoms on the other. Wells and Papageorgiou controlled for the overlap between worry and obsessive-compulsive symptoms in examining the metacognitive predictors of each cluster of symptoms in a sample of 120 nonpatients. Consistent with the findings of Cartwright-Hatton and Wells (1997), all MCQ subscales were significantly and positively correlated with obsessional checking and obsessional thoughts. Each of the MCQ subscales also correlated significantly and positively with the Penn State Worry Questionnaire (a measure of pathological worry) and with social worries measures by the Anxious Thoughts Inventory. Positive beliefs about worry as a strategy, negative beliefs concerning danger and uncontrollability of thoughts, and cognitive confidence were also positively associated with health worry. However, superstition, punishment and responsibility, and the cognitive self-consciousness subscales did not correlate with health worry in this particular study, suggesting that the relationship between these two MCQ factors and health worry may be unreliable. Correlations between the Penn State Worry Questionnaire and the MCQ subscales ranged from 0.22 to 0.57. The correlations of highest magnitude were for danger and uncontrollability ($r = 0.57$), and positive beliefs about worry ($r = 0.45$). To explore the independent metacognitive predictors of pathological worry and proneness to individual subtypes of obsessive-compulsive symptoms, a series of regressions were run. Two MCQ subscales, positive beliefs about worry, and negative beliefs (danger and uncontrollability), were significant positive predictors of pathological worry. MCQ negative beliefs about worry (danger and uncontrollability) were positively associated with washing rituals, whilst obsessional checking was associated uniquely and positively with MCQ positive beliefs about worry. Obsessional thoughts were predicted by MCQ positive beliefs, and negative beliefs concerning uncontrollability and danger. Health worries also made a significant contribution to this equation. Dressing and grooming compulsions were positively associated with cognitive self-consciousness, with a further marginally non-significant contribution from MCQ positive beliefs, and negative beliefs concerning danger and uncontrollability. Evidence from a different set of researchers also supports relationships between beliefs about worry and emotional disorder measures. Davey, Tallis and Capuzzo (1996) found that the belief that worry helps analytical thinking was significantly and positively correlated with trait anxiety, pathological worry, depression and anxiety.

The results of these studies show that metacognitive beliefs are positively associated with proneness to anxiety, pathological worry, and particular obsessive-compulsive symptoms. Relationships of both pathological worry, and obsessive-compulsive symptoms with metacognitive beliefs and processes remains when the overlap between worry and obsessive-compulsive symptoms is controlled. These data also show that whilst there is a high degree of commonality in the predictors of a range of measures of emotional disorder proneness, there appears to be some specificity in patterns of metacognitive predictors. Of interest in the Wells and Papageorgiou study was a lack of association between MCQ beliefs concerning responsibility, superstition and punishment and obsessive-compulsive symptoms when intercorrelations with other MCQ subscales and worry were controlled. This may be significant, because responsibility appraisals have been linked to obsessive-compulsive disorder in cognitive-behavioural models (Salkovskis, 1985, 1989). However, the metacognitive data suggest, as predicted by Wells and Matthews (1994, 1996), that responsibility appraisals may be a function of underlying metacognitions that are more important determinants of obsessive-compulsive symptoms. Data by Emmelkamp and Aardema (1999) that add further support to this assertion are reviewed later in this section. The data on metacognitive predictors of worry proneness are consistent with the S-REF model and also provide support for a particular metacognitive conceptualisation of generalised anxiety disorder (GAD; Wells, 1995, 1997; see Chapter 10).

Bouman and Meijer (1999) explored beliefs about worry in hypochondriasis. These authors addressed the question of whether hypochondriacal individuals are more concerned about their illness-related worries than they are about worrying in general. More specifically, do these individuals exhibit content-specific metacognitions? Measures of metacognition; the MCQ and a tailor-made metacognition about health anxiety inventory, the Penn State Worry Questionnaire, and a measure of hypochondriasis (the Whitley Index), were administered to participants. The authors report significant positive correlations between the Penn State Worry Questionnaire (a measure of proneness to pathological worry) and MCQ positive beliefs, negative beliefs concerning uncontrollability and danger, and negative beliefs concerning superstition, punishment and responsibility, confirming the reliability of these associations found in previous studies. For the first time, these authors showed that a measure of hypochondriasis was significantly positively correlated with two MCQ negative belief dimensions: (a) uncontrollability and danger, and (b) superstition, punishment and responsibility ($r = 0.42$ and 0.52). In regression analyses, MCQ negative beliefs about uncontrollability, interference of health anxiety worries (measured by the metacognition about heath anxiety scale), and MCQ cognitive self-consciousness, emerged as significant predictors of hypochondriasis. These preliminary data should be interpreted cautiously because of the heterogeneous nature of the sample used in the regression analyses, and because the psychometric properties of the specific metacognition about health anxiety questionnaire are not reliably established. Nevertheless, the data suggest that individuals with hypochondriacal concerns show specific metacognitive beliefs concerning the uncontrollability and interference associated with hypochondriacal worries, whilst showing a general tendency to believe that worries are uncontrollable and dangerous, and believe that thoughts should be controlled within a context of superstition, punishment or responsibility.

Metacognitive beliefs appear to relate to test anxiety. Matthews, Hillyard and Campbell (1999) showed that test anxiety scales of tension, worry, test-irrelevant thinking and bodily symptoms were significantly and positively correlated with MCQ uncontrollability and danger and cognitive confidence. In addition, MCQ positive beliefs were correlated with tension and bodily symptoms. Superstition, punishment and responsibility and the cognitive self-consciousness scales of the MCQ also correlated positively with tension, worry and bodily symptom subscales of Sarason's (1984) Reactions to Tests Scale (RTT). Moreover, the individual MCQ subscales showed some specific correlations with state test anxiety dimensions. Positive beliefs about worry were positively correlated with self-focus. Lower cognitive confidence was correlated with greater tension. Negative beliefs concerning superstition, punishment and responsibility were negatively and significantly correlated with motivation, but positively correlated with self-focus.

Cognitive-behavioural models of obsessive-compulsive disorder have recently begun to emphasise the role of beliefs about one's own thoughts in the development and persistence of the disorder. Early statements of this approach were couched in terms of inflated responsibility appraisals (Rachman, 1976; Salkovskis, 1985, 1989). In Salkovskis' model, obsessional subjects tend to appraise intrusions in a negative way, such that they are personally responsible for the harmful consequences of the intrusion. Such responsibilities for the intrusion are thought to emerge from particular beliefs, for instance "having a thought about an action is equivalent to performing the action". Whilst metacognitive beliefs are implicit in this approach, by grounding this model largely in terms of inflated responsibility, the area of metacognition has not been explored in detail. More recently Shafran, Thordarson and Rachman (1996), introduced the concept of "thought–action fusion" (TAF), as a possible source of inflated responsibility appraisal. This places the theoretical analysis of obsessions more explicitly in the realm of metacognition, coinciding with the proposed role of metacognitive beliefs in OCD presented by Wells and Matthews (1994) and Wells (1997). Rachman and Shafran (1999) state:

> The term Thought Action Fusion is now used to describe the belief that (one's) specific intrusive thoughts can directly influence the relevant external event and/or the belief that having these intrusive thoughts is morally equivalent to carrying out a prohibited action. (p. 80)

There are two forms of TAF: (1) *Probability TAF*, in which the intrusive thought is believed to increase the probability that a specific negative event will occur; and (2) *morality TAF* in which experiencing intrusive thoughts is believed to be morally equivalent to carrying out a prohibited action. In psychometric studies of the structure of responsibility, TAF emerged as one of four factors in addition to responsibility for harm, positive responsibility and responsibility in a social context, (Rachman, Thordarson, Shafran & Woody, 1995). The TAF subscale correlated significantly with measures of obsessionality and guilt and these relationships remain significant after controlling for depression.

The relationship between specific obsessive-compulsive beliefs and obsessive-compulsive behaviours was investigated by Emmelkamp and Aardema (1999). The Obsessive-Compulsive Beliefs Research Inventory was used to explore beliefs associated with obsessive-compulsive behaviours in 305 community inhabitants. The measure was partly based on an early attempt of the Obsessive-Compulsive Cognitions Working Group to construct a questionnaire. The initial item pool for this instrument was based on 15 other questionnaires available at that time (Obsessive-Compulsive Cognitions Working Group, 1997). Of the 14 subscales eventually used for analysis, several of them assess TAF and metacognitive beliefs. These subscales measure TAF ("having violent thoughts is almost as unacceptable to me as violent acts"), over-importance given to thoughts ("if a thought repeatedly intrudes into my mind, then it must have special significance"), consequences of having the thoughts ("I believe that if I lost control over my thoughts, I might eventually develop a psychological problem"), control ("I believe that having control over one's thoughts is a sign of good character") and inverse inference ("whenever I feel anxious it must mean that danger is near"). Results of multiple regression analyses demonstrated that obsessional beliefs were related to specific obsessive-compulsive behaviours and most of these results held when depressed mood was controlled. Evidence emerged that specific obsessional beliefs were related to specific obsessive-compulsive behaviours. However, the data suggests that metacognitive beliefs in particular were important, irrespective of specific obsessive-compulsive behaviours. The metacognitive beliefs of inverse inference, and to a lesser extent, TAF, were related to nearly all specific obsessive-compulsive behaviours. Inflated responsibility explained only a small part of variance in obsessive-compulsive behaviour, namely precision, and did not account for any unique variance in the other obsessive-compulsive behaviours measured. This result is consistent with the position of Wells and Matthews (1994) and Wells (1997), who suggest that metacognitive beliefs concerning the danger and power of intrusive thoughts are relevant to understanding obsessive-compulsive symptoms, and responsibility appraisals are emergent properties of metacognitive beliefs.

PREDICTION 1(b): EFFECTS OF METACOGNITIVE BELIEF MANIPULATION

Rassin, Merckelbach, Muris and Spaan (1999) conducted an experimental investigation of the effects of experimentally induced TAF on obsessive intrusions in non-patient subjects. In this study, a novel paradigm was used to manipulate TAF. When participants arrived at the laboratory, they were led to believe that the EEG apparatus to which they were connected would detect the occurrence of the thought "apple", and on detecting this thought, the apparatus would send a signal to an adjacent room, where it would be transformed into an electric shock applied to another participant the subject had just met. Subjects were informed that they could interrupt the electric shock by pressing a button within 2 seconds after the word "apple" had surfaced in their stream of consciousness. In the control comparison condition, subjects were connected to the

EEG apparatus and were informed that the apparatus could detect specific thoughts such as "apple" but no information about delivery of electric shocks to another participant was given. Compared to the control condition, the TAF manipulation resulted in significantly more intrusions, greater discomfort, more internally directed anger and greater efforts to avoid thinking. These preliminary data show that manipulations of TAF can influence the frequency of intrusions and responses to intrusions. It remains to be established whether the effects of TAF manipulations are mediated by emotion or strategies such as attempts to suppress or not think about target thoughts. Elsewhere, thought suppression has been linked to an increase in target thoughts (e.g. Wegner, Schneider, Carter & White, 1987).

In this section, we have seen that self-report indices of metacognitive beliefs are associated with measures of stress vulnerability and specific measures of worry and emotional disorder. There is some evidence of specificity in the metacognitive correlates of worry versus obsessive-compulsive symptoms. However, there is considerable commonality in patterns of predictors suggesting that particular metacognitive beliefs may be more generally linked to emotional disturbance and disorder. It is only recently that studies have begun to explore metacognitive belief factors in emotional vulnerability and disorder. Much of this work is correlational, probably because of the inherent difficulties in effectively and ethically manipulating metacognitions. However, we saw that in one study a manipulation of TAF increased intrusive thoughts and distress. This result is consistent with a causal effect of specific metacognitions on intrusive thoughts and subjective responses.

PREDICTION 2: METACOGNITIONS AND MALADAPTIVE COPING

Matthews, Hillyard and Campbell (1999) tested whether metacognition relates to test anxiety in a student sample. Their study compared metacognition, coping and worry as predictors of test anxiety. This study is notable in the present context because the data-analytic procedure used allows an examination of the link between metacognition, worry and adaptive and less adaptive forms of coping.

There were two phases to testing in the Matthews *et al* (1999) study. First, student subjects completed Sarason's (1984) Reactions to Test scale (RTT), which assesses an individual's usual reactions to tests and examinations. Its scales are tension, worry, test-irrelevant thinking and bodily symptoms. Students also completed a range of cognitive measures at this testing interval. These measures consisted of the MCQ, a measure of coping (CITS-D, Matthews & Campbell, 1998)[1], and a measure of worry proneness (Anxious Thoughts Inventory; AnTI, Wells, 1994b). In the second phases of testing, subjects completed a multi-dimensional measure of stress state immediately after an examination. Initially, the intercorrelations between the cognitive and metacognitive scales were simplified by factor analysis. Parallel analysis (Horn, 1965), showed that two factors should be extracted from the correlation matrix. Two factors were extracted and subjected to an oblique rotation. The first factor appeared to be a general metacognition factor, with substantial loadings for all MCQ scales, AnTI worry scales and an emotion-focused coping scale. The highest loadings were for MCQ uncontrollability and danger and AnTI meta-worry (worry about worry). The second factor, labelled "Adaptive coping", consisted of the use of task-focused coping which loaded most highly on this scale. It also had two loadings greater than 0.40 for the MCQ scales: low cognitive confidence loaded negatively and high cognitive self-consciousness loaded positively on "Adaptive coping". The factor results show that metacognitive beliefs are associated with worry and emotion-focused coping, both of which can be viewed as maladaptive forms of coping with examinations. Moreover, this appears distinct from a more adaptive coping factor.

The score on the general metacognitive maladaptive coping factor correlated positively with all RTT scales. These results showed that trait test anxiety is associated with metacognition, worry and emotion-focused coping. Further analysis by regression was conducted to test whether the cognitive trait measures were independently related to the test anxiety scales. Metacognition was a significant independent predictor of tension, worry, test-irrelevant thinking and bodily symptoms accompanying test anxiety. This was independent of adaptive coping or the residualised coping subscales. These results show that a general metacognition factor, defined most strongly by beliefs that thoughts are uncontrollable and dangerous, and use of emotion-focused coping are associated with test anxiety traits.

In summary, these data suggest that vulnerability to test anxiety is related to metacognition and worry, which appear to load with emotion-focused coping, and this can be distinguished from adaptive coping.

In terms of the present S-REF predictions, this study shows that metacognitions are associated with trait test anxiety, adding further support to

---

[1] (Dispositional Coping Inventory for Task Stress, CITS-D: Matthews & Campbell, 1998).

Prediction 1. However, they also support Prediction 2, that metacognitions are associated with coping strategies which are maladaptive. In particular, a general metacognition factor, defined strongly by a belief that thoughts are uncontrollable and dangerous, and use of emotion-focused coping appears to be closely related to vulnerability to test anxiety.

PREDICTION 3: METACOGNITIVE THOUGHT CONTROL STRATEGIES

One dimension of metacognition that is linked to psychological problems in the S-REF model is the use of particular thought control strategies. Studies of thought suppression, which involve subjects attempting not to think particular target thoughts, indicate that thought suppression of this kind can lead to an immediate and/or delayed increase in the target thought occurrence. This work has been pioneered by Wegner and colleagues (Wegner, Schneider, Carter & White, 1987; Wegner, Shortt, Blake & Page, 1990; Wenzlaff, Wegner & Roper, 1988). In an early study of this kind, Wegner et al. (1987) asked subjects not to think of a white bear but to report their stream of conscious thought for 5 minutes and ring a bell each time the target thought occurred. Subjects were unable to suppress the thought as instructed, and when subsequently asked to think about a white bear for 5 minutes they reported significantly more thoughts about the bear than subjects who were asked to think about the bear from the outset. Using paradigms based on this original suppression methodology, others have sought to investigate the effects of suppressing more emotional and idiosyncratic thoughts. However, the paradoxical effects of suppression have not been consistently detected (e.g. Merckelbach, Muris, van den Hout & de Jong, 1991; Purdon & Clark, 2000a,b). Overall the results of studies are inconsistent (see Purdon, 1999, for a review). Much of this work is in its infancy and has not used clinical samples or even examined the effects of suppression during particular emotional states.

The effects of suppression following exposure to stress or in post-traumatic stress reactions have been explored by a number of researchers. These studies have observed a rebound effect of suppression on thought frequency in non-patients exposed to stressful material, and in a clinical sample of individuals diagnosed with acute stress disorder (e.g. Rassin, Merckelbach & Muris, 1997; Davies & Clark, 1998; Harvey & Bryant, 1998a,b). The results of studies investigating the effects of suppressing obsessional thoughts have once again produced mixed data. Some studies detect a paradoxical effect of suppression whilst suppression is in operation (Salkovskis & Campbell, 1994; Trinder & Salkovskis, 1994), others show a trend towards rebound (McNally & Ricciardi, 1996) or no paradoxical effects (Purdon & Clark, 2000a). In her review, Purdon (1999) concludes that the results of thought suppression studies have been vastly inconsistent. This inconsistency may be due to methodological differences across studies, individual differences in willingness to report thought occurrences, the availability of distracters in experimental settings, and individual differences in motivation to suppress.

Suppression studies have tended to use general instructions not to think about a particular thought or to use a specific target distracter. However, according to the S-REF model, some thought control strategies may be more effective than others and their effectiveness or impact on emotional well-being will be influenced by the context in which they are used and the purpose they serve. In particular, it has been suggested that some individuals, particularly those with GAD, use worry in order to distract from more upsetting images (Borkovec & Inz, 1990) or as a means of coping with anticipated threats (Wells, 1995, 1997). Under specific conditions of short exposures to worry, worry tends to lead to an increase in intrusive thoughts as demonstrated experimentally (Borkovec, Robinson, Pruzinsky & DePree, 1983; Butler, Wells & Dewick, 1995; Wells & Papageorgiou, 1995). Thus, consistent with the S-REF-based prediction, some thought control strategies may be more deleterious under some circumstances for mental and emotional self-control. Furthermore, the context in which thought control is used may well be important. For example, if individuals suppress or control their thoughts in an attempt to avert a feared catastrophe such as a mental breakdown, a non-occurrence of this catastrophe can be attributed to use of the thought control strategy, thereby preserving maladaptive beliefs concerning the likelihood of this catastrophic event.

Wells and Davies (1994), developed the Thought Control Questionnaire (TCQ; see Appendix V) to assess individual differences in the use of a range of thought control strategies and the relationship between these strategies and emotional vulnerability. Four published studies have so far investigated relationships between individual differences in thought control strategies and stress vulnerability, acute stress disorder, obsessions, PTSD depression, the responsiveness of the thought control strategies to treatment and their ability to predict treatment outcome. The TCQ is reviewed in detail in Chapter 7. Briefly, the scale comprises five subscales that measure thought control strategies of distraction (e.g. "I do something that I enjoy"); social control (e.g. "I ask my friends if they have similar thoughts"); worry (e.g. "I focus on different negative thoughts"); punishment (e.g. "I punish myself for thinking the thought"); and re-appraisal (e.g. "I try to reinterpret the thought"). The TCQ has a replicable factor structure, both in non-patients (Wells & Davies, 1994) and in patients diagnosed with depression or PTSD (Reynolds & Wells, 1999). The tendency to use worry and punishment as control strategies is positively associated with measures of pathological worry, neuroticism and introversion. The other TCQ subscales of distraction, social control and re-appraisal showed non-significant but negative correlations with stress vulnerability measures in the Wells and Davies study. Wells and Davies concluded that these results suggest that the use of worry and punishment to control unwanted thoughts is associated with proneness to emotional problems. It is possible that other TCQ subscales, i.e. social control, re-appraisal and distraction, which appear not to correlate with neuroticism or trait anxiety significantly, may be positive psychological health markers that, under some circumstances, buffer against emotional vulnerability.

Amir, Cashman and Foa (1997), investigated individual differences in TCQ thought control strategies employed by individuals with a diagnosis of obsessive-compulsive disorder (OCD) and 27 non-patient controls. OCD participants used significantly more punishment, worry, re-appraisal and social control than control subjects. In contrast, control subjects used significantly more distraction than OCD patients. Punishment was the strongest discriminator between OCD patients and non-patients. The next strongest discriminator was the use of worry as a control strategy. The results are consistent with Wells and Davies, who showed that worry and punishment were strategies associated with measures of vulnerability to psychopathology. Similar differences in preferred use of control strategy have been found in a comparison of patients with acute stress disorder (ASD) and matched non-patient controls (Warda & Bryant, 1998). Warda and Bryant investigated thought control strategies in survivors of motor vehicle accidents who had either ASD or no ASD. ASD participants used more punishment and worry than non-ASD patients. Correlations showed that punishment and worry control strategies were significantly and positively correlated with Beck Depression Inventory score, Beck Anxiety Inventory score and a measure of intrusions and avoidance. Re-appraisal was positively and significantly correlated only with depression score. Distraction correlated negatively with all psychopathology measures but these correlations were non-significant. Similarly, social control showed an overall pattern of negative correlations with pathology, and the negative correlations with depression, anxiety and intrusions were significant.

Reynolds and Wells (1999) explored relationships between thought control strategies and psychiatric symptoms in patients with major depression and patients with PTSD, with or without major depression. This study is notable, since it included a prospective component in which TCQ predictors of recovery from PTSD and depression were investigated. The sample consisted of 124 psychiatric inpatients and outpatients who met DSM-IV (APA, 1994) criteria for major depression and/or PTSD. In order to assess the sensitivity of the TCQ subscales to recovery, 35 patients completed the TCQ again approximately 6 months later. Criteria for recovery was based on DSM-IV. A comparison of groups based on primary diagnosis, PTSD versus depression, revealed only one significant difference in TCQ scores. The PTSD sub-group scored significantly higher on distraction than the depressed group. In the PTSD group, avoidance was negatively correlated with TCQ social control. Similarly, depression and anxiety were negatively correlated with distraction. In the depressed group, depression was negatively correlated with TCQ re-appraisal and distraction, and positively correlated with punishment. Anxiety was positively associated with TCQ worry and TCQ punishment. Intrusions were positively correlated with punishment and negatively associated with reappraisal. In this group there was a significant negative association between avoidance and social control. The PTSD and depressed groups were combined in order to analyse the sensitivity of the TCQ to recovery. In the recovered group, the ability to use distraction was higher at baseline and improved at follow-up, whilst the unrecovered group had a lower score at baseline which did not change at follow-up. In the recovered group self-punishment decreased, whilst in the unrecovered group it increased. In the recovered group there was a lower score in reappraisal at baseline compared to the unrecovered group, and an improvement in this strategy, whilst in the unrecovered group there was a decrease in re-appraisal. Finally, there was a main effect of recovery status for the worry subscale in which the unrecovered patients had higher scores at baseline and at follow-up. Degree of change in strategies for recovered and unrecovered patients are depicted in Figure 3.0.

Multiple regression analyses were run to explore relationships between thought control strategies and anxiety and depression whilst partialling out the overlap between these emotional states and between TCQ subscales. Regressions were run for the PTSD and depressed groups separately. The use of distraction emerged as a negative predictor of depression scores in both the PTSD and depressed patient groups. In the

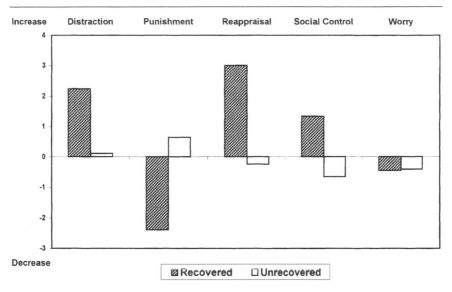

Figure 3.0 Change in TCQ strategies in recovered and unrecovered patients with PTSD or depression

depressed group, punishment was positively associated with depression and re-appraisal was negatively associated with depression. Whilst punishment and re-appraisal predicted intrusions in the depressed group, no TCQ subscales independently predicted the intrusions in the PTSD group.

Overall, the studies reviewed in this section, particularly those that have used the TCQ, show that particular control strategies, namely worry and punishment, appear to be elevated in some clinical disorders and are associated with particular measures of psychopathology. The TCQ sub-scales are sensitive to differences between patient groups and to recovery. In particular, there is preliminary evidence that recovery from depression or PTSD is associated with increases in the use of both distraction and re-appraisal and decreases in the use of worry and punishment strategies. In summary, worry and punishment appear to emerge consistently as strategies that are elevated in psychopathology and as strategies predictive of vulnerability. These strategies appear to decrease in frequency whilst other strategies increase in recovered patients, at least in the case of depression or PTSD. These data are consistent with the prediction that particular control strategies, especially worry and negative self-directed appraisal/behaviour (punishment) are closely associated with psychological disturbance. Unfortunately, the nature of these data precludes conclusions concerning causal relationships between control strategies and emotional symptoms or disorder. However, as we will see in the next section, evidence from experimental manipulations of thinking lend support to the idea that particular thinking strategies, such as worry, may lead to an incubation of stress symptoms in the form of intrusive images.

PREDICTION 4: DELETERIOUS EFFECTS OF WORRYING/ RUMINATION

We saw in the previous section how worry and punishment thought control strategies are related to psychopathology. In this section, I will review evidence that suggests that worrying may be problematic for cognitive self-regulation. Therefore, consistent with S-REF predictions, individuals who use worrying as a thought control strategy or as a means of coping with stress may be engaged in an activity that has deleterious consequences under some circumstances. That is to say, worry may be a maladaptive coping strategy in many situations. In particular, the S-REF model predicts that worrying may bias cognitive processes for the detection of threat, is capable of maintaining the activation of maladaptive beliefs, and may distract from processing new information capable of modifying beliefs or supporting emotional processing following stress.

Borkovec, Robinson, Pruzinsky and DePree (1983) examined the effects of periods of 30, 15 or 0 minutes of worry on high or low worriers and then asked subjects to focus on their breathing for a further 5 minutes. During the breathing task, thought content reports were obtained every minute. Compared to non-worriers, the worriers reported more anxiety and depression, less task-focused attention and more negative thoughts during the breathing task. When the worrier and non-worrier data was combined, the data revealed that for the 15 minute worry period negative thought distractions increased, whilst for the 0 and 30 minute worry groups distractions decreased. In a subsequent study, York, Borkovec, Vasey and Stern (1987), demonstrated that subjects had more negative thought intrusions after the induction of worry than after a neutral condition. These results suggest that brief periods of worrying can increase subsequent negative thinking.

Two studies have explored the relationship between worrying and intrusive images following exposure to stressful stimuli. If worry diverts attention from distressing images, as suggested by Borkovec and Inz (1990), then worrying could block emotional processing. A symptom of failed emotional processing would be an increase in the frequency of intrusive images following stress. In a preliminary study, Butler, Wells and Dewick (1995) asked three groups of subjects to watch a gruesome film about a workshop accident. Subjects were then asked to do one of the following for a 4 minute period: (a) settle down; (b) image the events in the film, and (c) worry in verbal form about the events in the film. Participants who were asked to worry about the film reported significantly more intrusive images related to the film over the next 3 days compared to subjects who had imaged or settled down. In a subsequent study, Wells and Papageorgiou (1995) replicated and extended these finding by testing for possible mechanisms underlying the incubation effects of worry on intrusive images. They used four post-stress manipulations that theoretically varied in the extent to which they blocked emotional processing and produced tagging. "Tagging" refers to the accessing of information concerning the stressor and engaging in elaborative processing, such that a wider range of material serves as a retrieval cue for stress-related intrusions. This study showed that worrying about the film resulted in the highest frequency of intrusions over a subsequent 3-day period. Moreover, there was an incremental pattern of frequency of intrusive images across manipulation conditions that were consistent with a co-joint tagging and blocked emotional processing mechanism.

Hazlett-Stephens (1997) investigated the effects of worrying in speech-anxious participants asked to give five consecutive speeches. Whilst individuals in the control conditions displayed habituation of subjective anxiety over repeated exposures, individuals in the worry condition did not. Thus, participants who worried prior to each exposure failed to benefit subjectively from it. The negative consequences of worry and rumination have been discussed by Clark and Wells (1995) in their Cognitive Model of Social Phobia, which is grounded in S-REF theory. Here, negative post-event thinking is thought to contribute to problem maintenance. Mellings and Alden (2000) examined post-event worry or rumination in highly socially anxious subjects. High-anxious subjects reported more post-event rumination than low-anxious subjects. Moreover, rumination predicted the recall of negative self-related information, negative bias in self-judgements, and recall of anxiety-related sensations on a subsequent occasion involving anticipation of a social interaction.

Studies of the effects of rumination on depression provide further data that are consistent with the S-REF prediction concerning deleterious effects of negative perseveration. The S-REF model is consistent with Nolen-Hoeksema's (1991) response styles theory of depression, which proposes that individuals who engage in ruminative responses to depressed mood will experience amplification and prolongation of the mood[2]. Several studies have been conducted on the effects of induced rumination on dysphoric subjects. These studies reliably show that rumination leads dysphoric subjects to a worsening of mood (Lyubomirsky & Nolen-Hoeksema, 1993; Morrow & Nolen-Hoeksema, 1990; Nolen-Hoeksema & Morrow, 1993). Most individuals over a 30-day period show consistent styles of responding to depressed mood and after controlling for initial severity of mood, rumination predicts duration of depression for more severe and long lasting depression days (Nolen-Hoeksema, Morrow & Fredrickson, 1993).

Nolen-Hoeksema, Parker and Larson (1994) conducted a longitudinal study of 253 bereaved adults interviewed 1 month following the death of their loved one and again 6 months later. Rumination at time 1 was significantly and positively associated with depression at 6 months. In a hierarchical regression with depression at 6 months as the dependent variable, depression at 1 month accounted for 26% of the variance, rumination at 1 month predicted a significant additional 8%. When rumination at 6 months was forced into the equation, it explained a significant additional 7%. Thus, ruminative coping at 1 month and 6 months predicted depression at 6 months.

In summary, the data reviewed in this section support the prediction that perseverative forms of negative processing, namely worry or rumination, can bias cognitive processes and affect self-regulation, as predicted by the dynamics of the S-REF model. Studies that have directly manipulated worry or rumination and a prospective study of ruminative coping styles are supportive of a causal effect of negative perseverative processing on emotional and cognitive disturbance.

PREDICTION 5: COGNITIVE EFFICIENCY

The S-REF model states that individuals with emotional disorder are "locked-into" cycles of maladaptive self-processing, with consequent loss of resources and impaired flexible control over processing. If this is the case, emotional disorder should be associated with meta-appraisals of lowered cognitive efficiency. This should be most pronounced in disorders characterised by prolonged bouts of S-REF processing.

---

[2] The S-REF model differs from the response styles theory in offering a detailed multi-level and multi-component information processing account of the causes and consequences of perseveration.

Consistent with this prediction, low confidence in one's cognitive abilities appears to be linked to emotional disturbance. However, this may reflect accurate metacognitive judgements of actual impairment or inaccurate metacognitive appraisals. Cognitive confidence is measured on a trait level by one of the MCQ subscales. As depicted in Table 3.0, low confidence in memory and attention is correlated with a range of measures: trait anxiety, obsessive-compulsive checking, and worry.

Wells and Papageorgiou (1998a) demonstrated significant positive correlations between MCQ cognitive confidence (a high score denotes greater inefficiency/low confidence) and obsessive-compulsive symptoms of checking, washing, dressing, impulses and obsessional thoughts. MCQ low cognitive confidence was also associated with greater pathological worry. However, confidence did not independently predict these symptom measures when overlaps between worry and obsessive-compulsive symptoms and all MCQ factors were controlled. The emergence of other MCQ dimensions as predictors of these symptoms suggest that other metacognitive factors mediate associations between confidence and the vulnerability measures used. In contrast, Cartwright-Hatton and Wells (1997) showed that low cognitive confidence predicted total worry score on the Anxious Thoughts Inventory, Padua Impaired Control of Mental Activities (obsessions), and checking when co-variances with trait anxiety and other MCQ factors were controlled. This different pattern of results across studies may be a consequence of controlling for worry in the Wells and Papageorgiou analysis. When worry is controlled, the relationship between confidence and particular obsessive-compulsive symptoms may be weaker. Cartwright-Hatton and Wells (1997) showed that patients with GAD and those with OCD reported significantly lower cognitive confidence than a group of non-patients. In comparison, a mixed group of patients with other anxiety disorders showed intermediate confidence scores, not differing significantly from non-patients, GAD or OCD patients. In their analysis of the cognitive and metacognitive predictors of state and trait test anxiety, Matthews et al. (1999) found that proneness to dimensions of test anxiety were associated with lower cognitive confidence. Low cognitive confidence was also positively associated with a state measure of tension following an examination.

Slife and Weaver (1992) suggested that lack of confidence in cognitive skills is related to depression. They attempted to distinguish depressive effects on cognitive and metacognitive skills. They examined the effects of depression on cognitive skill (ability to answer maths problems), metacognitive knowledge about cognition (ability to accurately predict one's ability to answer the problems) and metacognitive monitoring of performance (ability to rate accurately one's performance after answering the problems). In Study 1, they induced elation and depression and in Study 2 depression was measured with the Beck Depression Inventory (BDI; Beck, Ward, Mendelson, Mock & Erbaugh, 1961), using college students as samples in both studies. Students were shown a difficult arithmetic test and were asked to rate how many problems they would be able to answer accurately within 10% (knowledge of skills). Subjects then performed the speeded arithmetic test (cognitive skill) and afterwards judgements of accuracy in performance were assessed (metacognition monitoring). In Study 1, the predictions of depressed subjects were significantly less accurate than predictions of elated subjects, suggesting metacognitive deficiencies in knowledge about cognition in depression compared with elation. However, there were no effects of mood on actual performance. Turning to metacognition monitoring, depressed subjects were less accurate at rating their performance than elated subjects. Correlations between cognitive and metacognitive ratings showed that metacognitions were not associated with actual performance, supporting the view that these abilities are separate. Study 2 compared groups of students with mild and severe depression with non-depressed individuals. The subjects with severe depression showed lower skill than the other two groups. All three groups differed significantly in knowledge about skill, with the severely depressed students showing the least accurate predictions and the non-depressed subjects the most accurate. Finally, severely depressed subjects were the least accurate in monitoring, followed by mildly depressed and then non-depressed subjects. Each of these differences was significant. Correlations of cognitive skill with each of the metacognitive dimensions were not significant. The results of these studies suggest that severe depression is associated with actual performance deficits, and also with deficiencies in metacognitive knowledge and monitoring of performance. Milder forms of depression appear to be associated with metacognitive deficiencies but not necessarily actual cognitive inefficiency. The lack of correlations between metacognitive dimensions and actual performance suggests that efficiency in metacognitive and cognitive skills can be separated. Only the severely depressed students showed impaired cognitive performance on the task. Mild BDI depression and induced mood were associated with a decreased accuracy of pre-test and post-test ratings of accuracy and confidence. These data indicate metacognitive deficiencies in the knowledge and/or monitoring or regulation of cognition.

Cognitive deficit has been explored in OCD patients and in non-patients prone to obsessive-compulsive symptoms. Some studies show that obsessional checking is associated with reduced memory performance (Sher, Frost & Otto,1983; Sher, Mann & Frost, 1984). However, there are several failures to obtain these effects in patient groups (Sher, Frost, Kushner, Crews and Alexander, 1989) and the results of deficit studies are inconclusive. Clinically, checkers report uncertainty about events that stimulate checking. However, it has been suggested that checking may be linked more with metacognitive judgements, such as doubts in the accuracy or efficiency of memory, although objective memory accuracy may show little or no impairment (Wells & Matthews, 1994). Radomsky and Rachman (1999), found that OCD patients with contamination fears had better memory for contaminated objects than clean ones, but anxious controls and student controls did not show this bias. Thus, any actual memory deficit, if it does indeed exist in obsessive-compulsives, may not be global across different presentations of obsessive-compulsive symptoms. That is, it may be more relevant to checking than contamination fears. Unfortunately, these studies have focused on exploring potential deficits in memory rather than general metacognitive appraisals of cognitive efficiency and control. However, studies that have used measures of self-reported cognitive efficiency can possibly shed light on the present prediction of an association between lowered metacognitive efficiency appraisals and emotional disturbance. Much of the questionnaire data on naturally occurring cognitive errors may be explained by supposing that negative beliefs about personal cognitive deficiency are primarily anchored in the person's metacognitions, rather than in objective performance, i.e. cognitive skill level (Wells & Matthews, 1994, p. 193). Beliefs do partly reflect objective levels of performance, but only on some specific tasks. The Cognitive Failures Questionnaire (CFQ: Broadbent, Cooper, Fitzgerald & Parkes, 1982) and the Attentional Experiences Questionnaire (AEQ: Davies, Matthews, Wells, Holley, Taylor, Blanco & Westerman, submitted), have been used to assess everyday errors in memory and/or attention. The CFQ, in particular, has been studied in relation to measures of stress and psychopathology. The CFQ is a reliable positive predictor of trait anxiety, neuroticism and depression assessed by the BDI (Broadbent et al., 1982; Matthews & Wells, 1988; Maylor, 1990). CFQ score is also related to measures of obsessional symptoms, such as compulsive checking (Broadbent, Broadbent & Jones, 1986). There may be some degree of specificity to these relationships. Gordon (1985) found that obsessional patients obtained high scores on the CFQ but phobics did not.

In summary, the research examined in this section provides general support for the prediction that emotional disturbance is associated with metacognitive experiences (appraisals) of reduced cognitive efficiency.

The direction of relationships between such experiences and S-REF perseveration remains to be established. Moreover, it seems that some emotional disturbances may be associated more with appraisals of reduced efficiency than others. This can be explained in terms of disorders differing in the frequency or chronicity of "locked-in" S-REF processing.

CONCLUSIONS

The evidence reviewed in this chapter is generally supportive of S-REF predictions concerning relationships between metacognition, coping and emotional disorder[3]. Meta-cognitive traits associated with emotional vulnerability include a range of positive and negative beliefs about worrying, beliefs and judgements of cognitive confidence and a tendency to focus on and monitor thought processes. Similarly, metacognitive strategies, particularly worry and punishment, can also be linked to stress vulnerability and appear elevated in patients suffering from obsessive-compulsive disorder, acute stress disorder, depression or PTSD. The study by Reynolds and Wells (1999), of the effects of recovery on thought control strategies in PTSD and depressed patients, shows that recovery is associated with changes in the usage of control strategies.

Much of the data at the present time is correlational in nature with only a few manipulation studies, therefore it is necessary to be cautious in drawing causal inferences concerning the effects of metacognitions and perseverative coping. Those studies that have manipulated beliefs such as thought–action fusion (TAF) and have manipulated worry and rumination strategies, suggest a causal relationship between metacognitive beliefs and strategies and particular emotional symptoms. A longitudinal analysis of rumination and depression, in particular (Nolen-Hoeksema et al., 1994), is suggestive of a causal link between rumination and subsequent depression following bereavement.

---

[3] This chapter has focused on predictions of the S-REF model concerning metacognitions, other data reviewed elsewhere (e.g. Wells & Matthews, 1994) on attentional processes in particular, provide further support for the S-REF model.

Chapter 4

EMOTIONAL PROCESSING, THE S-REF AND TRAUMA THERAPY

The concept of emotional processing has been used to explain the ameliorative effects of exposure based interventions on anxiety and abnormal post-trauma reactions such as post-traumatic stress disorder (PTSD). The nature and theoretical basis of emotional processing is considered briefly in this chapter. Later in this chapter the S-REF perspective on emotional processing is described and implications for treating post-trauma reactions are discussed. A central idea is that emotional processing normally consists of development of a general plan for appraisal and coping with acute threat. However, several internal and external factors lead to a failure to develop such a plan because they focus resources on maladaptive thinking and coping strategies and on "fragmented" memories of trauma. The mechanisms linking such strategies to failures of emotional processing are considered in detail. Failure to generate coping options for encoding in the trauma memory, replaying negative fragments of the trauma memory, perseverative thinking (worry/rumination), threat monitoring, and negative appraisals of symptoms restrict the flow of new information into the processing system, so that there is a limited database on which to develop an adaptive plan for dealing with threat. Moreover, these processes lead to the reverberation of a danger perspective, so that the anxiety programme does not decay or is not replaced by a more adaptive programme or plan. A central idea is that symptoms of intrusive images provide an impetus and vehicle for running *mental simulations* of trauma, which in turn are a means of revising knowledge and developing plans for coping. However, this adaptive process is disrupted in abnormal post-stress reactions.

EMOTIONAL PROCESSING

The term "emotional processing" has been used to refer to decreases in fear and anxiety during successful therapy, typically exposure-based interventions. Rachman (1980, p. 51) defined emotional processing as "a process whereby emotional disturbances are absorbed and decline to the extent that other experiences and behaviour can proceed without disruption".

Foa and Kozak (1986) adopted Lang's (1977) network model of fear, and argued that in order for effective treatment to occur, fear structures have to be accessed and incongruent information incorporated in them. This process of emotional processing is indicated by within-session and between-session reductions in anxiety and by evaluating objective changes in psychophysiological responsivity to feared stimuli. Lang's (1977) analysis of fear structures as networks stored in memory suggests that they consist of three different types of inter-related information: (1) information about the feared stimulus situation; (2) information about verbal, physiological and overt behavioural responses; and (3) interpretative information about the meaning of the stimulus and response elements of the structure. This informational structure is viewed as a programme for escape or avoidance behaviour. Foa and Kozak (1986) suggest factors that distinguish the fear structures of normal fears from those of pathological fears. More specifically, pathological structures involve excessive response elements (e.g. avoidance, physiological activity, etc.), and are resistant to modification. Persistence of fears is, at least in part, due to impairments in mechanisms for processing of fear-relevant information. In this framework, emotional processing is defined as the modification of memory structures that underlie emotions. It is argued that two conditions are necessary to reduce pathological fear and facilitate emotional processing: (1) first, the fear structure must be activated; (2) then, incompatible information must be incorporated in it. It is suggested that a number of factors may interfere with emotional processing, such as high arousal and cognitive and behavioural avoidance. These factors may result in a failure to incorporate fear-incongruent information in the fear structure.

In their initial analysis, Foa and Kozak (1986) discuss several mechanisms for the emotional processing of fear. As a result of exposure, the process of short-term within-session habituation constitutes information that changes a fear structure. When physiological responses decline during confrontation with feared situations, interoceptive information about the absence of physiological arousal is generated. This information is available for encoding as new response propositions that are inconsistent with those of the structure. In this way, pre-existing links between stimulus and response elements are weakened. Weakening of linkages between stimulus and response elements may occur automatically through habituation processes, and may involve conscious strategies, such as the use of relaxation practice during repeated imaginal exposure. Apart from short-term habituation effects, confrontation with feared stimuli is also likely to change its meaning. In particular, Foa and Kozak argue that changes in the meaning of stimuli and responses resulting from confrontation with feared situations weaken associations between the stimulus and response elements of a fear structure. More specifically, repeated exposure without catastrophe incorporates information that the probability of catastrophe is low. This information replaces erroneous representations in the fear structure about the likelihood of threat. In addition, emotional processing involves changes in beliefs about harm associated with anxiety responses. It is suggested that two kinds of information may require modification. First, many patients report a fear that, once initiated, anxiety responses will persist indefinitely. This threat of perpetual anxiety requires disconfirmation. Second, some patients report a belief that anxiety will produce a disaster such as insanity or cardiac arrest. In these instances, the proposition that persistent anxiety is dangerous must be disconfirmed. Foa and Kozak argue that short-term habituation changes representations of threat concerning fear responses. Habituation leads to incorporating information that anxiety reactions are of limited intensity and duration. In this approach, patients need not be consciously aware of the components of a fear structure. Thus, associations between stimuli, responses and their meanings can exist in the absence of conscious knowledge about them. However, individuals are able to report some beliefs and evaluations that reflect aspects of their fear structures.

Clearly, behavioural and cognitive behavioural therapy can be construed as leading to emotional processing. The concept has useful heuristic value but it appears to be a description of effective fear reduction rather than a model of the mechanisms underlying change processes. For instance, how does waning arousal become incorporated in the fear structure? Moreover, the use of a memory network-based model for accounting for fear reduction or other emotion effects is open to question. As we will see later, the network model has been criticised on a number of grounds.

The original emotional processing construct appears to relate most closely to automatic cognitive processes, such as the waning of arousal during habituation, which somehow becomes automatically associated with elements of the fear structure, thereby producing change. The involvement of upper-level processes is predominantly restricted to factors that interfere with emotional processing. The use of avoidance-based coping strategies are posited as central interfering agents in this respect. If the emotional processing concept is to be more useful, it will be important to specify the range of mechanisms underlying emotional processing effects and thereby specify in detail the processes that facilitate emotional processing. The traditional fear network approach is based predominantly on the decay of arousal in fear networks produced through habituation, and an automatic encoding of this new response information in the fear network. Although top-down processes of avoidance are implicated in failures of emotional processing, it is likely that other forms of coping also facilitate or impede emotional processing. For instance, metacognitions that influence choice of coping strategy, so that it is characterised by worry or rumination, may impede the acquisition of new information for incorporating in the fear structure following stress. For example, Wells and Papageorgiou, (1995) showed that worrying following stress led to an increase in intrusive images over a subsequent 3 day period.

The emotional processing concept is limited by the network level of structural representation adopted. Two particular limitations of network models outlined by Wells and Matthews (1994) are: (1) network approaches do not appear to distinguish between the role of automatic spreading activation in the network and of controlled or strategy-driven processing in cognitive emotional change; (2) individuals may differ in properties of networks other than the level of network activation. Ingram (1984) draws attention to the possibility that there may be differences in the strength and extent of excitatory links between emotion and other nodes in networks. In addition, Matthews and Harley (1993) have shown that there are a range of specific network parameters that may account for individual and group differences in information processing, including rates of decay of activation, levels of random noise in networks, and the strengths of different connections between units.

It is unlikely that emotional processing can be fully explained in terms of changes in representations that are automatically produced as a consequence of exposure and habituation. Moreover, such a model seems to be restricted in the range of cognitive information represented, and does not specify the factors that lead to the control of emotional processing. For instance, what factor(s) determine the cessation of emotional processing, that is, how are the goals of emotional processing represented? Moreover, there have been few attempts to link emotional processing to the nature of the individual's knowledge base that guides the selection and execution of particular coping strategies, some of which may be counterproductive. These and similar issues can be resolved by structural models that link knowledge stored in long-term memory with lower-level processing activities in a dynamic way. The S-REF model presented in Chapter 2 provides a framework of this kind, and the perspective on emotional processing provided by this approach will be discussed later in this chapter. However, in the next section the review of network models is broadened and some of the problematic issues that have been identified with the use of this construct are given further consideration.

BOWER'S NETWORK MODEL OF MOOD AND MEMORY

In his original network model, Bower (1981) suggests that emotions may be represented by discreet nodes in memory that are interconnected by associated links to form a semantic network. Emotions are viewed as distinct nodes in the network, such that emotions like joy, depression and fear have their own specific nodes. Each node is connected to nodes representing events and concepts that have previously been activated in parallel with that emotion. Activation spreads through the network from the emotion node to other nodes that are associated with patterns of autonomic response, expressive behaviours and verbal labels corresponding to the emotion. When activation in the network reaches a particular threshold, information becomes conscious. A general prediction is that emotional states prime processing that is congruent with the emotion. This effect is considered to account for *mood-dependent retrieval* and *mood-congruent retrieval*. In mood state-dependent retrieval, nodes for the material to be remembered become associated with nodes for contextual features including the person's emotional state. When retrieval occurs in the same emotional state, the emotion node partly activates the nodes for the material to be remembered, rendering it more or less accessible. In mood-congruent retrieval there are stable associative links between emotion nodes and nodes for related concepts or events. Thus, if an individual is in a depressed mood, he/she is more likely to remember events that were previously associated with that mood. The model has intuitive appeal but has been criticised on a number of grounds. One of the problems is a general failure to find mood congruence in simple perceptual and encoding tasks in both mood induction studies and in anxious and depressed patients. Furthermore, the model predicts that mood-congruent biases in memory should be seen in depression and anxiety. However, mood congruent recall of threat- or danger-related material in anxiety has been difficult to demonstrate reliably (Mogg, Matthews & Weinman,1987), although some researchers have found anxiety congruence in recall (Cloitre & Liebowitz, 1991). It is possible that methodological factors may account for the inconsistency between studies.

A number of theoretical difficulties with the network model have also been articulated. Bower and Cohen (1982) point out that spreading activation implies that people will always feel a particular emotion when they refer to concepts associated with that emotion. However, individuals can discuss emotions in a cool non-emotional way, without feeling emotions at all. In order to overcome this problem, they suggest a distinction between a "cold node" and a "hot node". The cold node represents the concept of a particular emotion, whilst the hot node represents the experience of the emotion itself. A further difficulty, raised earlier in this chapter, is that it is not clear how top-down influences of processing may lead to a modification of characteristics of the network—individuals are clearly able to modulate their emotional responses.

INGRAM'S NETWORK MODEL OF DEPRESSION

A network theory of information processing in clinical depression has been advanced by Ingram (1984). Consistent with Bower's framework, depression is viewed as associated with activation of a depression node caused by appraisal of life events associated with loss. Ingram suggests that the depression node becomes associatively linked in a loss-associated network with nodes representing recent events and cognitions related to prior episodes of depression. In non-depressives the activation level of the network decays over time, so that moods are of short duration. In clinical depressives there are various factors that tend to prevent decay of network activation. For example, if the loss-associated network is large and interconnected, neutral events may be appraised as depressing. Recycling of activation through the network is described as "automatic" but generates conscious cognitions that demand attention.

SUMMARY OF NETWORK LIMITATIONS

Network levels of explanation have been used to explain treatment effects of emotional processing, to account for mood memory bias effects, and in explaining the persistence of depression. These models identify a range of factors that prevent the resolution of emotional disturbances. These are: in the case of fear, use of avoidance-based coping strategies and negative appraisals; and in depression, properties of networks, such as their interconnectedness.

We have seen that network models have several critical limitations: (1) difficulty explaining a person's ability to think about an emotional event in an unemotional way; (2) experimental data on mood-congruent recall is less compelling in anxiety compared with depression (although many of the failures to replicate mood congruency and mood state dependency effects may be due to methodological factors); (3) there has been little consideration of higher-level strategic cognitive factors in the network approach to emotional processing of fear; (4) the role of beliefs in processing is overlooked. To overcome criticisms of lack of integration with higher levels of cognition, some network theorists have linked networks to higher-level processes. Bower and Cohen (1982) suggested a working memory or "blackboard" that integrates emotional information from a variety of sources. It allows the strength of emotion to be modified automatically or deliberately by interpreted rules, so that a person's emotional response is appropriate. More recently, Bower (1992) proposed that emotion may activate not only isolated semantic concepts but also rule-based action plans that have proved useful in similar previous situations. This view is closer to the specification presented in the S-REF model in its linking of lower-level reflexive (network) processing to higher action plans and self-regulatory cognitive mechanisms, which are strategic rather than only automatic.

THE S-REF PERSPECTIVE ON EMOTIONAL PROCESSING

We have seen how emotional processing, as described by Foa and Kozak (1986), involves the accessing of fear structures and the assimilation of corrective information. Emotional processing can be viewed as a subset of S-REF processing activities that functions to produce a meaningful general plan for appraisal and coping with threat. Differences in the specification of system architecture, emphasis on multiple levels of control of processing and the involvement of metacognitions lead to a different account of emotional processing. In the S-REF model, fear and emotion are not represented structurally as discreet networks. Indeed, as we have seen, network models of emotion are limited in a number of respects. In the S-REF model, the "hot" and "cold" thinking issue is not a problem, since emotions are generated only when the S-REF is activated and it is possible to think about emotional topics without activating the S-REF processing configuration. For example, if emotional stimuli are processed as non-relevant to the self, in a detached way that is irrelevant for self-regulation, then emotions will not be raised.

Several points of contrast between the S-REF model and network models of emotional processing can be highlighted. These include: (a) architecture; (b) representations of information; (c) goals and coping strategies; (d) the role of metacognitions and attention.

Architecture

Architecturally the S-REF model is based on three interacting levels of processing, whilst fear network approaches are based on networks of interlocking nodes that support spreading activation. The modelling of emotional processing in terms of three levels, as in the S-REF model, implies that so-called failures of emotional processing could emerge from maladaption at any one or combination of three levels. Thus, there may be maladaption in lower-level processing networks that support automatic processing. For instance, repeated exposures to specific traumatic experiences (e.g. early in life) may lead to strong stimulus–response connections leading to arousal responses largely independently of upper-level involvement. Maladaption may occur at the on-line level, in that attentional strategies and coping strategies may interfere with the restructuring of negative material in memory. For example, after being attacked and robbed, an individual may be hypervigilant for "suspicious looking individuals in his/her environment". This type of strategy will maintain a trauma-related processing mode that emphasises danger. Finally, there may be maladaption at the upper belief level, which is intrinsically linked to the strategies used by the individual to cope and may lead to exaggerated threat appraisals. Certain types of knowledge are 'likely to underlie exaggerated fear and arousal responses, such as negative beliefs about anxiety symptoms, and one's vulnerability. For example, the individual may negatively interpret and become fearful of the symptomatic sequelae of stressful encounters.

Level of representation

Another important point of departure that has conceptual and clinical implications is the nature in which information is represented in models of emotional processing. In the network approach, information is stored as propositions in particular nodes and there are specific nodes corresponding to meaning-based, arousal and behavioural response aspects of fear. In the S-REF model, fear and other emotions are not represented in propositional network form. Emotions are emergent properties of self-regulatory processing and signal discrepancies in self-regulation. Propositional information may be stored, but it is likely that information is represented as general purpose plans (procedural knowledge) for responses to threat. Propositions may be the outputs of running a particular plan for processing. If knowledge is highly proceduralised in this way, it will be necessary not only to modify the content of propositional knowledge but also to focus on the processing strategies that individuals use in dealing with the consequences of trauma. Attention, behavioural and ideational processes will have to be modified in order to develop replacement processing routines and plans that facilitate emotional processing. It does not follow from the S-REF analysis that repeated and prolonged imaginal exposure alone to trauma-related memories is sufficient or necessary to process trauma. We will return to this issue later.

Goals and coping

In the S-REF model, cognitive processing is guided by the individual's explicit goals and by more implicit metacognitive self-regulatory goals. A central goal for self-regulation is the reduction or elimination of personally significant threats. This is achieved through the development of coping strategies and/or by modification of unrealistic negative beliefs. Self-regulatory processing is terminated when self-discrepancies are eliminated. In the S-REF, symptoms of failed emotional processing are indicative of on-going unresolved discrepancies in self-regulation. Symptoms of failed emotional processing are an indication that coping strategies that restructure maladaptive self-knowledge and/or meet the systems goals of generating a plan for coping have not been met. In particular, symptoms such as flashbacks, anxiety, re-experiencing and dwelling on negative aspects of a trauma can be viewed as indicators of an on-going discrepancy in self-regulation. Since these are normal symptoms following stress, they are likely to represent cognitive responses that have functional significance in terms of emotional processing. Whilst a continuation of these symptoms may be indicative of failed emotional processing (e.g. Rachman, 1980), such intrusions are likely to be adaptive in their normal form, since they interrupt on-going activity and stimulate selection and modification of upper-level beliefs and plans for dealing with threat. In normal form, these intrusions act as motivationally significant interrupts that prompt the individual to revise knowledge about the world and, most significantly, prompt the selection and execution of on-line strategies that facilitate the acquisition of new plans for coping (dealing with threat). A clinical implication of this proposal is that symptoms of failed emotional processing, such as those characteristic of PTSD, may be amelio-rated by interventions that enable patients to develop a plan or script for coping with similar events in the future. The development of an escape or active coping plan is most probably an in-built system goal that has provided survival in the evolutionary past. Such a plan can be represented as a narra-tive or script for dealing with threat. In PTSD the individual fails to generate a personally acceptable narrative or script for coping. Memories of trauma may be fragmented or "frozen" in time because the individual is engaging in subsequent cognitive avoidance or because of the attentional priorities and coping strategies adopted during the trauma or post-trauma. For example, dwelling on one salient aspect of a memory does not provide an efficient strategy for processing information that can modify negative beliefs and provide a plan for coping.

The present approach suggests particular circumstances under which failures of emotional processing are likely to occur. In particular, situa-tions that lead to a failure in developing a coping plan will contribute to the development of PTSD and other abnormal post-stress reactions. An important implication is that the nature of an individual's appraisal of the manner in which he/she coped during a trauma and afterwards will be an influence on the maintenance or resolution of self-discrepancies, thereby influencing the nature of stress reactions.

Metacognitions and attention

Metacognitions are implicated in emotional processing and trauma reac-tions in terms of (1) effects of metacognitive knowledge and strategies on belief change, and (2) the interpretation of particular symptoms such as intrusive thoughts.

At the knowledge level, negative beliefs about intrusive thoughts under-pin negative appraisals and negative emotional responses to such symp-toms. Beliefs of this kind are likely to add to a spiral of intensified negative emotions, as the individual fears emotional symptoms them-selves. In another vein, beliefs that lead to thinking strategies, such as worry or dwelling on past events in order to "work things out" or avoid threat, give rise to problematic patterns of appraisal and unhelpful diver-sion of processing resources. As demonstrated experimentally, worrying following exposure to stressful stimuli leads to an increase in intrusive stress-related images over a 3-day post-stress period (Butler, Wells & Dewick, 1995; Wells & Papageorgiou, 1995). More generally, worrying for brief episodes appears to be associated with an increase of negative thought intrusions during a subsequent non-worry period (Borkovec, Robinson, Pruzinsky & DePree, 1983). Thus, the particular ideational strategies adopted by individuals may block emotional processing or contribute to negative thought intrusions. Other strategies, such as attempts to suppress thoughts or distract from more upsetting topics by diverting attention to more minor worries, are likely to be unsuccessful and/or interfere with emotional processing. As we saw in Chapter 3, the use of worry- and punishment-based thought control strategies are positively associated with vulnerability to psychological disorder (Amir et al., 1997; Warda & Bryant, 1998; Wells & Davies, 1994) and are inversely associated with recovery from depression or PTSD (Reynolds & Wells, 1999). Beliefs and strategies that load attention can prevent activation of relevant knowledge structures, and interfere with the development of a prospective plan for coping with trauma. Dysfunctional strategies are those that are likely to maintain self-regulatory discrepancies, and thereby contribute to symptoms of failed emotional processing.

In the S-REF model, attentional strategies, aside from worry-based (rumination) strategies, are central to emotional dysfunction. Specifically, emotional disorder is linked to a "threat-monitoring" strategy guided by the active plan for processing. Following trauma, an individual's attention is likely to be dominated by monitoring for specific trauma-related threats. However, in chronic post-trauma reactions the model predicts that attention will be bound up with processing of threats, self-focused on worry, and prone to be captured by threat-related memories and arousal symptoms. Because of restrictions and biases imposed by such processing the distressed individual is locked into processing threat-congruent information. Thus, plans for processing threat and danger-related beliefs are strengthened. This restricts the flow of information into processing that is capable of disconfirming over-predictions of danger. Moreover, strategies for accurately judging the likelihood of threat and developing coping responses are not practised under these conditions.

FAILURE AND SUCCESS IN EMOTIONAL PROCESSING

In order to understand emotional processing, it is necessary to examine the inherent purpose and goals of normal emotional processing following trauma. As a starting point, I assume that emotional processing is a naturally occurring cognitive activity in which the cognitive system is engaged in recalibration processes and knowledge is modified through experience. The goals of emotional processing are to modify self-knowledge, so that discrepancies between current state and desired state can be resolved. These discrepancies may exist in the domains of levels of arousal, sense of safety, sense of self, or discrepancies between current perception of self and some desired state. In these instances the discrepancy can be resolved through the revision of self-knowledge, development of coping strategies and a plan for coping that can be subsequently evoked.

Following stress, emotional responses are typically transient. Several factors contribute to the prolongation of stress responses. They will be prolonged when individuals lack appropriate coping strategies for dealing with threat or when inappropriate coping strategies are implemented. Moreover, self-discrepancies are more likely to be activated when the nature of threat is beyond normal experience or situational factors lead to failures in coping or negative self-appraisals of coping effectiveness. Threats that are difficult to bring under personal control are also likely to activate discrepancies. Threats that are beyond normal experience are problematic because the individual will lack a plan for controlling cognition and action in these circumstances. In these circumstances, greater demands are placed on in-situation processing to tailor some general-purpose plan to deal with threat and the demands of the situation. This provides greater room for failure and negative appraisal of one's performance.

Following exposure to threat, cognitive functioning will be determined by the metacognitions and plans that are activated. The cognitive responses of PTSD, such as re-experiencing and hypervigilance for threat, can be explained in S-REF terms by supposing that they result from the activation of basic metacognitive monitoring and control operations. These responses serve a self-regulatory purpose. Hypervigilance facilitates the detection of threat, so that self-preservation may be readily implemented. It also increases the selective flow of information into processing, so that knowledge compilation on salient topics can be enhanced. Re-experiencing responses can vary in form and intensity. The S-REF model attributes particular functional significance to intrusive recollections in the form of images in normal emotional processing. A core objective of emotional processing is to strengthen plans for dealing with threat, and imagery provides a "programming environment" in which information and behaviours are combined to form a rudimentary plan. Imagery can depict dynamic relationships between events and behaviour over a time course, and can link information about situations (stored in memory) with a range of cognitive and behavioural responses.

In the natural environment it is safer to build or "fine-tune" a basic plan through the use of imagery than it is to accomplish this through repeated trials with threat. During the normal course of emotional processing, intrusive images are linked with procedures for the control of cognition and action until a coherent imaginal script for interpreting and dealing with a threat is established. This script constitutes a basic plan for cognition and behaviour.

Several factors may impede the compilation of a plan. Following a traumatic event, negative metacognitive beliefs about intrusive imagery may promote active avoidance or deleterious control over mental events. Thus, the traumatised individual fails to run mental simulations of events and coping. The use of worry or rumination that is predominantly verbal will divert attention away from processing imagery, and therefore a plan will not be compiled. The nature of processing during trauma is also likely to be of importance in plan development. More specifically, if the individual's in-situation coping was characterised by mental planning and/or the execution of actively mediated coping responses, it is more likely that a plan will be strengthened. Appraised failure to cope, however, will lead to continued activation of the S-REF supporting cycles of self-monitoring and implementation of coping which may or may not be adaptive.

In summary, the model suggests that several factors contribute to failed emotional processing. These are: (1) use of unhelpful coping responses; (2) maladaptive self-knowledge (including metacognitions); and (3) situational variables that lead to failures to revise maladaptive self-knowledge (self-discrepancies) and acquire plans for coping. These will be considered in turn.

Coping strategies

Unhelpful coping responses include the range of responses normally associated with failures of emotional processing, such as emotional and cognitive avoidance. However, as we have seen, they also include coping strategies characterised by changes in attention and ideation. In particular, strategies of hypervigilance or monitoring for threat and rumination/worry as coping strategies are particularly problematic. Worry and rumination may block the accessing of trauma memories in imaginal form and thereby interfere with the development of more adaptive self-knowledge and plans for coping. Aside from worry, strategies of avoidance are problematic, since individuals fail to encounter situations that can lead to modification of negative beliefs. For example, a person who, after being attacked, avoids walking alone in the street, does not encounter experiences that can disconfirm over-perceptions of the likelihood of danger.

Metacognitions

The use of particular coping strategies is intimately linked to the individual's self-knowledge, especially metacognitions that direct attention and thinking strategies in potentially counter-productive ways. For instance, the use of worry to anticipate and avoid danger, or the use of hyper-vigilance, is intimately linked to metacognitive beliefs concerning the usefulness of such strategies. Metacognitions that lead to negative appraisals of the symptoms of stress (e.g. intrusions) are especially likely to contribute to problems of emotional processing. In this instance, cognitive resources are diverted to negative self-evaluative processes that do not contain information that can contribute to an adaptive mental simulation of events. Negative appraisal of symptoms perpetuates threat-related cycles of processing that strengthen mental associations between trauma-related stimuli and loss of coping. Post-event processing of stress and trauma may also be influenced by metacognitive events, such as subjective feelings, other than the symptoms of stress, such as confidence in one's memory for the event, and confidence in one's mental abilities. These metacognitive "feelings" may be affected by post-event social circumstances, or by the individual's stable theories about the meaning of these feelings.

Situational factors

Situational variables also exert an impact on emotional processing. More specifically, the coping strategies that an individual was able to execute during the stressful episode, and the extent to which salient self-discrepancies were created, will have an impact on subsequent emotional and cognitive responses. If the individual appraises personal coping strategies as ineffective, discrepancies will be created. Despite effective coping with the situation, selective retrieval of instances of failed or inefficient coping and/or subsequent situational factors that lead to a reappraisal of one's coping efforts in a negative way will contribute to subsequent failures of emotional processing. For example, a rape victim who was raped at knifepoint "gave in" to her attacker, as she reasoned during the attack that she might otherwise be murdered. After the event, she appraised her coping strategy as inadequate, despite the fact that it had probably saved her life. This situation was compounded by the fact that her strict religious family refused to talk about the trauma. This was appraised by the victim as an indication that her family thought that she was to blame. In this instance, a negative self-discrepancy persisted as the individual failed to revise self-knowledge concerning the appropriateness of her behaviour in the situation[1]. This case illustrates how appraisal of coping strategies in-situation, and subsequent situational factors, can lead to a re-evaluation of threat and responses in a way that contributes to self-discrepancies, strengthens maladaptive self-knowledge and undermines plans for coping.

Symptom appraisals

Situational factors that lead to negative appraisal of the symptoms of stress, or pre-existing beliefs that lead to negative appraisal of PTSD symptoms, can provide an obstacle to effective emotional processing. In particular, negative appraisal of symptoms as a sign of failure to cope, or of emotional or mental weakness, will increase self-discrepancies as the individual appraises the self as deficient in coping and self-regulatory skills. Thus, pre-existing unrealistic attitudes and goals concerning emotional symptoms will, in some instances, predispose the individual to experience stress symptoms as profound instances of personal inadequacy and failure. Such an event is likely to activate self-regulatory (S-REF) processing aimed at discrepancy reduction. The nature of self-regulatory attempts will determine the effectiveness with which such discrepancies are eliminated.

LOW-LEVEL MALADAPTION

So far, we have concentrated on the role of upper-level processes in emotional processing and the development of maladaptive stress

---

[1] In this case, therapy focused on re-evaluating the in-situation coping strategy, pointing out how this was probably the best strategy under such life-threatening circumstances. Treatment also focused on reducing the amount of time engaged in rumination, reducing behaviour avoidance of social situations, and increased attention to safety cues in the environment.

reactions. It is possible in a multi-level system, like the S-REF, to experience maladaption at the lower level, although it is more likely to be an interaction between this level and upper levels that leads to a particular expression of symptoms. Maladaption at the lower level may exist as over-sensitivity of lower processing components to particular types of stress or stimuli. For example, abusive early learning environments or repeated exposure to uncontrollable stresses will produce certain strong and automatic stimulus–response associations. Such responses may be particularly difficult to modify in therapy. Wells and Matthews (1994) suggest that the lower level may be more sensitive to innate fear stimuli than to the complex and ambiguous social stimuli which often generate depression and anxiety. Whilst the lower level may be tuned via experience and innate factors to generate particular types of responses (e.g. intrusions and arousal) in response to trauma, it is assumed that the lower level generates feedback to the upper level, which executes self-regulatory processing. Thus, lower-level activity or maladjustment is intermeshed with upper-level S-REF dysfunction. Wells and Matthews suggest that it is likely to be S-REF dysfunction that prevents maladaptive activity in lower-level pathways from decaying as the lower-level network re-tunes to a more normal environment. In particular, monitoring for threat, self-attention and active worry may bias the lower-level network to continue regeneration of symptoms such as intrusions, enhanced startle responses and other forms of arousal.

S-REF TREATMENT GUIDELINES FOR OVERCOMING TRAUMA REACTIONS

Habituation is not the central means of emotional processing in the S-REF model. It does not follow from the present theoretical analysis that prolonged imaginal reliving of trauma, in itself, is necessary for resolving abnormal trauma reactions. Indeed, in circumstances where imaginal exposure does not lead to development of plans for coping and a correction of faulty self-beliefs, it may strengthen the processing of danger signals. Moreover, imaginal exposure is poorly tolerated by some patients. When exposure does work, it is likely to do so because it facilitates the reappraisal of danger and leads to the development of a coping plan. As suggested by Foa and Kozak, repeated experience of emotion during exposure will provide evidence that emotional symptoms are transient and non-dangerous. However, it seems likely that there are alternative pathways to cognitive change of this kind, such as cognitive restructuring methods that do not involve imaginal exposure.

The present model suggests that abnormal post-trauma reactions are linked to a failure to revise one's beliefs and develop a satisfactory plan for coping. Several specific factors responsible for locking the individual into cyclical preoccupation with threat were outlined. These include the use of worry-based coping strategies, threat monitoring/ hypervigilance, strategies of avoidance of trauma-related situations and preoccupation with one's performance in the traumatic situation. Therapeutically, it is important to block and modify these maladaptive processes. In particular, a central problem is the individual's tendency to repeatedly process emotional response components of the post-traumatic reaction and to dwell on fragments of the trauma memory, without engaging in more complete processing to produce a mental simulation. Treatment should focus on blocking conceptual worry-based responses, focus on modifying negative self-beliefs, and focus on running mental simulations through guided imagery, so that coping narratives and plans can be established. In addition, *in vivo* exposure to trauma-related situations (in the absence of trauma) should be undertaken with use of external attentional strategies that over-ride threat monitoring (e.g. focus on safety signals instead to facilitate updating of threat-related trauma images and memories). In summary, there are two general clusters of strategies that can be used to facilitate emotional processing. The first involves blocking worry-based activity following trauma and allowing intrusions to occur without negative appraisal of them. This is intended to allow normal emotional processing to take its course. The second consists of strategies supporting the active assimilation of knowledge and plans for coping. This will involve running mental simulations and/or reinterpreting negative judgements of the effectiveness of coping when coping has been appropriate. Several specific treatment implications are suggested:

1. Worry-based and ruminatory coping strategies should be reduced and preferably eliminated early in treatment. A discontinuation of ruminatory strategies should free-up attentional processes for cognitive restructuring. Moreover, a reduction of rumination should allow lower-level processing activity time to decay in its own right. Therapists should explore the patient's purposes and goals of retrieving trauma-related information from long-term memory and of dwelling on this material. Maladaptive metacognitive beliefs supporting such processes should be challenged using behavioural and verbal reattribution methods.
2. Factors leading to a failure to emotionally process should be assessed in detail. It will be necessary to assess in-situation variables and post-

situational and personality factors that lead to the activation of self-discrepancies. Key influences are likely to be:

(a) Negative beliefs and appraisals concerning stress symptoms.

(b) Appraised failure to cope adequately in the trauma situation. This will lead to a preoccupation with aspects of the trauma in which such a discrepancy was activated. Under favourable conditions, such preoccupation would culminate in developing new coping options and accepting the past failure as irrelevant for self-perception/concept. Several factors may prevent such acceptance, for example stigmatization, rigid pre-existing attitudes, ego-dystonic nature of one's reactions in trauma situations.

3. Unhelpful post-trauma coping strategies, namely avoidance, should be modified with a view to restructuring maladaptive negative self-knowledge. In particular, exposure to feared situations should be used in conjunction with attentional refocusing strategies that enable patients to re-evaluate the presence and likelihood of threat in trauma-related situations.

4. Since the model assumes that an implicit goal of cognitive activities underlying normal emotional processing is the establishment of a plan for coping, patients should be encouraged to evaluate their coping efforts in a positive way and to develop a plan for coping with similar threats in the future. This will consist of "finishing out" images of trauma and running *mental simulations* of coping. In some cases, modification of small aspects of the memory through shifting attention to features stored in memory that can correct dysfunctional interpretations and beliefs can be effective in eliminating discrepancies. Alternatively, mental simulations should develop an imaginal narrative that finishes out memories in a non-fragmented way, with specific coping responses. These responses may be pre-existing but ignored aspects of the memory or may be new elaborations if necessary.

5. In order to prevent negative post-event processing of behavioural responses and/or symptoms of stress, education of patients should be undertaken to normalise affective and stress symptom experiences.

6. When unrealistic goals for self-regulation (e.g. "Only weak people are affected by stress—I must not be affected") appear to underlie vulnerability to adverse stress reactions, these personal standards for self-regulation will need to be conceptualised and modified in treatment.

A central assumption of the present model is that normal emotional processing is likely to occur if maladaptive and unhelpful coping strategies,

maladaptive metacognitions and environmental factors that sustain negative post-event processing are removed, and the individual has the basic
general metacognitive knowledge and flexibility of processing to support
emotional processing. Factors such as a negative model of one's own
cognition, and concurrent psychological disturbances that diminish cognitive control and attentional resources (e.g. worry or depression), are
likely to impair emotional processing. In particular, the present model
predicts that concurrent emotional disturbances involving perseverative
conceptual activity and diminished cognitive flexibility, such as worry or
rumination in depression, will contribute to the development of persistent stress reactions. Thus, the development of chronic stress reactions
may be prevented by strategies that interfere with the S-REF maladaptive
cognitive-attentional syndrome following trauma.

CONCLUSIONS

In this chapter, the concept of emotional processing has been examined
and the network formulation of emotional processing in trauma briefly
evaluated. The S-REF model has been applied to conceptualising emotional processing and the factors that contribute to adaption or maladaption following trauma. This approach avoids the conceptual problems
associated with network models, and provides specific predictions concerning the treatment of stress reactions. An important idea is that emotional processing involves generating a plan for processing, interpreting
and coping with threat. Intrusive symptoms, namely imagery, provide
the impetus for running mental simulations that form the basis of plan
revision or compilation. Several factors have been identified that can
interfere with this process and activate discrepancies in self-regulation.
The concept of mental simulation in plan development is discussed further in Chapter 8.

Chapter 5

S-REF, SCHEMA THEORY AND INTERACTIVE COGNITIVE SUBSYSTEMS (ICS)

This chapter focuses discussion on the principal differences between the S-REF model, Beck's schema theory (e.g. Beck, 1976), and Interactive Cognitive Subsystems (ICS: Teasdale & Barnard, 1993). Conceptual limitations of schema theory and ICS are considered within this context.

Beck's schema theory is a descriptive clinical account of emotional disorder that has proved to be hugely influential. If we judge theories predominantly in terms of their conceptual and practical utility, schema theory has performed impressively. However, the theory has limitations, like all theories, but the present thesis is that these can be overcome and significant progress made by theoretical advances that consider the role of levels and varieties of cognition, and the mechanisms of metacognitive control of processing. The S-REF model provides a detailed and integrated account of this kind. In the next section I will briefly elucidate some of the key similarities and differences between the S-REF model and schema theory. However, for the most part, this chapter focuses on the similarities and differences between the S-REF model and another recent multi-level model: Interacting Cognitive Subsystems (ICS: Teasdale & Barnard, 1993). The reason for comparing these two approaches is that several similarities appear to exist in the clinical implications derived from them. Moreover, both approaches have points of theoretical convergence in describing the roles of perseverative ruminatory processing and multiple levels of cognitive representation in disorder.

S-REF AND SCHEMA THEORY

As reviewed in Chapter 1, schema theory links emotional disorder to activation of dysfunctional beliefs held by the individual. These beliefs or schemas influence processing by directing attention to threat and introducing other forms of bias or distortion that maintain maladaptive beliefs and emotional disorder. Beliefs are represented in declarative form and concern themes of danger, vulnerability, loss, failure, etc. The occurrence of appraisals in the form of "negative automatic thoughts" in the stream of consciousness indicates the activation of underlying schemas.

The S-REF model is consistent with schema theory in as much as emotional disorder is considered to derive from the self-relevant knowledge base or beliefs. However, one of the unknowns of schema theory is the mechanism by which beliefs affect or control cognitive processing. In the S-REF model, the knowledge base consists partly of metacognitive knowledge that directs the activities of the individual's processing system. In particular, emotional disorder is associated with metacognitive knowledge that directs attention to threat and supports the use of ruminative strategies. Rather than selective attention emerging solely as an incidental or "automatic" result of schema activation, in the S-REF model attention to threat is largely a function of the person's motivated coping strategy, consisting of monitoring for threats. In addition, the use of active worry (rumination) as a processing strategy may further bias threat detection by lower-level processing.

In schema theory, knowledge (beliefs) is represented solely in declarative form, and there is no specified role of metacognitive knowledge. This causes difficulty in explaining the effects of knowledge on processing operations. It may be beneficial to consider knowledge in proceduralised form as adopted by the S-REF model, such that negative beliefs and appraisals like "I'm vulnerable" and "I'm boring", are the outputs of running particular processing plans.

The schema approach lacks an architecture for processing. There is no attempt to distinguish between voluntary and involuntary processing and there is no description of factors that contribute to the dynamics of cognitive control. By focusing predominantly on the content of appraisals and knowledge in declarative form, it is not specified how other multiple components of processing may be involved in the maintenance of psychological disorders. More specifically, it is not clear if disorder results predominantly from automatic or strategic attentional processes, and the involvement of metacognitive knowledge, self-regulatory goals and perseverative styles of processing are largely ignored. By characterising emotional disorder appraisals as rapid and telegraphic "negative automatic thoughts", schema theory fails adequately to describe and account for the perseverative nature of thinking in emotional disorder, which is better typified by worry or rumination. Moreover, several varieties of thought can be distinguished, and each may be related to emotional disorder in functionally different ways. The S-REF model avoids these problems because an architecture is specified and the role of strategic attentional processes is described in detail. Metacognitive knowledge (incorporating self-regulatory goals) is linked to disorder by the concept of coping, and perseverative thinking is considered central to disorder maintenance. Worry and rumination are viewed principally as coping strategies resulting from activation of metacognitive beliefs.

The schema concept itself has been criticised on a number of grounds. One problem is that when a new cluster of symptoms or disorder arises, it is possible to account for this by proposing the existence of another particular schema. There is a problem of circularity, in which any particular affective response can be attributed to a new schema that appears to represent the content of the patient's negative appraisals. On first sight it appears that this criticism can be levelled at the S-REF model, too; it is easy to attribute any specific feature of disorder, such as cognitive bias or worry, to whatever hypothetical plan (metacognitive knowledge) that seems to fit the data. However, this problem is avoided by proposing that a range of anxiety and depression effects can be explained by a specific pattern of cognitive-attentional responses, and thus the plan on which they draw. At a rudimentary level, disorder is generally identified with a plan and metacognitions that specify worry/rumination-based processing, monitoring for threat, negative appraisal of thinking and self-relevant goal-directed processing. Such a plan consists of self-knowledge in the metacognitive domain that specifies the advantages of worry and perseverative types of processing, but also appears to represent dysfunctional negative beliefs about thoughts such as beliefs about uncontrollabilty and danger. We saw in Chapter 3 how data from studies of metacognitive belief provide support for the proposition that a common set of positive and negative metacognitions and strategies are associated with a wide range of psychopathology indices.

In summary, the S-REF model is consistent with schema theory, but advances schema theory by combining aspects of cognitive architecture, levels of control of attention, and multiple process and metacognitive components of cognition with the individual's schema or knowledge base.

S-REF AND INTERACTING COGNITIVE SUBSYSTEMS (ICS)

Teasdale and Barnard (1993) have advanced a multi-level model of cognitive processing in depression aimed at overcoming some of the limitations of schema theory. In this model, qualitatively distinct types of information or mental codes are distinguished: sensory codes representing basic visual, acoustic and propreoceptive stimuli; intermediate codes representing recurrent patterns in sensory codes and object codes; propositional codes representing specific meanings; and, at the deepest level, implicational codes representing holistic and generic meanings. In ICS, only this deepest level of implicational codes is directly linked to emotion. The knowledge present in implicational codes can be viewed as mental models of experience. This knowledge is implicit, but explicit general knowledge can be derived from it (e.g. predictions, attributions, etc.). In ICS, emotional reactions occur when emotion-related schematic models are produced. Maintenance of depression relies on repeated production of depressive schematic models by the generation of self-perpetuating processing configurations. In this manner, it is suggested that "depressive interlock" is produced and this is experienced as a stream of negative automatic thoughts. Depressive interlock refers to a mode of processing in which resources are devoted to repetitive, rumination-like processing cycles directed at attaining personal goals that can be neither attained or relinquished. It is suggested that the ease with which interlock is maintained determines vulnerability to depression onset or relapse (Teasdale, Segal & Williams, 1995). In this model, other types of information, i.e. propositional information represented as negative thoughts, and the processing of bodily information can maintain depressive schematic models.

The ICS model appears to share some similarities with the S-REF perspective. The S-REF and ICS models have developed independently of each other and in parallel. Whilst the ICS perspective is intended to expand the conceptualisation of depression maintenance and of depression relapse, the S-REF model is more widely focused on general vulnerability to emotional disorders and was the first to place attentional bias/self-focused attention and metacognition in centre stage. More recently, these components have been discussed in ICS (Teasdale, 1999), but the main emphasis in ICS remains on levels of meaning and representation in depression.

Architectural considerations

The S-REF model consists of an architecture of three interacting levels of cognition rather than interactions between informational codes as specified in ICS. In contrast to ICS, the S-REF model views processing as a continuous interaction between three levels of cognition, namely self-beliefs, controlled processing and automatic processing. Whilst some highly learned activities are largely automatic, they still require monitoring and regulation by a supervisory system. In addition, automatic processes can be influenced by an input of attention. The contents of consciousness and focus of action at any one time is controlled by a combination of automatic and strategic processes. The S-REF can exert an influence on automatic processing by increasing the sensitivity of processing units for particular patterns of activity, as, for example, in deliberate attempts to increase hypervigilance for particular bodily sensations in hypochondriasis. Similarly, the activity of the strategic processing system can suppress the capture of attention by automatically generated intrusions, for example by diverting attention to other demanding processing operations. Because the S-REF model has a cognitive architecture, it can account for a wide range of cognitive phenomena associated with emotional disorders. It can account for attentional bias and performance deficits, and it can link thinking styles in emotional disorders with other concepts, such as emotional processing and the return of fear. In using multiple informational codes rather than levels of cognition, it is unclear in ICS how controlled and automatic processes dynamically interact with self-knowledge and can be shaped by appraisals and behaviour.

Limitations of implicational codes

The idea that emotional responses are linked to implicational codes is the most novel feature of the ICS model. Other aspects of the model, such as central processing resources and rumination (interlock), are already familiar features in cognitive accounts of emotional disorders. For example, repetitive processing cycles in depression have already been discussed in detail by Ingram (1984) and Nolen-Hoeksema (1991). Arguably, this aspect of the S-REF model is also not new, although in the S-REF model these components are seen as part of a general emotion disorder syndrome, rather than specifically being linked to depression. Moreover, both ICS and the S-REF model provide an account of mechanisms giving rise to rumination, which is less developed in these other models.

In the S-REF model, metacognition and attention are placed in centre stage, in contrast ICS places implicational meanings at centre stage. The contribution of ICS therefore depends on the usefulness or predictive power of the concept of implicational codes. In some respects, the implicational code hypothesis is an interesting attempt to deal with a number of well-known theoretical difficulties: (1) that dissociations appear to exist in therapy between an individual's intellectual and emotional beliefs; (2) that propositions do not necessarily generate emotion (Bower & Cohen, 1982); (3) that emotions may be generated from a range of stimuli including non-verbal cues and stimuli, of which the person has limited awareness; and (4) that emotions may be difficult to convey to others in propositional form. In the S-REF model, these phenomena are explained by the concept of procedural knowledge stored in memory. This knowledge is generic and not directly verbally expressible. Procedural knowledge comprises personally significant goals, so that when it is activated the knowledge represents a plan. Emotion may be generated irrespective of whether or not running this plan happens to produce explicit declarative beliefs. Thus, a "felt sense" or emotion can occur even though the knowledge associated with this emotion may not be directly expressible in propositional form. Emotion is not directly derived from self-relevant procedural knowledge, but it is an output of the processing activity of the S-REF, which indicates the current status of the plan for processing, as in Oatley and Johnson-Laird's (1987) model. Plan status is computed from prior knowledge and current circumstances, although in familiar situations appraisal of plan status may be rapidly accomplished. Depression is generated in the S-REF model by the failure of a personally important plan rather than by production of a "depressive schematic model", as in ICS. In some cases, consciously accessible propositional information, such as "I will never accomplish anything", may be sufficient to lead to an appraisal which generates depression. In other cases, the person may be unaware of the computations contributing to the appraisal.

One of the difficulties in the ICS model is circularity in the implicational code hypothesis. The definition of depressogenic implicational codes is circular in that they can only be identified through the occurrence of their defining features, such as limited reportability, together with actual symptoms of depression, such as negative emotions and beliefs. Teasdale et al. (1995, p. 29), state that "depressogenic schematic models produce depressive emotional reactions . . ." thus, we can identify a schematic model as depressogenic only because it elicits depressive emotional reactions. The S-REF model avoids this type of circularity because emotional dysfunction is not an identifying feature of the occurrence of maladaptive plans for processing and the antecedents of emotion are specified in greater cognitive-attentional detail.

Perhaps one of the greatest limitations of the implicational code concept is difficulty in defining precisely what it means and hence locating this in information processing. The implicational subsystem appears to be like the other subsystems identified in the ICS model in having its own memory store and processing operations. However, no experimental evidence is provided to indicate how these storage and processing functions may be distinguished from those related to other codes. Implicational codes have a small number of features that appear to discriminate them from other codes. More specifically, they convey meaning that is "holistic and implicit". However, it is unclear what "holism" and "implicitness" are and what their roles are in generating emotion. Unfortunately, the two properties concerned "holism" and "implicitness", are defined mainly by exclusion. Both properties are inferred from the person's inability to express implicational codes propositionally or in single sentences. However, this criterion is too weak. There are several reasons why expressing cognitions in propositional form is impaired. For example, people are frequently unable to report on their cognitive processes (e.g. Nisbett & Wilson, 1977). Moreover, other processes, such as cognitive and emotional avoidance and lack of metacognitive awareness, may provide barriers to expressing emotion-related knowledge in propositional form.

Dynamics of cognitive control

Unlike ICS, the S-REF model specifies how voluntary and involuntary processing influence the contents of consciousness and action at any one time. The ICS approach says little about the dynamics of control of attention and cognition. Whilst voluntary control of processing appears to be equated with a "central engine" supporting controlled processing, the central engine is not described in detail. The central engine is deemed to be capacity-limited, but capacity limitation and voluntary control are logically distinct. The model does not represent levels and shifts in levels of control that are characteristic of information processing (see Norman & Shallice, 1985). The S-REF model therefore possesses a detailed architecture that is lacking in the ICS model. In the S-REF model, control of cognition frequently shifts between executive and lower-level processing to fulfil goals which then allow control to be returned predominantly to the lower level of control. Emotional disorder is associated with a loss of this flexibility of control, which in the S-REF model is seen as essential for normal adaptation.

The S-REF model identifies several other failures of flexibility of control of processing in addition to the depressive cycle identified by Teasdale and Barnard (1993), Ingram (1984), and Nolan-Hoeksema (1991). Wells and Matthews (1994), describe:

1. An anxiety-related perception–action cycle consisting of threat monitoring, in which individuals maintain attention on threat cues— a strategy which in turn increases stress sensitivity.
2. A cycle of monitoring for somatic cues characteristic of panic disorder.
3. A cycle of monitoring for negative thoughts, which may generate disorders characterised by intrusive thoughts, e.g. obsessive-compulsive disorder.
4. Cycles of maladaptive behaviour and coping that prevent belief change.

Simplistic view of self-awareness

Teasdale (1999) relates three modes of central engine processing to three distinct clinically recognisable modes in which patients process emotion-related material. In one mode (mindless emoting), individuals are immersed in and identify with emotional reactions with little self-awareness, internal exploration or reflection. In another mode, emotional processing corresponds to "conceptualising/doing", in which awareness is dominated by relatively impersonal detached thoughts about the self or emotion (as objects). Depressive interlock is characterised by this mode of thinking about the self, about depression, and about its causes and consequences. A third mode of processing, which corresponds to "mindful experiencing/being there", is an integrated cognitive affective inner exploration and use of feelings and felt senses as a guide to problem solution and a non-evaluative awareness of subjective self-experience. The mindful experiencing mode is equated with good psychological/therapeutic outcomes and one of the aims of therapy is to help individuals learn skills to disengage central engine modes that support depressive interlock. This means helping individuals learn skills to enter mindful experiencing mode. However, the description of "mindful experiencing" indicates that, at least partially, it comprises the use of a felt sense and inner exploration to guide problem solving and resolution. This seems to resemble reasoning processes in psychological disorder. In particular, we have seen in the S-REF model that disorder is associated with inner self-processing, and use of a felt sense to guide processing and behaviour. This type of processing may be maladaptive because it fails to revise the individual's knowledge base and lead to the production of more appropriate processing routines. Moreover, feeling states are not necessarily good indicators of how close the individual is to achieving important personal goals or problem-solving. For instance, social phobics use a felt sense or image of the self to determine how they think they appear to others (Clark & Wells, 1995; Wells, Clark & Ahmad, 1998; Hackman, Suraway & Clark, 1998; Wells & Papageorgiou, 1999). Similarly, some GAD patients and obsessionals use a "felt sense" as a stop signal for worry or rituals. ICS seems to be advocating the development of a "mindful" mode of processing in therapy that resembles some parameters of dysfunctional processing. This problem most probably arises because the ICS prescription for treatment is not derived specifically from a detailed self-regulatory model, but represents a fusion of theory with meditation and mindfulness philosophy and practices (e.g. Kabat-Zinn, 1990).

By equating a healthier mode of mind with greater self-awareness and experiencing of the present moment, there is a failure to adequately address the data supporting a link between heightened self-awareness and disorders such as depression (e.g. Ingram, 1990). ICS has adopted the Buddhist notion that self-awareness and present-moment experiencing are positive experiences. The S-REF model, backed up by an extensive literature on self-awareness, clearly indicates that heightened self-awareness is a non-specific feature of emotional disorders. The concept of self-attention/awareness requires a more sophisticated treatment than that provided by ICS, so that the precise components of self-awareness involved in disorder maintenance *and* disorder resolution can be specified. In the S-REF model, self-attention is problematic when it is inflexible and adhesive, and when it depletes resources necessary for belief change or diverts resources away from processing information that could modify maladaptive beliefs. Self-awareness is helpful for disorder resolution when it can be used flexibly to process disorder-related information in a detached way without triggering worry or rumination (typically in metacognitive mode).

Modifying problematic processing modes

The construction of treatments that lead to lasting modification of problematic processing modes requires a specification of how maladaptive modes may be replaced. The prescription derived from ICS is to teach distraction from depressive thoughts by focusing on one's breath and on the here and now (teaching mindfulness) in a meditative way. This appears too simplistic, as it is not clear how such processing will lead to replacement strategies or beliefs. In contrast, in the S-REF model it is important to generate replacement strategies and to increase the person's ability to switch between stimulus-driven and executive control of processing appropriately in response to external demands. The ICS model offers little guidance on how to ensure that replacement strategies endure over time and over-ride ruminative strategies. The S-REF model is more explicit about the roles of knowledge or beliefs in long-term memory and more specific about the roles of on-line self-relevant processing, resource limitations and interactions between involuntary and voluntary levels of cognition.

Worry/rumination cycles

In the S-REF model, self-focused processing of an inflexible and perseverative type (active worry) is problematic for emotional self-regulation. Similarly, in ICS, depressive interlock which resembles this type of processing is problematic. Both models agree that perseverative self-focused processing can deplete processing resources, can maintain disorder and that it is desirable to shift out of this processing. The S-REF model further emphasises that loss of attentional resources due to ruminative processing may interfere with the processing of belief-incongruent information. Unlike ICS, the S-REF model indicates how perseverative processing (active worry/rumination), develops and may be modified. Generic metacognitive beliefs about the advantages of worry/rumination, about thought control and the personal significance of intruding thoughts are of special importance, so that metacognitive knowledge is a key vulnerability factor in emotional disorders. Emotional disorder may develop when social, somatic or environmental cues generate intrusions that trigger metacognitive plans. In summary, the S-REF model and ICS have different accounts of the generation of streams of negative thinking in psychological disorder. In the S-REF these streams are generated on-line under the influence of metacognitive knowledge and plans and typically represent strategies aimed at coping and eliminating self-discrepancies. In ICS, these streams of thinking are generated by continuing interactions between the propositional and implicational sub-systems, i.e. the central engine of cognition. However, the mechanisms by which this reciprocal interaction between types of meaning maintains streams of negative thought is vague. Explanation is further compounded by the difficulties in defining the meaning of implicational codes. Processing code, as a concept, as presently defined does not lead to understanding the architecture underlying cognitive processing. In contrast to the view that streams of negative thought are produced by interactions between codes, the S-REF model hypothesises that streams of negative automatic thoughts (i.e. active worry or rumination), are the consequences of activating maladaptive meta cognitive knowledge (beliefs) about the usefulness or desirability of such strategies in particular circumstances. Moreover, in accessing this type of knowledge the individual is accessing a plan for guiding cognitive processing which is executed and modified on-line in particular situations. The use of worry and rumination as processing strategies may be viewed as one form of coping. The concept of coping links the activity of the individual's on-line processing in the behavioural and cognitive domains to the store of self-knowledge or beliefs in long-term memory. Metacognition and plans for processing do not figure in ICS.

Interruption of worry cycles

The S-REF model suggests a variety of ways in which the processing cycle may be interrupted. Cues which initiate S-REF activity may be removed (as in relaxation therapies that reduce arousal cues). Activation of alternative plans through external cues may be elicited (as in distraction therapies) or cyclical maladaptive processing may be interrupted by active coping efforts (problem-solving) and slow effortful modification of knowledge that takes place in cognitive restructuring. It has been proposed that establishment of "detached mindfulness" (Wells & Matthews, 1994) may be a useful prerequisite for interrupting cyclical and problematic modes of self-focused processing. This is a metacognitive processing mode in which thoughts are viewed as events that do not necessitate continued personal involvement. However, mindfulness in the meditation sense, as suggested in the ICS analysis, borrows from Buddhist tradition and consists of focusing on one's breath as an anchor for the "here and now" and non-evaluative processing. It is not apparent how such self-attentional exercises could reduce heightened or excessive self-consciousness—a feature of the maladaptive cognitive-attentional syndrome in psychological disorder. Whilst this may be less of a problem in depression, emotional disorders involving hypervigilance for bodily sensations may be less likely to respond to this type of self-focused manipulation as a means of establishing alternative processing strategies.

The choice of a self-focused distraction strategy in ICS (mindfulness meditation) may shift individuals away from processing negative self-relevant material but it maintains self-regulatory executive functioning. It is likely that under some circumstances other strategies for processing could be more beneficial for performance. For instance, in test or performance anxiety, external attentional strategies that enhance performance and/or focus attention on disconfirmatory experiences are more likely to be beneficial for generating alternative and more positive beliefs.

A central aim of S-REF treatment that is not directly specified by ICS is to increase control over processing and reduce self-focus of attention. Residual self-focus/inflexibility is a marker of vulnerability to relapse. Mindfulness meditation may alter the content of self-attention but does not necessarily influence the intensity of self-focus or increase the metacognitive control of attention. In contrast, as we will see in Part II of this book, a range of attentional strategies have been designed within the context of the S-REF model of attention processes that aim to reduce self-focus and increase the metacognitive control of processing.

COMPARATIVE TREATMENT IMPLICATIONS OF S-REF VERSUS ICS

In this section, treatment implications of the S-REF and ICS approaches are compared. First, the respective goals of treatment are considered, and in a subsequent section specific means of achieving these goals are contrasted.

Treatment goals

A central goal of psychological treatment based on ICS is the replacement of depressogenic implicational schematic models. How this is achieved depends on the mechanism maintaining the depressogenic model in each case. For instance, when this is persistent aversive environmental factors, some form of problem-solving may be appropriate. When this is associated with relationship difficulties, marital therapy may be effective. However, when the schematic model depends on the establishment of depressive interlock, the central aim of such interventions should be to interrupt resources that maintain depressive interlock. This may involve establishing an alternative processing configuration that competes for the same resources as interlock, thereby disrupting it. However, effects of distraction are likely to be short-lived and the more enduring alleviation of depression depends on the establishment of non-depressogenic schematic models. This might be achieved by extended processing on topics unrelated to depression. However, this may be difficult to sustain because it requires effortful controlled processing. The schematic models that maintain depression represent dimensions of aversiveness, uncontrollability and anticipated persistence of the depressed emotional state. Thus, vicious cycles of depression about depression are involved in problem maintenance. It is suggested that change in schematic models maintaining depression about depression is a central process in many effective psychological treatments. Since the implicational subsystem has its own memory store, Teasdale and Barnard (1993) suggest that in therapy it may be possible to exploit memory records that modify schematic models. An example would be to psyche oneself up to tackle a difficult task by accessing the "feel" of a previous experience of mastery. More recently, Teasdale et al. (1995) have advocated the adaptation of mindfulness-based meditation, a stress reduction programme, for preventing depressive relapse.

Several of the treatment implications of ICS correspond to the implications derived from the S-REF model. The goal of therapy based on the S-REF perspective, like ICS, is to generate replacement modes of processing. In the S-REF model this is conceptualised as developing new processing configurations that promote the acquisition of replacement self-knowledge, which subsequently guide information processing in problematic situations. This is a more specific and detailed specification than that offered by ICS with its stated aim of modifying implicational meaning and depressogenic schematic models, both of which are difficult to define and to falsify experimentally. The specification of ICS in terms of levels of codes, rather than in terms of a detailed architecture, limits the specific design of cognitive attentional strategies in treatment. Both the ICS and S-REF model advocate the necessity to block rumination. Treatment based on the S-REF model suggests that patients should be encouraged to develop "detached mindfulness", a metacognitive state in which they are aware of their thoughts but can observe them without entering into or triggering full-blown rumination and elaborative appraisal. Detached mindfulness should then be followed by attentional and behavioural strategies that support disconfirmatory processing. Detached mindfulness differs from the ICS concept of mindfulness, which is merely awareness of the "here and now" without specific reference to disconfirmatory processing or increasing control over attention allocation.

The distinction in the S-REF model between two types of belief or self-knowledge (declarative and procedural/plans) is significant for the design of treatment strategies, as it suggests that the metacognitive plans supporting processing are as important as the content of declarative knowledge about the self in emotional dysfunction. A central goal of S-REF-based treatment is modification of the knowledge (plans) that guide processing. Wells and Matthews (1994) advocate the use of "metacognitive profiling" (see Chapter 7), in which patients' processing routines are examined in detail during experiences of anxiety and depression. Those routines that support dysfunctional knowledge, or are likely to promote reinstatement of subsequent dysfunctional knowledge, are identified and cognitive and behavioural components are modified to facilitate disconfirmatory processing and reduce the likelihood of relapse. In the S-REF treatment framework, it is helpful for patients to repeatedly practise alternative processing strategies in order to strengthen new plans for processing.

One of the goals of ICS-based treatment is to shift people away from thinking that their models of themselves and the world are a reflection of reality and to generate the model that their problem is one of thinking. This is similar to the shift from an object to metcognitive mode in the S-REF. However, the ICS prescription does not offer a detailed formulation of the constituents of an alternative metacognitive mode or model that are necessary for rewriting maladaptive beliefs. Merely knowing that one has a problem with thinking does not equip one with the knowledge or ability to change thinking. Thus, the notion that a shift in a model of reality is important for therapeutic effectiveness, as expressed in the ICS framework, is important but is likely to have limited power in restructuring maladaptive self-knowledge. In the S-REF, this problem is resolved by delineating the essential components of the metacognitive mode. This takes us beyond socialising patients to the idea that thoughts don't reflect reality, and has a goal of activating metacognitions, appraisal and behavioural strategies directed at changing knowledge.

Specific strategies: mindfulness training and attention training

Teasdale et al. (1995) suggest the use of mindfulness training to overcome depressive interlock. This strategy involves disengagement of appraisals of stimuli or cognition in order to block ruminative thinking about one's situation. Mindfulness training is a meditative procedure based on the programme of Kabat-Zinn (1990), involving focusing attention on breathing and letting go of thoughts as they occur, followed by redeployment of attention on breathing. In everyday practice, focusing on breathing is used as an anchor for bringing attention back to the "here and now" whenever attention is diverted to streams of thought or general lack of awareness. It is argued that this procedure, when combined with more traditional cognitive therapy, should lead patients to alternative models of their problem (i.e. that the problem is one of mental events rather than realities). Building on this, Segal, Teasdale & Williams (cited in Teasdale, 1999) have more recently developed mindfulness-based cognitive therapy. The mindfulness-based cognitive therapy programme combines mindfulness meditation with aspects of cognitive therapy for depression, explicitly designed to foster a de-centred relationship to negative thoughts (thoughts aren't facts). Techniques that are designed to change belief in specific negative thoughts or assumptions are not included. The programme is designed for patients who have recovered from recurrent major depression who wish to learn skills to reduce relapse. Initial mindfulness training involves daily 45 minute exercises guided by tape-recorded instructions, in which attention is intentionally deployed to specific parts of the body in succession. Subsequently, exercises focus on directing awareness on breathing. In the course of the exercise, the patient's mind inevitably wanders away from the focus on the breath or body to streams of thoughts or feelings. These occasions are to be recognised and welcomed as opportunities to become mindful of the movements of the mind and of the contents to which attention is drawn. After briefly acknowledging these contents, attention should be gently returned to focus on the breath.

The S-REF also supports the use of strategies that facilitate a disengagement from negative thoughts and symptoms. This is conceptualised as training in alternative plans for dealing with threat. Moreover, such procedures can interrupt unhelpful strategies characterised by worry and rumination. Rather than training merely in greater awareness of the here and now, as specified in mindfulness training, the S-REF model underscores the importance of also working on reducing excessive and uncontrollable self-focused attention. For this purpose, Wells (1990) developed an Attention Training Treatment (ATT) designed to modify dimensions of attention considered to be important in the maintenance of emotional vulnerability. Attention training, as we will see in Chapter 9, is based on the principle that intense and adhesive self attention contributes to maintenance of anxiety and other disorders and represents an emotional vulnerability factor. Attention training involves externally-focused auditory attention exercises requiring progressively greater involvement of attentional resources. It consists of training in metacognitive skills of selective attention, attention shifting and divided attention. By modifying attention with methods such as AT, it is argued that it should be possible to disengage the influence of dysfunctional self-beliefs (metacognitions) and interrupt perseverative processing cycles. This should increase capacity available for disconfirmatory processing and also lay the foundations for strengthening metacognitive plans for the control of attention. Both the S-REF and ICS models support the use of attentional control strategies. However, the ICS prescription of meditation offers a means of controlling the content of conscious cognition but does not explicitly aim to modify higher-order cognitive factors, such as the metacognitive attentional control plans that drive dysfunctional processing.

SUMMARY AND CONCLUSIONS

Treatment implications based on ICS and the S-REF clearly have a number of overlaps, but key differences also exist. Both ICS and the S-REF attempt to overcome limitations of schema theory from different conceptual frameworks. Several limitations also appear to exist in ICS. These include definitional problems with implicational codes; circularity, in that implicational codes can only be identified with the occurrence of depression; lack of a processing architecture in which to locate levels of control of processing; little consideration of metacognition; and a simplistic view of self-awareness and mindfulness.

As illustrated in this chapter, some of the treatment specifications of the S-REF model appear similar to those proposed by Teasdale et al. (1995). The key similarities can be summarised as follows:

1. Both approaches advocate focusing on cognitive representations/processes other than stimulus-based propositions or declarative knowledge.
2. Both models identify a maladaptive processing configuration, but with slightly different specifications and levels of detail. Both identify problems with recurrent patterns of negative thinking, i.e. rumination/active worry.
3. The models concur that individuals should develop alternative mental models (beliefs, knowledge) about their experience.
4. There is agreement that strategies that suspend ruminative-based processing can be used beneficially in treatment.
5. Both models point to the use of attentional control training, although the nature of this training differs in several respects.
6. The models agree that an aim of treatment should be the establishment of a higher level of meta-awareness, i.e. an ability to relate to thoughts as events rather than facts. However, the models differ in

the suggestions of how this might be achieved or what precisely this should consist of.

The differences between the ICS and S-REF treatment specifications can be summarised as follows:

1. The S-REF treatment advocates the use of attention training exercises that disrupt perseverative negative processing, reduce self-attention and increase the flexible control of attention. The ICS prescription similarly aims to disrupt perseverative processing, but by focusing more on the here and now in a way that does not necessarily aim to strengthen attentional control processes or reduce general self-focused attention tendencies.

2. Attentional, metacognitive and behavioural strategies are advocated by the S-REF model that are explicitly directed at modifying dysfunctional beliefs. This component appears not to have been developed in the ICS treatment prescription.

3. In specifying two distinct forms of self-belief (declarative and procedural/plans), the S-REF approach directs the clinician to examining basic processing characteristics activated in distressing circumstances that contribute to the establishment of the cognitive-attentional syndrome, a component of which is prolonged worry or rumination. The ICS perspective says little about dimensions of self-belief and their contribution to the development or maintenance of maladaptive modes of processing.

4. The S-REF model offers implications, not only on what should be done in therapy but also on how cognitive change may be achieved, that are different from ICS. More specifically, the S-REF treatment suggests that it is essential to manage the patient's internal processing in a way that facilitates unambiguous disconfirmation of negative beliefs, leads to the development of replacement processing routines, and modifies dysfunctional non-metacognitive and metacognitive knowledge.

5. Goals for processing should be specified clearly, and unrealistic and counter-productive goals modified in S-REF based treatments. Thus far, the role of goals and the necessity to modify them have not featured predominantly in the ICS treatment prescription.

6. The identification of automatic and strategic levels of processing, and the concept of proceduralisation of knowledge in the S-REF, imply that repeated practice of alternative attentional and processing strategies in problematic situations is required in order to develop new plans for processing. However, ICS has not explained how alternative mental models or modes might be developed that over-ride dysfunctional processing operations (plans).

PART II

CLINICAL APPLICATIONS

Chapter 6

METACOGNITIVE FOCUSED THERAPY: BASIC CONSTRUCTS

Cognitive therapy based on schema theory is proving to be one of the most effective approaches to a range of psychological disorders, such as panic disorder, social phobia, depression and generalized anxiety. Although the best treatments in this tradition are theory-based, general schema theory provides few specific pointers on how cognitive-affective change may be best accomplished in treatment. Schema theory implies that we should modify the individual's beliefs and appraisals, which includes intervening at the level of cycles of behaviour that maintain maladaptive cognition. However, the model does not directly generate a wide range of predictions concerning *how* cognitive change may be facilitated. In order to do this we require a model that is based on a discrete cognitive architecture and specifies the dynamic and multi-component aspects of processing that are involved in disorder. In particular, we should concern ourselves not only with the content of cognition but also the role that beliefs have on processing style, attentional factors such as attentional bias, the control of cognition, and transient load-dependent limitations in processing. Above all, we should be attempting to find an answer in therapy to questions about self-regulation, such as "What is the role of beliefs in maintaining the stability of maladaptive processing in each case?" An aim should be to develop cognitive therapy in a way that exploits the capacity of the human information processing system to modify its own organisation and control processes.

These objectives are not beyond reach if we have models of psychological disorder that are based on a cognitive architecture, specify the dynamic disturbances that are involved in disorder, provide a framework for conceptualising cognitive change processes, and generally supply a model of the maintenance of maladaptive cognitions. In this chapter, the clinical implications of the S-REF model are presented with a view to advancing the conceptual and technique base of cognitive therapy practice. Many of the procedures that are already used in cognitive therapy are supported by the S-REF analysis, although in some instances the model suggests particular revisions to existing procedures.

A central concept in the S-REF approach is that maintenance of emotional disorder results from a wider range of information-processing functions than those that have been attributed to "schema activation" in cognitive therapy. These information-processing functions include attentional processes, self-regulatory goal states, metacognition and modes of processing. Cognition is explicitly viewed as dynamic rather than static, and is modifiable by behavioural and cognitive responses, the effectiveness of which are modulated by particular operating characteristics of the processing system.

A further elaboration provided by the S-REF model is that the processing operations associated with the occurrence of depressive and anxious negative thoughts and beliefs are linked to metacognitive knowledge and plans, and attempts to modify the content of thought alone, by positive thinking for instance, may not be sufficient to change underlying metacognitions and their associated processing operations. For example, individuals with generalized anxiety disorder (GAD) present with multiple worries which change in content. Addressing the content of fluctuating worries does not modify the underlying processing characteristics that repeatedly generate the pattern of oscillating worries. We will see in Chapter 10 how a particular model of GAD (Wells, 1995, 1997), which is grounded in S-REF principles, aims to conceptualise and modify underlying metacognitive characteristics.

GENERAL TREATMENT PRINCIPLES

The S-REF model, like schema theory, assumes that we should attempt to modify the patient's maladaptive knowledge base by generating and facilitating the acquisition of replacement self-knowledge. To accomplish this we need to explore and understand the knowledge and self-regulatory processes that are linked to disorder maintenance. The S-REF model implies that we should consider beliefs in psychological disorder as multidimensional. On one level, beliefs can be viewed as declarative knowledge about the self and world, and on another level as metacognitions that guide processing. Two types of belief are important in disorder maintenance: general non-metacognitive beliefs (e.g. "The world is a dangerous place"), and metacognitive beliefs (e.g. "Worrying helps me cope"; "Having bad thoughts can make bad things happen"). Metacognitive beliefs or knowledge have two components, a declarative component as expressed above, and also a procedural component. Procedural metacognitions are plans that control the processing system and vary in their accessibility to verbal report. In some instances, this type of knowledge can be marked by the presence of instrumental assumptions concerning the effects of particular cognitive coping responses (e.g. "If I worry about my health, I'll be safe"; "If I think of the worst that can happen, I won't be taken by surprise"; "I must be vigilant or I could be attacked"; "the world is bad—if I don't ruminate about it I am out of touch"). In each case, metacognitions of this type are linked to plans that direct the controlled processing system in activities such as worry, rumination, hypervigilance and memory search, etc.

It follows from the S-REF analysis of beliefs that it is necessary in assessment and treatment to target and restructure maladaptive metacognitions in addition to the more general beliefs that are a focus in traditional cognitive-behavioural therapy (CBT). The plans or knowledge that we are interested in from the clinical standpoint are those that are recurrently activated in situations that the individual experiences as problematic. In these situations maladaptive metacognitive plans can be inferred from the exploration of attentional strategies, behaviours and the nature of appraisals that are implemented.

Cognitive therapy based on the S-REF model is one in which the individual is encouraged to modify belief or self-knowledge in long-term memory. According to this model, this can be more effectively accomplished if therapists are sensitive to the interacting and dynamic aspects of processing which can be used to facilitate belief change. Since the nature of the S-REF processing configuration is responsible for maintaining emotional disorder and effecting metacognitive change in self-knowledge, the S-REF has to be used in a particular way to restructure self-knowledge. Use of the S-REF to restructure self-knowledge comprises activation of a metacognitive mode and, within this mode, utilisation of a processing configuration that directs cognitive resources to the disconfirmation of existing knowledge and the construction of replacement self-knowledge. If a distressed individual's S-REF is dominated by the object mode, it is unlikely that disconfirmatory experiences will modify self-knowledge. An aim of metacognitive therapy should be to present the setting conditions under which an active metacognitive mode can be established within the S-REF. The next step is to reduce perseverative processing, control the allocation of cognitive resources, and manipulate coping behaviours in a way that promotes the restructuring of maladaptive self-knowledge. The shifting from object mode to metacognitive mode is equivalent to helping the patient construct an alternative model of his/ her experience. Rather than merely eroding belief, individuals should be assisted in acquiring or strengthening a general-purpose metacognitive plan and skill that can be used as a resource for the modification of cognition.

COGNITIVE AND BEHAVIOURAL RESPONSES CHANGE COGNITION

A key tenet of the present theory is that specific effortful processing strategies can lead to changes in cognition, both at the level of stored self-knowledge and in the strengthening or weakening of more reflexive and automatic processing activities. However, psychological disorder is associated with processing configurations and coping behaviours which "lock" the individual into maladaptive emotional experiences that fail to restructure self-knowledge and do not lead to the acquisition of alternative coping responses (e.g. new attentional responses, styles of appraisal, and behavioural strategies). A marker for the activation of maladaptive processing is heightened self-focused attention and perseverative forms of appraisal and coping, such as active worry or rumination, and threat monitoring. In order to re-write self-knowledge and the plans for processing, it is important that the S-REF configuration is active, that is, the individual should be experiencing negative affect and/or showing signs of the cognitive attentional syndrome outlined above. Under these circumstances, therapy should proceed to train the patient in the execution of alternative attentional, ideational and coping strategies that restructure maladaptive self-knowledge. Only if these strategies are practised under typical threat conditions will the patient be able to override dysfunctional processing and construct new plans for guiding attention, emotion and behaviour in future encounters with threat. Thus, the activities of the limited capacity S-REF configuration have to be managed in a way that leads to changes in multiple components of the emotional response. This requires therapist skill, as the activities of the S-REF must be prioritised or time-shared in a way that produces change in beliefs, metacognitive plans and new coping strategies, in conjunction with a workable level of affective experience.

STRESS MANAGEMENT STRATEGIES

CBTs have tended to emphasise the control or management of particular symptoms, such as anxiety responses, and the questioning or interrogating of negative appraisals (automatic thoughts). Challenging thoughts, generating rational responses and using anxiety control strategies such as relaxation require considerable attentional resources, and do not necessarily modify dysfunctional beliefs or facilitate optimal control over S-REF function. However, training in relaxation skills may in some circumstances provide new strategies for responding to threat. In the S-REF analysis, these strategies have several potentially useful effects of: (1) reducing worry/perseverative processing; (2) reducing arousal, thereby freeing up valuable processing resources; (3) providing alternative online strategies for guiding processing in stressful situations; (4) weakening the activity of lower-level processing that generates intrusions of body-state and other information. Thus, relaxation techniques may provide a means of disrupting maladaptive S-REF perseveration and of influencing plan development and lower-level processing. However, different forms of relaxation may produce different effects and the conditions under which relaxation is applied are likely to influence its effect on cognition. In particular, the mode of processing activated during relaxation will be important. If relaxation is practised in object mode, in which the individual has little meta-awareness and personal goals are to escape from or reduce non-existent threat, relaxation may prevent the individual from developing metacognitive skills and will not unambiguously modify negative beliefs about threat, particularly if threat is attributed to arousal symptoms.

Relaxation effects may be useful when such procedures inherently strengthen a metacognitive processing mode. Some forms of meditation procedure may be particularly prone to activate and strengthen a metacognitive mode of processing. However, establishing a metacognitive mode is insufficient to produce changes in processing necessary to over-ride the maladaptive cognitive-attentional syndrome in emotional disorder. More specifically, patients should learn new plans that guide attention to disconfirmatory experiences, increase the control over attention, and reduce self-focused processing in stressful situations. A limitation and potential problem with relaxation and meditation procedures is that they increase self-focused processing and do not aim to increase the control over processing. In some situations, self-focused procedures of this kind may run the risk of contributing to the maladaptive cognitive-attentional syndrome. An alternative technique that avoids some of these limitations is to train patients in direct attentional control. Attentional procedures are discussed in Chapter 9.

Whilst some forms of relaxation may facilitate meta-awareness and control, an important therapeutic consideration concerns the effect of such procedures on beliefs. In particular, relaxation does not typically convey unambiguous information that contradicts negative beliefs. For example, in disorders where anxiety and distress is maintained by the belief that anxiety is dangerous (i.e. there is a fear-of-fear component), relaxation does not present evidence that may be used to revise this knowledge. It is more likely that under some setting conditions, stress management strategies convey the idea that anxiety *is* dangerous and *should* be controlled. Similarly, if a patient fears loss of control due to anxiety, the teaching of control skills may increase the person's belief in self-control, but it does not lead to evidence that anxiety does not lead to loss of control. A potential danger is that some control and coping strategies, whilst they may lead to reductions in affect, do not present the conditions necessary for belief change. Some strategies may become additional coping behaviours that compromise revision of beliefs. The non-occurrence of catastrophe can be attributed to use of the coping strategy, and the individual therefore fails to discover that general beliefs about catastrophe are inaccurate. The reduction of emotional arousal through self-control strategies can potentially present a further problem for the modification of self-knowledge if it removes internal triggering conditions for the activation of negative beliefs. Thus, maladaptive beliefs and plans may remain unmodified and dormant, awaiting subsequent activation.

DEVELOPING METACOGNITIVE CONTROL

Metacognitive therapy comprises enabling distressed individuals to relate to their thoughts in a different way. This calls for the instatement of a metacognitive mode, increased flexible control over attention, and an ability to disengage from ruminative (active worry) processing. Wells and Matthews (1994, 1996) have suggested that the establishment of "detached mindfulness" will be a useful way of achieving these aims. This is a metacognitive detachment from thoughts while maintaining objective awareness of them. Here, individuals are encouraged to disengage further processing and behaviours from intrusions (thoughts, symptoms, etc.) and to merely observe such events over time. Such strategies are intended to facilitate: (1) the development of a metacognitive mode; (2) control over the selection of strategies for appraisal; (3) the development of new plans for regulating S-REF activity; and (4) the freeing-up of resources for disconfirmatory processing and the modification of beliefs. This type of detached mindful processing may be useful in preventing full S-REF activation and may be developed as an adaptive coping strategy which can be used to facilitate disconfirmatory processing. That is, patients are first encouraged to disengage from continued processing of intrusions, and this is followed by redirection of attention to disconfirmatory information and behaviours. Consistent with the idea that this type of processing may be beneficial, Roger, Jarvis and Najarian (1993) demonstrated that detached processing, which involves not taking things personally, feeling clear-headed about situations, deciding it's useless to get upset and just getting on with things, is an empirically distinct mode of coping which may be more adaptive than emotional coping and avoidance.

As discussed in the previous chapter, Teasdale and colleagues (e.g.Teasdale, 1999) have used mindfulness meditation techniques as prevention strategies for depressive relapse. Such a strategy, which involves focusing on breathing, counting breaths and reacting to thoughts as events appears to be effective in preventing relapse in individuals with recurrent depression. However, the analysis provided by the S-REF model suggests that the way in which mindfulness is accomplished may be an important determinant of its general effectiveness and may determine for whom it is specifically effective. The model suggests that mindful procedures will be most effective if they strengthen alternative plans for dealing with thoughts (e.g. detached mindfulness), increase the flexible control over attention, interrupt rumination, and reduce self-focused attention tendencies. The danger is that some procedures, such as meditation-based strategies involving heightened body-focused attention, could strengthen self-focused processing tendencies and thus maintain or strengthen individual susceptibility to S-REF activation. Particular individuals may be more susceptible to these negative effects. Individuals whose S-REF processing is characterised by hypervigilance for bodily sensations and catastrophic misinterpretation of such sensations may not benefit, because the procedure strengthens hypervigilance and does not contain information that can correct faulty catastrophising appraisals. For example, the depressive who misinterprets symptoms of lethargy as a sign that he/she is "not coping", and the panic patient who misinterprets a racing heart as sign of an imminent heart attack, may benefit less than individuals who do not show bodily hypervigilance. More generally, the model would predict differences in response to self-focus procedures, depending on the chronicity of the problem. For individuals who have experienced only one episode of anxiety or depression, self-focusing procedures may generally run the risk of strengthening the S-REF configuration, whilst for individuals with chronic problems or multiple episodes of disorder, it is likely that the S-REF configuration is more inflexible and hypervalent. Therefore, it is less likely that self-focused procedures will be strengthened, and such individuals may obtain some benefit from the strengthening of the metacognitive mode provided by these techniques. Overall, the S-REF model implies that mindful procedures that rely on non-self-focused strategies and achieve attentional control may be particularly useful in the general treatment of a range of disorders. However, in the present analysis, mindfulness procedures are seen only as a prerequisite to, or component of, knowledge modification.

A DYNAMIC VIEW OF COGNITIVE-BEHAVIOURAL MODIFICATION

The S-REF model implies that we should view cognitive disturbance in psychological disorder in a dynamic rather than a static way. Traditional cognitive therapy approaches focus on disconfirming the content of patients' beliefs and appraisals through asking questions such as: "What is your evidence for believing that? . . ."; "What is your counter-evidence?"; "What type of thinking error can you identify in that thought/appraisal?"; "What is another way of looking at the situation?", etc. These questions predominantly question the content of cognition and may be seen as merely asking the patient to make a logical (metacognitive) appraisal of his/her belief. These questions do not elucidate the nature of the individual's processing and coping operations that maintain dysfunctional knowledge. Moreover, they do not explicitly change dynamic aspects of processing (and the plan), such as selective attention, threat monitoring, use of particular thinking styles (e.g. worry/rumination) and memory search.

The S-REF model suggests that verbal reattribution should contain questions aimed at exploring and modifying dynamic processes. Typical questions will include: "How are you thinking?"; "What are you paying attention to?"; "Where is your evidence coming from (e.g. self/external)?"; Are you using internal data rather than observable facts?"; "What memories are activated?"; "Are you evaluating your thoughts or the situation?"; "What is your goal—is it to modify your thoughts or to escape from threat?". This form of questioning may be undertaken whilst the patient is exposed to problematic situations/emotions in order to elucidate the in-situation dynamics of processing. The technique can be used to build a profile of the patient's dysfunctional S-REF processing configuration, which is linked to his/her plan. This process has been termed "*metacognitive profiling*" (Wells and Matthews, 1994). Once the profile has been established, individual components can be systematically modified so that the individual develops a new processing routine. The new routine forms the basis of a replacement plan that can be proceduralised through repeated practice. Similarly, the routine can be used to process new information that modifies dysfunctional declarative belief. Systematic modification will typically comprise elicitation of a metacognitive goal state that emphasises belief change rather than escape from (non-existent) danger, the initial disengagement of self-perseveration by employing a detached processing style, specific attention allocation strategies, and other behaviours that disconfirm key negative beliefs and provide an alternative plan for processing and behaving in-situation.

The effective implementation of new behaviours and processing strategies in modifying self-knowledge requires that patients become aware of when a maladaptive plan is operating. Therefore, therapists should aim to educate patients about the role of cognitive processes and behaviours in the maintenance of dysfunctional emotional reactions. In particular, information should be presented that shows how attentional strategies of monitoring for threat, use of internal sources of data (e.g. body state feelings) to make inferences, appraisal styles (e.g. worry) and unhelpful behavioural coping strategies maintain negative self-beliefs.

SUMMARY OF GENERAL TREATMENT IMPLICATIONS

Several treatment implications of the S-REF model have been summarised in this chapter and elsewhere by Wells and Matthews (1994, 1996). The general aim of treatment should be to create replacement self-knowledge which guides the S-REF in response to stress rather than just challenging negative automatic thoughts and beliefs. To this end, the following strategies are suggested:

1. Emotional disorders should be viewed in terms of an interaction between levels of cognition. This has implications for both assessment and treatment.

2. Cognitive processes, particularly those involving excessive self-focused attention, attentional monitoring of threat and active worry, as well as the content of cognition, should be modified as part of a dynamic conceptualisation of maladaptive self-knowledge.

3. Metacognitive beliefs and plans for processing, as well as general non-metacognitive beliefs, should be modified in treatment in order to enhance and sustain therapeutic change. Dysfunctional metacognitive plans that direct processing can be inferred from instrumental assumptions and/or inferred from observation of attention, memory and thinking processes during problematic situations. *Metacognitive profiling* (see Chapter 7) in particular may be used to identify problematic processing routines, which can then be modified to facilitate disconfirmation and the replacement of knowledge. It is important to modify these routines as well as the content of knowledge. Plans for processing specify both cognitive and behavioural responses that maintain dysfunctional processing and prevent disconfirmation of faulty knowledge. These cognitive and behavioural strategies should be identified and reversed in therapy.

4. Modification of self-knowledge and lower level processing is achieved by manipulating on-line S-REF activity. Because on-line activity is capacity-limited, perseverative processing should be blocked early in treatment in order to increase subjective control over processing and facilitate efficient disconfirmatory processing.

5. Patients should be encouraged to develop a higher metacognitive mode and learn to process information in a way that does not trigger full-blown dysfunctional S-REF activity. This may be achieved by training in detached mindfulness and/or attentional control skills.

6. Metacognitive plans contain goals for self-regulation. Unrealistic goals should be identified and altered during the course of therapy.

7. A general marker for the efficacy of treatment in modifying the dysfunctional S-REF syndrome, and developing replacement metacognitive plans, is the extent to which treatment reduces self-focused processing tendencies.

Wells and Matthews (1994) suggest that the locus of dysfunctional processing in some disorders may be more explicitly metacognitive. Disorders such as GAD and OCD, which are characterised by unwanted intrusive thoughts, are candidate disorders. It should be possible, therefore, to develop specific clinical conceptualisations and treatments of these disorders that rely almost entirely on metacognitive constructs and metacognitive focused treatment strategies. These approaches are described in detail in Chapters 10 and 11.

CONCLUSIONS

In this chapter, we have seen how the S-REF approach provides a range of basic implications for cognitive-behaviour therapy. Applying the model to emotional disorder treatment suggests new and important realms for assessment and a multi-component approach to conceptualising the influence of self-knowledge. It will be important to restructure maladaptive metacognitions as well as non-metacognitive beliefs. The manipulation of on-line processing offers the principal means of cognitive restructuring. Such restructuring would appear to benefit from strategies that lead to the strengthening of a metacognitive mode (and hence a metacognitive plan for processing) and the use of strategies that directly modify cognitive processes, specifically those linked to the allocation of attention. Whilst a range of existing procedures, such as stress management strategies, may impact on maladaptive components of self-regulatory processing, the effect of such procedures can be seen as more complex and less predictable than would be normally envisaged within a behavioural or cognitive framework.

In Chapter 8 we will continue the discussion of cognitive restructuring. We will consider in more detail the factors that influence a patient's ability to modify beliefs, and explore the strategies that can be used to facilitate belief change and the acquisition of replacement plans for processing. However, before proceeding with that, in the next chapter we will examine methods for the clinical assessment of metacognitions, including metacognitive profiling, and present a revised A–B–C model as a basic unit for case conceptualisation.

Chapter 7

CLINICAL ASSESSMENT OF METACOGNITIONS

In this chapter I will consider in detail the implications of the present model for the assessment of psychological disorders in clinical practice. Assessment should include an analysis of the nature of metacognitive control processes and knowledge that operate to guide thinking in psychological disorder. Two basic elements of the self-regulatory system can be partitioned for special attention. These are: (1) characteristics of on-line processing; and (2) the nature of the library of self-relevant knowledge and plans (beliefs) in long-term memory on which processing draws. Psychological disorder is associated with both beliefs that incorporate negative self-relevant information and with metacognitive beliefs that lead the individual to engage in maladaptive styles of processing, namely perseverative, self-focused, rumination or worry, and attendant biases of attention. Once the nature of such metacognitive components is established, the therapist should work toward modifying them in constructing new thoughts and new beliefs.

Metacognition-based assessment does not exclude the avenues of enquiry associated with more typical cognitive-behavioural therapy assessment. It aims to augment existing assessments by eliciting and exploring metacognitive beliefs and appraisals and the nature of coping strategies/processing routines operating in distressed states. The clinician is interested in questions such as, "What type of thinking strategies are being used in problematic situations?" and "What is the knowledge base guiding the selection of cognitive and behavioural coping strategies"? In standard cognitive-behavioural therapy (CBT), the therapist operates with a different set of questions, typified by: "What is the content of negative automatic thoughts?" and "What is the content of (non-metacognitive) beliefs associated with these cognitions?".

REFORMULATED A–B–C ANALYSIS

The A–B–C analysis forms the basic unit of assessment and conceptualisation in cognitive-behavioural approaches. Using this unit of analysis in cognitive-behavioural assessment, patients are asked to recall a recent distressing situation and are questioned about the nature of the antecedents (A) or triggers for distress. The content of thoughts and beliefs (B) activated in the situation, and also the emotional and behavioural responses or consequences (C) activated are elicited.

An A–B–C analysis can be simplistically represented as responses to three broad categories of questions:

A.   What was the trigger for anxiety/depression?
B.   What thoughts were activated when anxiety/depression occurred?
C.   What were the emotional and behavioural responses in the situation?

Antecedents or triggers for emotion (A) typically include internal and/or external stimuli. Examples of internal stimuli are bodily sensations, emotional responses, intrusive thoughts or other mental experiences. External triggers include the behaviour of other people, environmental stresses, exposure to feared situations, etc. The appraisal of such stimuli (B) is typically negative and represents themes of threat, danger or loss. An example of an A–B–C analysis is presented in Figure 7.0.

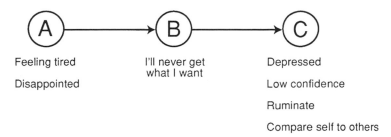

Figure 7.0   The A–B–C unit of analysis

The present approach argues for the use of additional questions that explore beliefs about one's thought processes and the nature of cognitive operations. More specifically, assessment should attempt to elucidate the nature of metacognitions. The metacognitions relevant to understanding disorder are:

1. Explicit[1] beliefs about the meaning of thoughts/feelings.
2. Explicit[1] knowledge (instrumental metacognitions) that underlie cognitive control (e.g. beliefs about worry, rumination, attention strategies).
3. Implicit metacognitions or plans for processing which may be inferred from self-report or observation of cognitive and behavioural processes during dysfunctional emotional states.

A reformulated A–B–C framework is required in which metacognitions (M) are a crucial determinant of consequences (C). Moreover, since metacognitive knowledge is a plan that controls appraisal processes, the appraisals and beliefs activated (B) are a function of the metacognitive plan activated. This calls for a reformulation of the A–B–C unit of analysis. The reformulated A–B–C is depicted in Figure 7.1. In this patient example, feelings of tiredness and an initial self-discrepancy in performance (disappointment in work), activates an explicit metacognition about the meaning of feeling tired (and the meaning of experiencing disappointment). This interpretation process relies on accessing a generic plan for processing and responding which consists of an explicit belief about rumination (2) and procedural metacognitions (3). The appraisal itself (B) is subject to similar metacognitive influences to the trigger, as depicted by the two arrows flowing between M and B. Thus, the output of on-line processing can become a further trigger that maintains a self-discrepancy and perpetuates the dysfunctional processing configuration. Additional feedback loops can also be considered for inclusion in the basic A–M–C analysis, since the consequences of processing (C) can become further triggers and are subject to metacognitive evaluation. Thus, a full model may incorporate the feedback cycles, as depicted in Figure 7.2.

Having presented the reformulated A–B–C analysis as a conceptual aid for framing assessment, in the next section we will consider how metacognitive information can be elicited through metacognitive profiling and questionnaire methods.

---

[1] (Note: the term "explicit" in this context refers to declarative knowledge, whilst "implicit" refers to procedural knowledge).

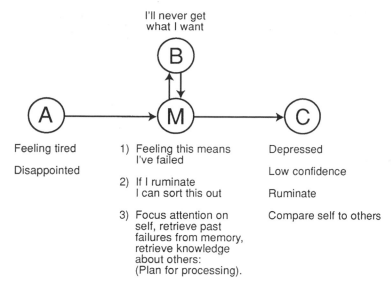

Figure 7.1   A reformulation of the A–B–C analysis: the A–M–C unit

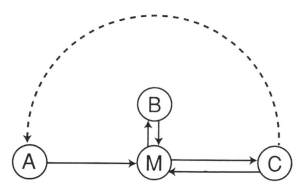

Figure 7.2   The A–M–C unit with feedback cycles included

METACOGNITIVE PROFILING

Wells and Matthews (1994) propose the use of "metacognitive profiling" to identify problematic processing routines and metacognitions that are activated under conditions of distress. Metacognitive components of cognition can be determined by particular questions used in tracing recent anxious or depressive episodes, or can be elicited during behavioural assessment tests (BATs), in which patients are instructed to observe what they do (prompted by therapist questions) in problematic situations. Several factors should be assessed in metacognitive profiling, namely declarative beliefs about the meaning of thoughts, beliefs about cognitive control strategies and the nature of goals and cognitive processes activated in-situation. The latter provides a basis for inferring the directives incorporated in the plan controlling processing. Basic questions for metacognitive profiling are presented below. These should be modified as appropriate to tailor them to specific patient experiences and to take into account whether the questions are directed at recounting a recent episode or are being used on-line during a BAT.

Profiling:

Meta-beliefs/appraisals

Question: When you felt anxious/panicky/depressed, did you have any thoughts about your mental state? What were these thoughts?

Probes: Did you have any negative thoughts about your own thinking? What thoughts did you have?
Did you notice that you were worried or ruminating about something? What was your rumination like?

Question: Do you think there are any advantages to worrying/ruminating/negative thinking?

Probe: What are the advantages?

Question: Do you think there are any disadvantages to worrying/ruminating/negative thinking?

Probe: What are the disadvantages?

Question: Can worrying/ruminating/thinking in certain ways be harmful or dangerous?

Probe: In what way could it be dangerous or harmful?

Coping strategies

Question: When you felt anxious/depressed, what did you do to cope with the situation?

Probes: Did you do anything to deal with the threat or danger? What did you do?
Did you do anything to control your thoughts? What did you do?

Did you do anything to deal with your feelings? What did
you do?

Question: What was your goal in using your coping strategies? That
is, what were you hoping to achieve?

Probes: How did you know that you had accomplished your goals?
How would you know when coping is effective?
What was the effect of your coping strategies on your feel-
ings and thoughts?

Cognitive processes, attention

Question: What were you paying most attention to in the situation?

Probes: What was most salient?
Were you focusing on your thoughts, on your feelings, or
the situation?
Were you self-conscious? What were you most conscious
of?
Are there any advantages to focusing your attention in that
way? What are they?
Are there any disadvantages to focusing your attention in
that way? What are they?

Cognitive processes, memory

Question: Were any memories activated? What were they?

Probes: Did you use your memory to try and work out what was
happening and/or how to deal with the situation?
How did you use your memory?

Cognitive processes, judgements

Question: How did you form your judgements in the situation?

Probes: What sort of evidence did you look for?
Where was your evidence coming from to support your
thoughts?
Were your judgements influenced by your physical
feelings?
Which feelings?

Were you influenced by mental feelings?
Were you influenced by your emotional feelings?
Question: If your feelings had been different, would you have judged the situation differently?
Question: How confident were you in your own mental abilities?

Mode

Question: Did you accept your thoughts and judgements as facts, based in reality?
Question: Could you see your thoughts as distortions of what was really happening in the situation?
Question: Can you keep your distance from these negative thoughts and feelings when they occur?

This line of questioning is not intended to displace more standard assessment of negative appraisals and behaviours. These questions should be used to supplement general assessment and provide data for conceptualising metacognitive and dynamic aspects of processing in emotional disorder.

The use of metacognitive profiling as an adjunct to general assessment has proved to be a useful tool for developing specific models of psychological disorder. In particular, profiling assessments based on this framework informed the development of the Clark and Wells (1995) cognitive model of social phobia, and facilitated the development of a specific cognitive model of generalised anxiety disorder (GAD) (Wells, 1995, 1997). The questions presented here can also be used to supplement the Socratic dialogue with the aim of verbal restructuring, and are not limited to assessment. Since the S-REF architecture and its constituents provide a generic framework for modelling psychological disturbance, it is likely that exploration of processing routines and metacognitions involved in psychological disturbance offers a means of developing specific cognitive models of a range of disorders.

THREE QUESTIONNAIRE MEASURES OF METACOGNITION

The development of measures of metacognition is important for research on metacognition in psychological disorder, and central to assessment and monitoring in treatment. Three recent instruments, the Metacognitions Questionnaire (MCQ), Anxious Thoughts Inventory (AnTI) and Thought Control Questionnaire (TCQ), have been developed to assess dimensions of metacognitive beliefs, monitoring, control and appraisal processes. Each questionnaire is reproduced in the Appendices, along with its scoring key.

Metacognitions Questionnaire (MCQ)

The MCQ (Appendix I; Cartwright-Hatton and Wells, 1997) was devised to assess individual differences in positive and negative beliefs about worry and intrusive thoughts, metacognitive monitoring and judgements of cognitive efficiency. The initial item pool for the questionnaire was derived from a semi-structured interview with 25 undergraduate students, and from transcripts of cognitive therapy conducted with outpatients attending treatment for GAD, obsessive-compulsive disorder (OCD), hypochondriasis and panic disorder. These participants were questioned about their experience of worry and intrusive thoughts, in particular, their reasons for engaging in this activity and the problems associated with it. Items were added referring to confidence in cognitive skills (as this is an important metacognitive experience that has been linked to anxiety and depression), and items tapping monitoring of thoughts were also included. The instrument has been subjected to systematic psychometric evaluation and development.

The final MCQ consists of five replicable factors assessed by 65 items in total. The five factors (subscales) measure the following dimensions of metacognition: (1) positive beliefs about worry (e.g. "Worrying helps me cope"), (2) negative beliefs about worry focusing on uncontrollability and danger (e.g. "When I start worrying I cannot stop"); (3) low cognitive confidence (e.g. "I have a poor memory"); (4) negative beliefs about thoughts, including themes of superstition, punishment, responsibility and need for control (e.g. "Not being able to control my thoughts is a sign of weakness"); and (5) cognitive self-consciousness (e.g. "I pay close attention to the way my mind works").

Each of the MCQ factors correlate meaningfully with measures of emotional vulnerability, and conceptually related constructs such as self-consciousness and cognitive failures, thus establishing the factors as substantive dimensions and not merely bloated specifics. The subscales appear to possess good reliability and validity. Psychometric properties of the MCQ are displayed in Table 7.0.

Table 7.0 Psychometric attributes of the Metacognitions Questionnaire (MCQ)

MCQ subscale	Items (n)	Alpha	Test-retest (5 weeks)	Correlations		Descriptives: mean (Sd)					
				Trait anxiety	PSWQ[1]	Non-clinical	GAD[2]	Panic[2]	Social[2] phobia	MDD[3]	OCD
		(n = 306)	(n = 47)	(n = 104)	(n = 105)	(n = 306)	(n = 21)	(n = 21)	(n = 21)	(n = 30)	(n = 17)
1. Positive beliefs	19	0.87	0.85	0.26*	0.45*	35.8 (10.9)	34.1 (10.9)	32.2 (6.7)	29.8 (6.4)	34.8 (10.3)	29.4 (11.1)
2. Negative beliefs	16	0.89	0.89	0.73*	0.57*	32.1 (9.6)	51.4 (8.5)	39.0 (11.1)	38.5 (9.4)	45.3 (11.2)	51.8 (8.2)
3. Cognitive confidence	10	0.84	0.84	0.50*	0.22+	17.9 (5.7)	24.4 (8.0)	17.1 (5.5)	19.3 (6.3)	22.3 (7.4)	21.4 (7.8)
4. Superstition, punishment, responsibility, etc.	13	0.74	0.76	0.47*	0.34*	21.8 (6.2)	31.1 (7.9)	24.2 (6.0)	25.5 (7.2)	30.9 (9.0)	31.1 (10.5)
5. Cognitive self-confidence	7	0.72	0.89	0.36*	0.26+	18.2 (4.6)	18.6 (5.4)	16.0 (4.2)	17.5 (4.0)	17.2 (4.5)	21.9 (2.6)

Note: * $p < 0.001$; + $p < 0.05$; PSWQ = Penn State Worry Questionnaire; MDD = major depression; OCD = obsessive-compulsive disorder; GAD = generalized anxiety disorder.

Sources: Cartwright-Hatton & Wells, 1997; [1]Wells & Papageorgiou, 1999; [2]Wells & Carter, 2000, interim data; [3]unpublished.

Anxious Thoughts Inventory (AnTI)

The AnTI (Wells, 1994b), is a multidimensional measure of worry. It comprises three subscales which measure proneness to social worry, health worry and meta-worry. The social and health worry subscales are content measures, whilst the meta-worry subscale measures metacognitive appraisals (worry about worry) and process dimensions of worry. Example items from the meta-worry subscales include: "I worry that I cannot control my thoughts as well as I would like to"; "I have difficulty clearing my mind of repetitive thoughts".

Items for the AnTI were generated from interviews with patients suffering from panic disorder and GAD, and additional items were based on items from the Beck Depression Inventory (BDI; Beck, Ward, Mendelsohn, Mock & Erbaugh, 1961) and the Maudsley Obsessive-Compulsive Inventory (Rachman & Hodgson, 1980). One item was used from the trait anxiety subscale (Speilberger, Gorsuch, Lushene, Vagg & Jacobs, 1983) linked to process dimensions of thinking. The instrument has a three-factor solution, and the factors are meaningful and reliable. Each factor constitutes a subscale and the subscales have good psychometric properties, as summarised in Table 7.1. The AnTI subscales appear sensitive to treatment effects in GAD (Wells, in preparation).

Thought Control Questionnaire (TCQ)

Wells and Davies (1994) developed the TCQ to measure individual tendencies to use particular metacognitive strategies to control intrusive and distressing thoughts. Five factorially derived and reliable domains of control strategy are measured by the TCQ: (1) Distraction (e.g. "I do something that I enjoy"); (2) social control (e.g. "I ask my friends if they have similar thoughts"); (3) worry (e.g. "I focus on different negative thoughts"); (4) punishment (e.g. "I punish myself for thinking the thought"); (5) re-appraisal (e.g. "I try to reinterpret the thought"). The initial item pool for this instrument was generated by an open-ended semi-structured interview with 10 patients with a range of anxiety disorders or hypochondriasis, and 10 non-patients. The scale was systematically refined across a series of factor analytic studies, and appears to have good reliability and validity. Psychometric properties are presented in Table 7.2.

The TCQ subscales appear sensitive to recovery from depression and PTSD, with main effects of recovery status for distraction and worry, and

Table 7.1 Psychometric attributes of the Anxious Thoughts Inventory (AnTI)

AnTI subscale	Items (n)	Alpha	Test-retest (6 weeks)	Correlations		Descriptives: mean (sd)				
				Trait anxiety	N	Non-clinical	GAD[1]	Panic[1]	Social phobia[1]	MDD[2]
		(n = 239)	(n = 64)	(n = 96)	(n = 96)	(n = 239)	(n = 21)	(n = 21)	(n = 21)	(n = 30)
Social worry	9	0.84	0.76	0.63*	0.62*	18.1 (4.5)	24.1 (5.3)	17.1 (3.0)	25.0 (5.5)	24.0 (6.3)
Health worry	6	0.81	0.84	0.36*	0.52*	8.8 (2.8)	14.6 (3.7)	14.9 (5.6)	9.3 (2.9)	11.0 (4.7)
Meta-worry	7	0.75	0.77	0.68*	0.60*	11.3 (3.2)	20.3 (3.8)	15.0 (4.6)	15.7 (4.7)	17.9 (3.7)

Note: * $p < 0.001$; N = Neuroticism.
Sources: Wells, 1994a; [1]Wells & Carter, 2000, interim data; [2]unpublished.

Table 7.2 Psychometric attributes of the Thought Control Questionnaire (TCQ)

TCQ subscale	Items (n)	Alpha	Test–retest (6 weeks)	Correlations			Descriptives: mean (sd)				
				Trait anxiety	N	PSWQ	Non-clinical	GAD[1]	Panic[1]	MDD[2]	PTSD[2]
		(n = 229)	(n = 33)	(n = 50)	(n = 50)	(n = 50)	(n = 229)	(n = 20)	(n = 20)	(n = 61)	(n = 63)
1. Distraction	6	0.72	0.68	-0.03	-0.15	-0.03	14.6 (3.0)	13.1 (3.4)	14.5 (3.0)	12.3 (3.3)	13.9 (3.1)
2 Social control	6	0.79	0.83	-0.09	-0.05	-0.02	14.0 (3.3)	10.6 (3.0)	13.1 (3.9)	11.6 (3.5)	11.1 (3.1)
3. Worry	6	0.71	0.72	0.50*	0.45*	0.49*	10.4 (2.7)	11.7 (3.5)	9.2 (3.0)	11.6 (3.4)	11.9 (3.9)
4. Punishment	6	0.64	0.67	0.53*	0.49*	0.50*	10.0 (2.9)	13.3 (3.3)	10.7 (3.6)	11.1 (2.8)	11.1 (3.6)
5. Re-appraisal	6	0.67	0.83	-0.13	-0.04	-0.01	14.4 (2.9)	11.3 (4.0)	12.3 (3.9)	12.3 (2.8)	12.7 (3.6)

Note: * $p < 0.001$; N = neuroticism; PSWQ = Penn State Worry Questionnaire; MDD = major depression disorder; PTSD = Post-traumatic Stress Disorder.
Sources: Wells & Davies, 1994; [1]unpublished; [2]Reynolds & Wells, 1999.

significant interactions between recovery status and time for the punishment and re-appraisal subscales (Reynolds and Wells, 1999).

CONCLUSIONS

Standard cognitive-behavioural assessment of emotional disorder can be augmented by including specific assessments of metacognitions. Such an approach permits the identification of beliefs, cognitive processes (plans), and beliefs about control strategies that contribute to a more comprehensive conceptualisation of factors supporting key components of emotional disorder. The reformulated A–B–C analysis provides a framework for linking metacognitive dimensions to the observed cognitive, emotional and behavioural responses manifested during exacerbations of emotion in particular situations.

Metacognitive profiling has been outlined as a technique for identifying and exploring metacognitive components underlying maladaptive emotional experience. The questions that constitute metacognitive profiling probe the individual's beliefs about thoughts, aim to build a description of the nature of cognitive processes activated during negative emotion, and elicit the nature of goals that modulate the continuation or cessation of coping strategies. Three questionnaire measures of metacognitions have also been reviewed. These measures provide a general coverage of metacognitive domains of beliefs, monitoring, appraisal and control strategies.

Chapter 8

MODIFYING BELIEFS

How do we modify beliefs? In the S-REF model, changes in self-knowledge or beliefs are achieved in psychological therapy by modifying processing at the on-line level. The extent of belief change is determined by the efficiency with which S-REF processing can be manipulated so that it activates appropriate dysfunctional self-knowledge, and leads to processing of information in a way that modifies self-knowledge in long-term memory. At the most basic level, the modification of beliefs requires: (1) activation of dysfunctional self-knowledge and processing routines; (2) a shift to metacognitive modes during dysfunctional processing; and (3) redeployment of processing activities to support declarative and procedural learning (i.e. disconfirmatory processing).

Activation of dysfunctional knowledge and processing is necessary so that individuals do not discount new disconfirmatory experiences as irrelevant to their concerns. It is also necessary so that new information may be incorporated within existing dysfunctional knowledge, so that dysfunctional knowledge is modified and this new modified knowledge is then activated in problematic situations. If this does not occur, newly acquired knowledge does not have the salience of maladaptive knowledge under idiosyncratic stress conditions. By activating problematic processing, the therapist can explore the full range of on-line processes that contribute to the maintenance of disorder, and can then manipulate cognitive processes with the aim of enhancing the acquisition of new plans and beliefs.

In order for belief modification to occur, a metacognitive mode of processing has to be established. More specifically, a general-purpose metacognitive plan for modifying cognition has to be activated and used to restructure specific components of dysfunctional self-knowledge. Thus, the individual's goal must be to examine and revise the knowledge base, and individuals must have sufficient knowledge of, and control over, strategies that can provide the basis for learning. Most individuals possess general metacognitive knowledge and strategies that influence learning processes. Here, general metacognitive self-knowledge and strategies practised within a metacognitive mode can be used to shape the nature of specific types of stored knowledge. It is clear from this analysis that there can be particular impediments to knowledge restructuring or composition. First, individuals may lack knowledge of the strategies that are effective for learning. Second, in emotional disorder, patients are in object-mode processing and may lack awareness of the fact that their knowledge requires modification. Third, individuals may show impaired flexible control over cognition and behaviour needed to support the execution of learning strategies.

MODULATING INFLUENCES ON BELIEF CHANGE

Several factors can interfere with the processing operations required for belief change. The ease with which beliefs are modified will be dependent upon the following factors:

1. *Awareness of the effect of beliefs on thinking and behaviour.* If patients are unaware of the influence of maladaptive beliefs on processing and behaviour, this will interfere with generation of a metacognitive processing mode. Through careful socialisation in a cognitive-behavioural case formulation, and by socialisation to a model of experience in which cognitions are a central problem and the goal is to modify cognition, metacognitive awareness may be enhanced.

2. *Availability of attentional resources.* If attentional resources are bound to threat or tied up with perseverative self-referent processing, there may be insufficient resources available for executive control operations and for modifying beliefs. Resources may be recovered by strategies that reduce rumination and active worry early in treatment. These strategies are also likely to be helpful when used prior to and following behavioural experiments that are intended to produce disconfirmatory data for encoding in long-term memory. Similarly, formal attention training procedures (see Chapter 9) may also be applied to counteract adhesive and locked-in self-focused processing.

3. *Availability of metacognitive strategies for cognitive restructuring/learning.*
    Patients with emotional disorders have reduced availability of strat-
    egies for restructuring negative self-knowledge. This diminished avail-
    ability may emerge from interference effects produced by maladaptive
    processing or a lack of alternative self-knowledge that can be called
    upon to direct cognitive-emotional change in threatening situations.
    Treatment should make available to patients specific strategies that are
    useful for modifying maladaptive beliefs. Thus, enhancing metacogni-
    tive skills and knowledge of unhelpful cognitive control strategies and
    the provision of replacement strategies for directing attention, discon-
    tinuing worry and retaining a metacognitive mode will be useful.

4. *The individual's goals for processing may impede belief modification.* If a
    patient persists in the object-level goal of avoiding (non-existent)
    threat, this will impair changes in coping strategies and behaviours
    that would facilitate disconfirmatory processing. In addition, some
    patients may wish to maintain certain maladaptive metacognitions
    because these are seen to provide advantages. For instance, a hypo-
    chondriacal patient no longer believed he had cancer following sev-
    eral treatment sessions, but continued to worry about his health
    because he believed this would keep him safe and enable him to
    detect potential signs of cancer in the future. The maintenance of this
    "anxious behaviour" can be seen as problematic because it fails to
    provide experience of alternative and more adaptive processing strat-
    egies that may be learned, and it repeatedly generates information
    that can re-establish negative declarative beliefs.

5. *Availability of new information.* A lack of new information will impair
    belief change. Information may be lacking because patients lack the
    cognitive set or basic knowledge necessary for selectively attending
    to new information or executing new behaviours that can strengthen
    new coping skills. Furthermore, some types of coping, such as avoid-
    ance and in-situation safety behaviours, restrict accessibility to infor-
    mation that can restructure negative beliefs.

6. *Flow of information.* Impediments to the flow of information into the
    cognitive system will impair the acquisition of new beliefs. Two types
    of flow are relevant. First, new information that can facilitate learning
    has to be processed. This will require orienting attention towards
    disconfirmatory information and experiences. Second, once this infor-
    mation is allowed access to processing, the output of on-line com-
    putations must flow into changes in knowledge stored in long-term
    memory. This second flow or transformational process can only occur
    if a plan for processing that facilitates belief change is activated.
    Overload of attention by worry, by maladaptive attentional

strategies, a predominance of object mode processing and inappropriate goals will impair such transformational processes.

7. *Compliance with behaviour modification.* Since on-line activity is the seat of belief modification and new learning, impairments in the patient's ability to modify behavioural repertoires will translate into a reduced propensity for belief change. Patients may be reluctant to give up particular coping behaviours, and in such instances therapy should focus on strengthening the advantages of behaviour change. Patients require an alternative mental model that emphasises the reasons for *not* engaging in particular maladaptive responses. When patients' maladaptive threat-related beliefs are strong, there are limited reasons for not acting in a way that is consistent with beliefs. Initial verbal reattribution may be required to weaken general declarative beliefs before patients are willing to engage in new behaviours that can support the acquisition of new plans for processing.

8. *Level of affect.* Weak or absent affect in therapy is likely to indicate a failure to activate beliefs and plans, thus modifications to on-line processing will have a reduced effect in rewriting maladaptive self-knowledge. In contrast, excessive affect may compromise executive control and narrow cognitive capacity to the extent that computations necessary for belief change are threatened.

Armed with the S-REF metacognitive model, it is possible to specify in detail a range of factors, as outlined above, that influence the active composition or restructuring of knowledge. It will be necessary to control these modulating influences during the course of treatment and in the implementation of behavioural reattribution strategies.

KNOWLEDGE ACQUISITION

The development of new plans for processing and new beliefs is accomplished through repeated controlled S-REF activity. The multi-level S-REF architecture and dynamic aspects of processing point to several therapeutic objectives as a means of facilitating the acquisition of new beliefs. In particular, during the course of treatment it will be necessary to:

1. Establish a metacognitive processing mode.
2. Promote on-line computations that modify self-knowledge.
3. Modify self-regulatory goals that are unrealistic or maladaptive. This includes the nature of signals (guides) that are used to activate or terminate maladaptive coping and thinking strategies.

4. Increase the reflexivity of new processing routines (i.e. restore some lower-level control over new processing).

Each of these objectives will be considered in turn.

Establishing a metacognitive mode

Characteristics of the metacognitive mode and object mode are depicted in Figure 8.0. The metacognitive mode is established by sharing with the patient a cognitive behavioural conceptualisation of the presenting problem. The emphasis should be on illustrating how negative appraisals are maintained by cognitive processes, coping behaviours, and situation-specific goal states. The rationale for treatment should emphasise a therapeutic goal of cognitive modification rather than the goal of escape from or management of threat/stress. Patients do not typically engage in therapy with the principle aim of changing their beliefs, but wish to enhance their coping with problematic situations or emotions. A potential problem with more eclectic CBT approaches is that they may promote emotion-control strategies or lack a coherent formulation of the role of

Object mode	Metacognitive mode
Metacognitions:	**Metacognitions:**
Thoughts depict reality (threat is objective)	Thoughts are events, not realities (threat is subjective)
Thoughts must be acted on	Thoughts must be evaluated
Goals:	**Goals:**
Eliminate threat	Modify thinking
Strategies:	**Strategies:**
Evaluate threat	Evaluate thoughts
Execute threat-reducing behaviours (e.g. worry, threat monitoring)	Execute metacognitive control behaviours (e.g. suspend worry, redirect attention)
Probable outcome:	**Probable outcome:**
Maladaptive knowledge strengthened	Knowledge restructured
	New plans developed

Figure 8.0   Characteristics of object-mode and metacognitive S-REF mode

cognition in disorder. As a result, the establishment of a metacognitive mode, or the setting conditions for multi-component belief change may be compromised.

Establishment of the metacognitive mode is dependent on the patient's ability to introspect and change processing and motivational priorities. Thus, the patient must possess a general-purpose metacognitive plan that can be called and used in stressful situations in order to examine and control cognitive processes. There are likely to be individual differences in the availability of such knowledge and the ability to influence on-line processes in stressful situations. For example, some patients show considerable difficulty in identifying negative thoughts in distressing situations. In these circumstances additional time in therapy should be devoted to training patients to recognise negative thoughts. The use of self-monitoring strategies in CBT, such as completing dysfunctional thoughts records, provide a means of enhancing patients' metacognitive monitoring skills, and in the present theoretical framework can be viewed as a technique that can be used to contribute to the development of the metacognitive mode.

Patients should be encouraged to examine their thoughts and feelings in a detached way. Detached mindfulness of this kind can be accomplished by instructing patients to "watch" their thoughts and feeling "as if from a distance", or "as if watching a movie screen". Negative thoughts that may occur in imagery or verbal form can be projected on an imaginal screen. In these instances, it is important that patients assume the role of "passive observer" and try not to interact with the thoughts or feelings in any other way. A strategy that has been particularly useful in individuals who are constantly bound up with controlling or manipulating their thoughts (e.g. obsessive-compulsive patients) is prescriptive "mind wandering". This strategy consists of asking patients to allow their thoughts to "roam free" for a specific period of time. Patients are instructed that during this time they should not attempt to control the course of their mental activities but merely watch thoughts and events "ebb and flow of their own accord". Once this basic ability is established, this can be strengthened by set homework practice, and applied to different situations. Some patients are reluctant to practise this exercise or find it too difficult to relax mental control. In these cases, an alternative strategy that may be attempted is "free association". Here the therapist asks the patient to free-associate in response to target words spoken by the therapist. Patients are asked to provide a word or brief description of an image that automatically comes to mind in response to different target words. Names of everyday objects provide the target words, so that associations are readily available, and cognitive censorship that may be linked to more personal stimuli is avoided. The goal in using this strategy is to train patients to observe cognitive events in a detached way without the need to actively engage with or resist thoughts.

Once a metacognitive goal is established and the patient is able to monitor cognitive events in a more detached way whilst maintaining control over attention allocation, the next step is to promote on-line processing that modifies self-knowledge. If cognitive control and meta-awareness remain problematic, strategies of Attention Training may be used to promote executive control. As we will see in the next chapter, Attention Training provides a means of strengthening metacognitive plans and controlling attention allocation, and has the advantage of reducing self-focused processing, thereby enabling the individual to switch out of the maladaptive cognitive-attentional syndrome.

Regulating on-line processing

Further manipulations of on-line processing are necessary to enhance the computations necessary to modify self-knowledge. Once the metacognitive mode is activated, the individual with emotional disorder has to regulate the flow of information in processing and the availability of processing resources.

Cognitive resources are drained by worry or ruminative activity and patients should be instructed to ban such activity. This is more readily accomplished than it might first seem, as perseverative processing of this type is most often a controlled coping strategy (although awareness of the degree of control may be diminished). At this stage, further strengthening of control over processing and reductions in adhesive self-processing (self-consciousness) can be accomplished by Attention Training.

A key component of belief modification consists of enhancing the flow of new information into the cognitive system. Two components of flow are important: (1) the accessing of disconfirmatory information; (2) the use of processing to compile new beliefs or plans. Individuals may fail to access new information that can potentially lead to revision of beliefs because attention is not directed towards new information. Cognitive strategies, such as inappropriate self-focused attention, monitoring for threat and coping strategies of avoidance or safety behaviours, can prevent access to disconfirmatory experiences or information. To overcome these problems, patients should be asked to engage in alternative attentional and behavioural strategies in stressful situations. These strategies should be directed at providing greater access to disconfirmatory data.

How can we maximise the potential for new attentional and behavioural strategies to modify beliefs? In the S-REF model, it is necessary to activate a metacognitive plan and execute on-line strategies that revise self-knowledge. This is accomplished by eliciting a cognitive set in which the patient's explicit goal is to practise specific new attentional and be-havioural strategies in emotional situations to test out maladaptive beliefs and predictions. Elsewhere, I have referred to this strategy for the con-duct of behavioural experiments as the P–E–T–S protocol (Wells, 1997). This refers to stages of implementing a behavioural experiment consisting of Preparation, Exposure to threat/emotion, Testing of belief, and Sum-marising the results and consolidation. This process is summarised in Figure 8.1.

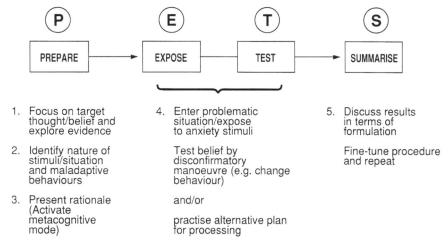

Figure 8.1 The P–E–T–S protocol (adapted from Wells, 1997)

In the preparation phase, negative beliefs should be elicited and the pro-cessing operations and behaviours that maintain such beliefs should be identified. Declarative belief level should be rated in this phase. A meta-cognitive goal should be activated in which the explicit aim of the ensuing experiment is to revise belief. In the next phase, the patient is exposed to anxiety-provoking situations or triggers of other types of emotion. In depression, this phase consists of asking patients to focus on depressive thoughts or feelings. In the test phase, patients are instructed to shift to external focused attention, and change their coping behaviours (e.g. decide to stop ruminating, engage in problem-solving, abandon unhelpful self-control behaviours). The aim of the test phase is to guide patients to behave and think differently, so that disconfirmatory experiences occur or new knowledge is compiled. For instance, in anxiety disorders this can be viewed as performing a disconfirmatory manoeuvre that is intended to test a specific belief or prediction. This approach is different from mere exposure, since attempts are made to directly manipulate processing and behaviour during exposure so that beliefs are restructured. The final phase consists of re-rating declarative belief level and summarising the results of the experiment in terms of the cognitive formulation. Homework strategies then consist of shifting to external focused attention and modifying behaviours the next time negative emotions are experienced. In anxiety disorders, specific exposure experiments can be suggested in which patients enter feared situations whilst practising new attentional strategies and behaviours. In depression, which is typically more chronically activated, homework consists of shifting to external attention, and stopping rumination (which can be achieved through cognitive control and activity scheduling) and problem-solving. Formal Attention Training (see Chapter 9) and activity scheduling provide two means of interrupting rumination and anchoring attention on external events.

In summary, the activation of a metacognitive mode and rescripting of attention and coping behaviours provides the basis for a new metacognitive plan for guiding processing and coping. Whilst such experiments can be used to weaken declarative beliefs/appraisals, repeated practice of new routines is advised in order to strengthen a new plan for processing. It is likely that strengthening of the plan is associated with changes in emotional belief, such that patients not only "intellectually know" that a negative belief is false, but begin to "feel" that this new knowledge is correct. Repitition of new propositions (e.g. rational self-statements) will help to strengthen replacement knowledge. Evidence suggests that repetition increases familiarity with propositional statements, and this increases the likelihood that such statements are judged to be true (Hasher, Goldstein & Topping, 1979).

Changing maladaptive self-regulatory guides

Self-knowledge consists of a representation of some "normative" or desired state of the self. In restructuring of beliefs it is necessary to take account of this representation, since pursuit of an unrealistic or inappropriate goal can maintain dysfunctional beliefs. According to the S-REF model, in psychological disorder, self-regulatory or coping efforts are guided by internal sources of information, such as feelings, a sense of knowing, or a self-image. The use of inappropriate internal sources of information to guide information processing, and the continuation or cessation of coping efforts, deflect the individual from engaging in behaviours that can restructure self-knowledge. Moreover, the ability to achieve an internal guide state (e.g. a particular feeling or state of cognition) may be unreliable, and often requires the use of metacognitive control and monitoring strategies that are incompatible with normal efficient self-regulation. For instance, an obsessional ruminator whose goal was to "always control my mind to prevent perverse thoughts", was locked in a constant and impossible metacognitive battle. Her self-regulatory strategy consisted of trying to "blank-out" her mind when in situations likely to trigger obsessions. This strategy was rarely effective. She also focused on her physiological feeling state to check that any "perverse" thoughts that did occur did not provoke an emotional reaction. On other occasions she would deliberately think a "perverse" thought whilst focusing and checking her bodily reaction, to determine if she was a "pervert". Unfortunately, having the thought provoked anxiety and this was misinterpreted as signalling the presence of sexual arousal. Here we can see how unhelpful guides (not experiencing emotional arousal) and regulatory (coping) strategies are prone to failure, do not provide data for modifying dysfunctional beliefs, maintain self-focused processing, and may provide information that is interpreted as supporting dysfunctional beliefs.

A key construct in understanding and dealing with maladaptive self-regulatory goals is the *mode*. Patients are operating in object mode when attempting self-regulation in emotional disorder. The therapist must shift the client to metacognitive mode, in which the goal is no longer to self-regulate by reducing threat/danger, but to self-regulate by modifying beliefs. Unrealistic goals for self-regulation such as aiming to abolish negative thoughts, or all anxious feelings must be challenged. Furthermore, new guides and linked strategies should be compiled that aim to *restructure beliefs*. This is accomplished by asking questions such as: "How will you know when (appraisal/belief) is false?"; "What type of information should you look for?"; "Do your feelings tell you this?"; "What are the advantages/disadvantages of using feelings to guide your judgements?"; "What alternative sources of data can you use?"; "What would happen if you stopped trying to cope and focused on the situation around you instead?".

When goals are unrealistic and involve the chronic control of emotional state, the therapist should examine the patient's attitudes and beliefs about experiencing unwanted emotions. Even when discreet catastrophic beliefs are not present, there may be a general intolerance of emotional responses. In these instances, the patient's predictions concerning the course of emotions should be explored. Maladaptive beliefs may concern themes of negative emotional states becoming permanent. Beyond this, it may be necessary to train patients to tolerate negative emotions. Strategies such as training in detached mindfulness, interoceptive exposure techniques, or transforming the meaning of emotional symptoms through imagery, can be useful in the context of anxiety responses.

Developing new processing routines

The S-REF model suggests that it may not be helpful to think of dysfunctional beliefs purely in declarative form, and it is important to consider the metacognitive belief domain. It is useful to think of declarative beliefs such as "I'm foolish", as data or output that is linked to procedural knowledge (plans) that guide coping and cognition. In this way, information and behaviour are integrated. It is necessary in treatment to develop procedural knowledge so that beliefs exert an influence on cognition and coping that is capable of sustaining adaptive experience.

In order for beliefs to exert a metacognitive influence, control and monitoring plans have to be committed to them. The practice of new processing and behavioural activities in-situation is the means of acquiring new skills for the metacognitive control over cognition and behaviour. Verbal and behavioural restructuring strategies of questioning the evidence for beliefs and exposure do not specify the control over processing necessary to restructure maladaptive knowledge/beliefs, or provide the practice of new responses that can be encoded as new plans for processing. More specifically, patients should be given instructions to regulate cognition and behaviour in a way that supports the acquisition of new knowledge. One way to understand this is to think of the provision of new information in CBT by verbal restructuring as simply changing declarative knowledge. However, this changed knowledge will have a limited effect on the control of cognition and behaviour unless new cognitive processes and behaviours can be linked to the knowledge. For instance, an individual troubled by low self-esteem and depression may concede during verbal restructuring: "I'm a success in some areas of my life", but this newly acquired knowledge will not exert control over attention, processing and behaviour unless a new plan for processing and behaviour is implemented in conjunction with it. The extent to which the process of verbal restructuring alone provides the basis for developing a new plan is questionable. Whilst verbal restructuring may enhance a metacognitive mode of processing, the mental operations required to sustain a more positive sense of self are not specified in detail. For example, if the person with low self-esteem and depression proneness continues to ruminate, recall past instances of failure, and engage in negative self-focus as a means of dealing with stressful life events, this will prolong negative mood and contribute to negative self-knowledge.

It follows from this that it is inefficient to focus predominantly on verbally challenging thoughts/beliefs or to focus only on exposure. Exposure and verbal reattribution must be combined with manipulations of cognitive processes and behaviours in order to develop and strengthen new plans.

In treatment, the acquisition of new plans and routines is achieved by asking patients to discontinue unhelpful cognitive processes and behaviours, and training in alternative processes and strategies. Patients should be encouraged to abandon worry and rumination strategies as a means of dealing with stress and life events. Alternative strategies, such as problem-solving, external-focusing, detached mindfulness, doing nothing, distraction (when appropriate), task focusing, positive self-talk, focusing on the present (rather than future), focusing on disconfirmatory information, and "doing" rather than "thinking" even in the face of uncertainty, can be used when appropriate.

Impediments to developing new plans for processing in therapy include metacognitive beliefs about the advantages of sustaining maladaptive processing, such as self-monitoring, rumination/worry and hyper-vigilance for threat. The presence of beliefs of this kind should be explored and they should be challenged when they exist.

STAGES OF KNOWLEDGE ACQUISITION

The S-REF perspective on treatment is consistent with a multi-stage theory of skill acquisition (Fitts, 1964; Anderson, 1982). The initial stage has been termed the "cognitive" or "declarative" stage, in which verbal mediation is often observed because the learner needs to maintain information in working memory to execute the skill. In the next phase, practice of the skill leads knowledge to be converted from declarative to procedural, in which there is a drop-out of verbal mediation. Declarative learning is a relatively slow and conscious process, and in cognitive therapy is most likely to correspond with presenting a rationale for therapy and using standard cognitive behavioural restructuring procedures. In terms of the S-REF approach, the aim during declarative learning is to: (1) increase awareness of maladaptive knowledge (increase meta-awareness); (2) provide a mental set for belief change (establish a metacognitive processing mode with its constituent goals); (3) use verbal and behavioural reattribution strategies to challenge the validity of declarative beliefs. In the second stage of belief modification, procedural learning is necessary. This involves practising new strategies: behaviours, thinking, and attentional strategies in problematic situations, so that "how to think and feel differently" configurations are strengthened. Thus, there needs to be specific training in how to use attention, memory, appraisal and behaviours in situations. Only through repeated practice of new combinations of attention, behaviour and thinking can alternative plans for processing be strengthened and some lower level of control over processing be restored. This stage will require repeated practice under disorder-related stimulus conditions in order to finely tune and strengthen new metacognitive procedural knowledge.

IMAGERY: A VIRTUAL WORLD PROGRAMMING ENVIRONMENT

We have seen in the previous section how information and procedures (behaviours) should be coupled to produce the cognitive "structures" that support self-regulatory processing. It is likely that some types of on-line activity in the S-REF provide a basis for developing new plans for processing without the execution of new behaviours. Cognitive activity that links information with behaviour in a "virtual environment" would satisfy this criterion. It is likely that some forms of imagery can provide both information and behaviour together, as a means of establishing a basic plan or procedure for cognition and action. One means of accomplishing this is by running *mental simulations* that provide information on the relationship between events over a time course, and couple this information with attentional and behavioural strategies in the imaginal simulation. Natural selection has most probably endowed humans with a mechanism for acquiring plans and procedures for handling threat that does not necessitate repeated and potentially hazardous real-life exposures to stressful circumstances. Plans can be acquired in a rudimentary form by imagining encounters with situations and imagining dealing with situations in different ways. Intrusive images following acute stress are likely to function as prompts for imaginal processing that should normally lead to development of a meaningful narrative that links information with adaptive behaviour. It may be failure of development of such a plan that contributes to the development of chronic stress reactions such as post-traumatic stress disorder, as described in Chapter 4.

WRITING NEW PLANS: A SUMMARY

In summary, how are we to write new plans and procedures for cognition *and* behaviour?

Since dysfunctional processing and behaviour in emotional disorder is plan driven, it is necessary to access a general-purpose plan that controls thinking and behaviour and to modify aspects of the plan to meet situational demands. These modifications rely on linking information with behaviour and should be undertaken in specific situations involving emotion. Modification of behaviour is considered in a wide sense to include manipulations of attention, thinking style, and other covert/overt coping behaviours. Imagery provides a potential vehicle for linking information and behaviour and laying the foundations of a plan, but this is probably not a complete substitute for actual behavioural practice of implementing alternative cognitive and behavioural strategies in "difficult" situations.

CONCLUSIONS

In spite of the importance of modifying beliefs in CBT, details surrounding the nature of beliefs that should be modified, and guidance on how to achieve restructuring has been limited. The importance of a multi-component conceptualisation of beliefs in the S-REF model, and a view of self-knowledge as dynamically linked to processing operations, provides a range of implications for understanding factors maintaining maladaptive beliefs and the factors that should be targeted during belief modification.

Belief modification requires activation of a metacognitive processing mode, dropping out of dysfunctional attentional, ideational and behavioural strategies, and instruction in alternative responses with repeated practice. In this chapter, a range of conceptual and practical guidelines for accomplishing belief modification have been described. A recurrent theme in the foregoing discussion is that a range of objectives in the process of modifying self-knowledge can be met by retraining attention in emotional disorder. Attention modification strategies can be used to reduce self-focus, disrupt worry/rumination, activate and strengthen attentional control plans and redirect attention to new information, thereby increasing the flow of disconfirmatory information in processing. We continue with a consideration of attentional strategies in the next chapter. A final concluding point of importance is that the maintenance and modification of beliefs, and perhaps the very nature of beliefs, is inextricably linked to metacognitive knowledge (plans) that control processing. This knowledge should be a central focus of cognitive-behavioural change.

A set of general summary guidelines for belief restructuring and knowledge (plan) compilation can be constructed. These are as follows:

1. Establish a metacognitive mode.
2. Promote on-line computations that modify knowledge:
   (a) Remove worry/rumination.
   (b) Increase availability of flexible attentional resources.
   (c) Increase flow of corrective information in processing (e.g. alternative routines/behaviours).
   (d) Use P–E–T–S protocol for behavioural experiments.
   (e) Use strategies that link information with behaviour (i.e. develop new plans).
3. Modify unrealistic self-regulatory goals, and shift attention away from using inappropriate internal sources of data for judgements.
4. Focus on modifying maladaptive declarative metacognitions and instruct patients in repeated practice of applying new cognitive processes and coping behaviours [this may be closely linked with activating (a)–(c) above].

Chapter 9

NEW PATHWAYS FOR COGNITIVE RESTRUCTURING: ATTENTION MODIFICATIONS (ATT AND SAR)

Distraction and attentional focusing strategies have been used thera-peutically in a range of contexts, as components of treatment in anxiety management and pain management interventions, and in the treatment of conditioned nausea. Task-focusing instructions have been used in the treatment of test anxiety and associated performance decrements. Gener-ally, attention procedures have tended to be used in a prescriptive way in the absence of a theoretical model of the nature of attention and its dy-namic relationship with beliefs and coping strategies in the maintenance of disorder. Furthermore, one of the complexities in developing process-oriented interventions that target attention directly concerns the multi-component nature of attention, and the possibility that several varying components may contribute to psychopathology. For instance, emo-tionally disordered individuals may selectively attend to information con-sistent with unrealistic beliefs, there may be a lack of flexibility in attention necessary for efficient self-regulation, or attention to the self may be so intense that it interferes with a sense of spontaneity in cogni-tion and behaviour.

A key contribution of the S-REF model to clinical practice is the idea that direct modifications of cognitive processes, particularly attention, should prove beneficial in cognitive-behavioural therapy (CBT). The task of developing attentional treatment strategies is simplified by information processing theories linking a range of attention phenomena to mechanisms of disorder maintenance. We saw in Chapter 2 that the S-REF model views attention phenomena, such as selective attention bias, attentional resource limitations and excessive self-focus, as manifestations of running particular plans for coping with threat, such as worrying and threat monitoring, which contribute to emotional vulnerability and disorder maintenance. In this chapter, attention modifications are discussed and two broad types of such strategy, the Attention Training Technique (ATT; Wells, 1990) and Situational Attention Refocusing (SAR) are presented in detail. Before proceeding with this task in the next section, the role of a different form of attention manipulation, namely distraction, in treatment is critically considered. It is necessary to make a distinction between distraction and the attentional strategies presented in the remainder of this chapter.

DISTRACTION

The experience of being distracted refers to the often involuntary capture of attention by task-irrelevant stimuli. For example, if the doorbell rings during a worry episode, the worrier may be momentarily distracted from worrying. However, individuals also use active and volitional distraction as a coping strategy. This typically consists of focusing attention away from threat or emotion. Patients with anxiety disorders report using distraction to divert attention away from feared bodily sensations, upsetting thoughts or disturbing external stimuli. In this context, distraction is used as a means of avoiding thoughts, feelings and emotions. It will be useful to distinguish different types of attentional strategy from "distraction". To the extent that distraction is a motivated strategy, we can consider it as a form of emotion-focused coping.

Studies of simple distraction

CBT strategies have used distraction in a variety of ways, as a means of educating patients about the cognitive model of disorder, and as a symptom management strategy. Distraction by pleasurable activities in the form of activity scheduling is used to interrupt depressive thinking and counteract depressive inertia (e.g. Beck, Rush, Shaw & Emery, 1979). The positive effect of such strategies on mood is typically used as evidence that thinking patterns and behavioural inactivity have an influence on depressive experiences. Laboratory-based studies have demonstrated that instructions to focus on and describe scenes reduces negative thoughts and reduces depressed mood in patients with depression (Fennel & Teasdale, 1984; Fennel, Teasdale, Jones & Damle, 1987). Empirical studies of distraction effects in anxiety have examined effects in test anxiety and its effects in conjunction with exposure interventions. For instance, Thyer, Papsdorf, Himle, McCann, Caldwell and Wichert (1981) failed to find an advantage of adding distraction to a CBT treatment for individuals with test anxiety. Wise and Hayes (1983) compared cognitive restructuring and task-focusing instructions with no treatment for test anxiety and performance deficits. Both treatments were superior to a wait-list condition in reducing anxiety and improving performance on digit-span tasks. The two treatments did not differ in effectiveness.

Under some circumstances it appears that the use of distraction may be disadvantageous. When used in conjunction with exposure, distraction has been associated with an increase in the return of fear responses following treatment. Sartory, Rachman and Grey (1982) showed that return of fear following exposure increased when distraction was used, compared with when subjects were instructed to think about the phobic object following exposure. It has been suggested that thinking about the phobic object following exposure is likely to extend exposure and therefore improve outcome. The effects of distraction versus attentional focusing instructions have been investigated in individuals with obsessive-compulsive symptoms undergoing exposure. Grayson, Foa and Steketee (1982) examined the effect of these attentional manipulations during exposure of individuals with washing rituals. Subjects received either exposure with distraction on day 1, followed by exposure with attentional focusing on the stimulus, or vice versa. Both conditions were associated with decreases in within-session anxiety; however, fear only remained lower on day 2 in subjects who had focused their attention on the stimulus during exposure when this was presented on day 1. In order to determine if this effect resulted from attention focusing facilitating habituation or from distraction impairing habituation, a further study was conducted by Grayson, Foa and Steketee (1986). This study compared attention focusing with distraction when both were used in conjunction with exposure to a most highly feared contaminant in obsessive-compulsive individuals with washing rituals. In the attention-focusing condition, the therapist engaged the subject in conversation about the contaminant that the subject was holding and the discomfort it aroused. The most feared contaminant was used, for example a subject fearful of contamination by urine held a paper towel dampened with urine. In the distraction condition, the subject held the contaminant in one hand while playing a video game with the other. The effect of these conditions on heart rate and subjective anxiety was evaluated. On the first day of exposure, distraction was associated with a greater reduction in subjective anxiety than attentional focusing but this was not statistically significant. However, the attentional focusing group showed significantly greater decreases in heart rate during the middle and later stages of exposure compared with the distraction group. These results suggest that attention to feared stimuli and responses may enhance heart rate habituation under some circumstances. However, as Wells and Matthews (1994) point out, since the attentional focusing condition used in this study incorporated instructions to focus on the external features of the stimulus and internally on discomfort, it is not known if it was external or internal attention focusing or their combination that was associated with heart-rate habituation.

Clearly, further studies are required to explore the effects of distraction in depression and anxiety. However, a potential difficulty for such studies rests with the ambiguity that surrounds the precise nature of feared stimuli in anxiety. The S-REF model asserts that internal responses and internal stimuli are a focus of attention in psychological disorder. For example, a claustrophobic fears confinement in small spaces because of the fear that he/she will suffocate or go crazy. Internal "feelings" are a predominant source of input for making distorted judgements in psychological disorder. Thus, distraction studies should endeavour to examine the relative effects of distraction from internal versus external events during exposure to threat. An important question in distraction research is whether distraction should be from features of the external situation, such as features of a spider in a spider phobic, or from thinking about or experiencing bodily reactions. Unfortunately, few studies in this area allow us to directly address this issue. In one study, Epstein, Rosenthal and Szpiler (1978) exposed subjects to bursts of aversive white noise under conditions of distraction (letter cancellation task), external attention (focusing on external features of the experiment) or internal attention (concentrate on feelings and inner reactions to the noise). External attention was associated with heart rate deceleration, while internal attention was associated with increased galvanic skin response (considered to be a measure of anxiety) during anticipation of the noxious stimulus. These data suggest that internal attention may intensify anticipatory anxiety; thus, under anticipatory stress it may be better to focus on external aspects of the situation rather than internal feelings, a finding consistent with S-REF predictions.

Other studies which shed some light on this issue have manipulated the intensity of self-focused attention during exposure to feared stimuli. These studies show that experimentally enhanced self-focus or elevated dispositional self-attention (self-consciousness) is positively associated with fear responses and avoidance in tasks involving exposure to feared stimuli (Carver & Blaney, 1977; Carver, Blaney & Scheier, 1979; Scheier, Carver & Gibbons, 1981). Moreover, instructions to focus externally appear to enhance the effects of brief exposure in patients with social phobia (Wells & Papageorgiou, 1998b). Craske, Street and Barlow (1989) studied the effect of focusing on feared somatic sensations and the effect of practising a distraction task during *in vivo* exposure of patients with panic disorder and moderate to severe agoraphobia. The distracted patients tended to show superior outcome post-treatment, but at six month follow-up the attention-focusing patients showed a tendency to improve over the follow-up period. However, none of these differences were statistically significant.

How might we explain these mixed effects of distraction? In the S-REF framework, distraction may divert attention away from processing threat and emotion, and thereby reduce emotional experience temporarily. It may also prevent activation of fear networks or anxiety "programmes", thereby reducing anxiety. It is likely that the longer-term effects of distraction will depend on whether or not the distraction has blocked or facilitated the encoding of new information that can modify maladaptive knowledge (beliefs and processing plans). It is possible that under some conditions attention diversion techniques will interfere with emotional processing because they prevent activation of maladaptive processing, and so the individual is unlikely to modify maladaptive components of specific processing routines. However, when distraction strategies reduce arousal, new information concerning arousal may become available for encoding. For instance, an individual may obtain evidence that arousal and bodily sensations are controllable, and this may challenge pre-existing negative beliefs about the uncontrollability and dangerousness of such responses. In an associative learning context, decreasing arousal intensity through distraction may weaken conditioned linkages between stimuli and arousal responses. However, complications emerge in predicting the effects of attention strategies or the circumstances under which specific strategies should be employed when we consider in more detail the potential impact of attentional strategies on beliefs. Whilst attentional strategies may reduce the intensity of arousal or emotion, they do not invariably provide access to unambiguous information that can disconfirm negative beliefs. In some circumstances, the use of distraction or attentional strategies may block the revision of negative beliefs. For example, if the individual uses distraction or attentional focusing to reduce arousal and the individual also believes that high arousal is potentially harmful, attentional strategies may prevent full exposure to disconfirmatory experiences. Because high arousal has been avoided, the individual has not encountered experiences demonstrating that high arousal is in fact harmless. In addition, even if arousal was experienced the individual may attribute the non-occurrence of catastrophe to use of distraction-based coping and so negative beliefs remain unmodified. On the basis of this analysis, it can be seen that distraction strategies may be helpful for reducing arousal and/or modifying beliefs under some circumstances. However, if these responses are linked to negative appraisals and beliefs that suggest that such responses are dangerous, distraction-based control strategies may prevent long-term reductions in fear, since fear-related propositions remain unmodified. Ideally, cognitive attentional strategies should be developed that facilitate reductions in physiological responses *and* provide information that modifies dysfunctional knowledge.

OVERSIMPLISTIC VIEW OF ATTENTION IN PSYCHOTHERAPY

On the basis of the foregoing review, it is clear that attention-based treatment strategies have not been based on a detailed theory linking attention to other important aspects of cognition in psychological disorder. Moreover, on a conceptual level, theories of attentional bias that emphasise selective processing of threat have focused chiefly on attentional bias for externally presented disorder-congruent material, and have ignored the role of self-focused attention. Studies of attention manipulations in treatment have used brief distraction or attention-focusing instructions as short-term coping strategies or in an exploratory way, without considering the multidimensional nature of attention or its links with maladaptive self-knowledge[1].

In contrast to earlier approaches, the S-REF perspective offers a more sophisticated view of attention. Here attention manipulations can have multiple effects on different components of cognition, depending on the nature of the attention manipulation used and the context in which it is used. Moreover, the S-REF model offers specific implications for

---

[1] "Self-knowledge" is used to refer to declarative beliefs and procedural knowledge (plans).

developing attention-based treatment strategies. Because the main-tenance of psychological disorder and vulnerability is linked closely with dynamic disturbances in processing, in which attentional processes are a primary substrate, modification of attention should facilitate thera-peutic changes. For instance, attentional strategies could be developed that have an important effect in counteracting heightened self-focused attention, provide a means of increasing the executive control over pro-cessing, and increase the flow of new information into processing to facilitate belief change. Since maladaptive processing is driven by meta-cognitive plans (procedural knowledge) stored in long-term memory, re-training attention provides a means of establishing and strengthen-ing alternative plans by consciously practising new attention strategies when dealing with threat or challenge. For example, individuals with performance anxiety can be instructed to focus away from themselves and onto key task parameters in order to reduce anxiety and improve performance.

Since attentional manipulations may impact on different aspects of cogni-tion and their effect may be determined by the individual's goals and contextual factors, it is assumed that a particular strategy will not always produce the same effects. As we saw earlier in this chapter, if attentional strategies are used to avoid unrealistic danger, the individual may fail to discover that his/her danger appraisals are false. Following from the S-REF model, it is reasonable to expect that attentional strategies can be developed that aim to effect the following maladaptive components of cognition: (1) reduce perseverative worry/rumination; (2) increase flex-ible control over processing; (3) reduce threat monitoring and unhelpful self-focus; (4) increase attention to disconfirmatory information. Thus, attention procedures may be used to write more adaptive plans for pro-cessing and free-up attentional resources needed for restructuring mal-adaptive beliefs.

The development of explicit theory-based attentional strategies for treat-ing emotional disorder is in its infancy but is already producing impres-sive preliminary effects which add impetus to continuing investigations in this area. One exciting possibility is that it may be possible to retrain attention in a way that interferes with the cognitive-attentional syndrome underlying emotional disorder maintenance, and increases flexible con-trol over processing (metacognitive control processes). The first attempt to construct a formal attention treatment strategy with this S-REF-based objective in mind was undertaken in the treatment of panic disorder (Wells, 1990). The ATT devised for this purpose has since been applied to a range of anxiety disorders and to depression.

ATTENTION TRAINING TECHNIQUE (ATT)

ATT was developed as an attempt to modify the perseverative self-relevant processing that is characteristic of emotional disorders. It was hypothesised that a technique that facilitated the interruption of repetitive self-attentional processing should switch off maladaptive processing routines that contribute to problem maintenance and stress vulnerability. The first published report of usage of the technique appeared in 1990 as a single case study of an individual with panic disorder and concurrent relaxation-induced anxiety (Wells, 1990). Since then, a series of further single cases have been published, replicating the findings with additional panic disorder cases and extending effects to modifying the cognitive and affective components of social phobia (Wells, White & Carter, 1997), hypochondriasis (Papageorgiou & Wells, 1998) and recurrent major depression (Papageorgiou & Wells, in press).

Effectiveness of ATT

The effects of ATT have been evaluated across a series of single case studies that have used formal single case methodology. These studies consistently show that the procedure is effective in reducing anxiety and depressed mood and is effective in modifying maladaptive beliefs in panic disorder, social phobia, hypochondriasis and recurrent major depressive disorder (Wells, 1990; Wells et al., 1997; Papageorgiou & Wells, 1998, submitted). The effect of attention training on beliefs is particularly interesting and is consistent with the view that direct modification of attentional processes can lead to synchronous changes in dysfunctional beliefs. This effect is clearly consistent with a dynamic view of cognition in psychological disorder.

Several mechanisms could underlie the clinical effectiveness of ATT. Candidate mechanisms include:

1. Attenuation of self-focused attention.
2. Disruption of ruminative and worry-based processing strategies.
3. Increased executive control over attention and processing.
4. The strengthening of a metacognitive mode of processing.

The attenuation of self-focused attention in emotional disorder is likely to be helpful since it will reduce the perceived intensity of affective and somatic responses. The use of attention procedures such as ATT could also imply that such responses are harmless and to be ignored. The procedure not only draws attention away from the physiological state and emotion, it is also likely to diminish selective attention to negative thoughts in emotional states. By diminishing self-focused attention, individuals are practising switching out of self-referent processing and are taking "off-line" the regeneration of negative self-knowledge.

ATT may exert a central therapeutic effect by disrupting perseverative processing activities, namely worry and rumination. Such processing is a central maladaptive component of the cognitive-attentional syndrome. In a series of patients with recurrent major depression treated with ATT, rumination clearly decreased during ATT (Papageorgiou & Wells, in press). There are benefits to interrupting perseverative processing of this kind. First, worry and rumination may be associated with the maintenance of dysfunctional patterns of attention, and memory retrieval that maintains threat appraisals and negative beliefs. For example, worrying about one's physical health may prime the detection of bodily symptoms. Similarly, ruminating on the unfulfilling aspects of one's current situation may be associated with the retrieval of previous failures and disappointments. Thus, ruminative and worry-based processing may lock individuals into negative processing configurations that sustain negative interpretations and beliefs. Second, the interruption of perseverative processing by ATT will switch off these cyclical processes and thereby free-up attentional capacity for other processing operations, required for executive control processes and/or the processing of new and potentially disconfirming information.

Attention control exercises constituting ATT rely on the use of metacognitive control strategies that initiate non self-referent processing and flexibly regulate object-level processing. ATT requires the development of demanding and flexible non-self-referent executive functions. The effect is to increase metacognitive control over attention allocation. Under these circumstances it is likely that attention becomes more flexible and is less bound to particular types of dysfunctional knowledge. Improved control allows the person to modify dysfunctional knowledge and process potentially threatening stimuli without triggering the full-blown dysfunctional configuration of cognitive perseveration and biased cognitive processes.

Similarly, it is likely that ATT augments a metacognitive processing mode. Intrusions of body state information or thoughts that occur spontaneously during ATT are treated as "noise" that should not be given attention. External focus may allow patients to reason about their condition in a detached problem-focused manner without being overwhelmed by their personal engagement with their difficulties. More specifically, the procedure may promote a "detached mindfulness" (cf. Wells & Matthews, 1994), in which individuals can view particular cognitions and other internal events in a non-self-relevant and non-threatening way.

The above considerations are not mutually exclusive, but each reflects a conceptually different effect. The finding that ATT appears to cause long-term improvement in anxiety and depression simply by periodically training attention rather than by explicitly modifying patients' beliefs, is challenging for cognitive theory that attributes psychopathology to the content of beliefs. However, if, as the S-REF model predicts, beliefs are the outputs of running particular processing routines, the modification of cognitive processes and of metacognitive control should influence beliefs.

Description of ATT

ATT consists of auditory attentional exercises. These exercises are conceptually classified as *selective attention*, rapid *attention switching*, and *divided attention* exercises. Each class of exercise is practised during the course of a single ATT session. The procedure lasts for 10–15 minutes. Participants are asked to focus on a visual fixation point and to remain visually fixated whilst practising the auditory attention exercises. At least three competing sounds are used in the immediate vicinity of the participant (i.e. in the same room). At least three sounds are also introduced or identified (if they pre-exist) outside of the room and within the near distance, and a further three sounds are identified in the far distance. If it is not possible to identify sounds outside of the practice room, a solution is to introduce several (e.g. nine) competing sounds of varying loudness in the immediate vicinity.

The attentional demands imposed by the technique are intended to be incremental within and across each phase. This is achieved by increasing task difficulty by progressively identifying less distinct sounds in the selective attention phase, increasing the speed of attention switching during the attention switching phase, and by completing the procedure with a sustained divided attention instruction.

ATT is intended to be practised in anxiety disorders when the participant is not in a state of anxiety or ruminatory self-focus. It is not intended to be a means of controlling anxiety symptoms or worrying thoughts. Usage as a control technique may be counterproductive in some instances where the non-occurrence of feared events may be attributed to use of the strategy, thereby leading to a failure to revise beliefs concerning the validity of fears. ATT is not principally conceptualised as a strategy to manage states of distress, but is considered to be involved in changing more stable maladaptive attributes of the cognitive system.

The rationale for ATT

As with most forms of intervention, a credible and acceptable rationale is an important component of ATT. The rationale used across single case evaluations has been modified across the different disorders that have been treated. However, an underlying theme in all rationales used to date is that self-focus intensifies internal reactions, increases the detection of such reactions, and contributes to the maintenance of negative beliefs and emotions. In using the technique with hypochondriacal patients, the effects of self-focus have been illustrated with self-focus experiments as a means of illustrating the basic principles central to the rationale.

Unrealistic patient assumptions about the technique should be elicited and dealt with prior to practising the technique. A common misconception is that the technique should lead to a complete unawareness of thoughts not related to the exercise. The therapist should emphasise that the aim behind the technique is not to "blank out" everything else from consciousness, but the aim is to practise directing attention in a particular way.

Examples of basic rationales

Panic disorder

> One of the factors that maintains anxiety is a tendency to focus attention on bodily symptoms. The problem with self-focus is that it intensifies emotional state and physical symptoms, and can increase difficulty in thinking. Focusing on symptoms and being overly aware of your body can make sensations seem alarming. An effective strategy for overcoming this problem is the reduction of high levels of self-focus. This can be achieved by practising a technique called "attention training".

The basic rationale is illustrated by discussion of the natural attentional modulators of anxiety that the patient has experienced, such as the effect of absorbing activities. Examples of attentional experiences reducing anxiety are used as evidence that reduced self-focus can reduce anxiety. In addition, specific symptoms for which the patient has become hypervigilant should be identified as an idiosyncratic example of heightened self-focus.

Hypochondriasis

People tend to become anxious about their health for different reasons. For example, someone close to them may become ill or die, or having your own symptoms can increase preoccupation with health and your body. Once you become worried about your health, it can be difficult to turn your attention away from monitoring your body. You may focus more on your body to make sure that symptoms do not get worse, and to ensure that bad things don't happen. However, focusing your attention in this way and becoming preoccupied with your symptoms has a number of negative consequences. First, it can intensify normal bodily sensations. Second, it increases your sensitivity to noticing bodily sensations. Third, it maintains worry about your health. It is normal for everyone to experience new symptoms from time to time. If you focus too much on your body you will begin to notice even more symptoms, which will make you worry more. To help you overcome your health anxiety, it is useful to reduce your body awareness. This can be done by practising a technique called Attention Training. This technique is not intended to distract you from your anxiety. It is designed to increase your control over attention, and allow you to develop more accurate beliefs about your physical symptoms.

The effect of self-focus on the awareness of bodily responses should be illustrated by an attentional focusing exercise in which participants can be instructed as follows:

Focus on the sensations in your fingertips. Concentrate on all of the sensations there. What sensations do you notice? You probably notice sensations that you were not aware of a few moments ago. These sensations are normal; but by focusing your attention on your body you have become more aware of them. If you thought that such sensations were a sign of serious physical illness, you would become anxious and even more preoccupied with them.

Depression

When people become depressed they tend to become highly self-conscious and to dwell on past problems, and present and future difficulties involving themselves. This form of self-preoccupation is problematic because it keeps low mood going. You can see this effect in action if you think about your own experiences of depression. When you dwell on your own negative thoughts and feelings, you probably notice that these become more intense and you feel worse. However, if something prevents or interrupts your dwelling, you may have noticed your mood improves. You will learn a technique called "attention training" which will allow you to prevent or interrupt self-focused thinking and reduce your overall level of preoccupation with your depressive thoughts and feelings.

Credibility check

Once the rationale has been presented, it is recommended that the therapist runs a credibility/expectancy check. This is achieved by asking the patient: "How helpful do you think this procedure will be in overcoming your problems? Can you give me a rating on a scale from 0 (not at all helpful) to 100 (very helpful)?".

If ratings of credibility are low, the therapist should examine the reasons for such judgements and attempt to enhance credibility. It may be necessary to repeat the rationale and use additional exercises to illustrate the role of self-focus in order to enhance ratings.

Self-attention rating

Following presentation of the rationale, a self-focus intensity rating should be made by the patient. This may consist of administering sub-scales of the Self-consciousness Scale (Fenigstein, Scheier & Buss, 1975) or consist of a specific Likert rating. A Likert rating is typically used in which patients are asked to rate current intensity of self-focus on a scale ranging from –3 to +3, as set out below:

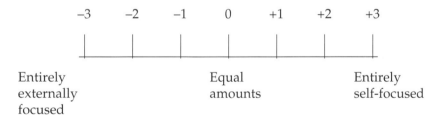

Self-attention ratings should be administered before and after sessional practise of ATT. Failure to produce a reduction in self-attention following the procedure should be explored. Following the first session of ATT, reductions in self-focus of at least two points are common.

OVERVIEW OF BASIC INSTRUCTIONS

The therapist should present the ATT in a slow, evenly paced and consistent tone. At least three competing sounds should be used in the consulting room. One of these can be the therapist's voice, a second sound is usually made by the therapist tapping on a desk or a book, and a further sound may be the sound of a clock, metronome or radio. Six sounds should be identified outside of the practice room. If naturally occurring sounds cannot be identified, an alternative strategy is to introduce further audible stimuli into the practice room of varying loudness to mimic low-level distant sounds. The selective attention and rapid attention switching phases of the exercise should occupy most of the 15 minute practice session (approximately 6 min each), with approximately 3 minutes devoted to divided attention. An example of a basic ATT instructional dialogue is presented below (the notation S3, S4, etc. is used to signify specific sounds that have been identified in each case):

Therapist dialogue

I am going to ask you to focus your gaze on a dot marked on the wall. I will sit slightly behind you so that I do not interfere with your fixed gaze. I would like you to keep your eyes open throughout the procedure. I will begin by asking you to focus on different sounds in this room and then other sounds outside of the room. After this first stage I will ask you to focus quickly on different sounds and shift your attention rapidly between them as I instruct you. The final stage consists of widening your attention and trying to attend to several sounds at the same time.

To begin, focus on the sound of my voice. Pay close attention to that sound, for no other sound matters. Try to give all of your attention to the sound of my voice. Ignore all of the other sounds around you. Focus only on the sound of my voice. No other sound matters, focus only on the sound of my voice.

Now focus on the tapping sound (S2), the sound that I make as I tap on the table. Focus only on the tapping sound, no other sound matters [Pause]. Closely monitor the tapping sound [Pause]. If your attention begins to stray or is captured by any other sounds, re-focus all of your attention on this one sound [Pause]. Give all of your attention to this sound [Pause]. Focus on the tapping sound and monitor this sound closely, filter out all of the competing sounds, for they are not significant [Pause]. Continue to monitor the tapping sound [Pause]. Focus all of your attention on that sound. Try not to be distracted [Pause].

Now focus on the sound of (S3, e.g. a clock in the room), focus all of your attention on that sound [Pause]. The other sounds do not matter. Focus on that sound, paying close attention to it and not allowing yourself to be distracted [Pause]. This is the most important sound and no other sounds matter [Pause]. Give all of your attention to that sound. If your attention strays, re-focus on the sound of (S3) [Pause]. Focus only on the sound of (S3). Give all of your attention to that sound [Pause]. Continue to monitor that sound closely, pay full attention to that sound [Pause]. Try not to be distracted.

(The above instructions should be repeated for three sounds (S4–6) in the near distance then three sounds (S7–9) in the far distance).

Now that you have identified and focused on different sounds I would like you to rapidly shift your attention between the different sounds as I call them out [Pause]. First, focus on the tapping sound, no other sound matters, give all of your attention to that sound [Pause]. Now focus on the sound of (S4) outside of this room, pay attention only to that sound [Pause]. Now switch your attention and focus on the sound of (S8) outside of this room, focus only on that sound, no other sound matters [Pause]. Now switch your attention to the tapping sound [Pause]. Re-focus on the sound of (S3) [Pause] now back to the tapping sound [Pause]. Now the sound in the far distance (S9) [Pause]. Focus back again on the sound of (S3) [Pause]. The sound of (S6) [Pause]; (S9) [Pause]; the sound of (S3); [Pause]: (S4).......(S8)......(S5).........etc.

Finally, expand your attention, make it as broad and deep as possible and try to absorb all of the sounds simultaneously. Try to focus on and be aware of all of the sounds both within and outside of this room at the same time [Pause]. Covertly count the number of sounds that you can hear at the same time [Pause]. Try to hear all of the sounds simultaneously. Count the number of sounds you can hear at the same time.

This concludes the exercise.

How many sounds were you aware of at the same time?

Eliciting feedback

Immediately following ATT, the therapist should elicit client feedback and ask the patient to re-rate the intensity of self-attention. A failure to reduce self-attention is a marker for difficulties which should be explored fully, and if necessary the procedure should be practised again with the necessary adjustments. The therapist should also ask how the client generally feels after the procedure, and normalise any concerns about perceptual or sensory experiences that occasionally follow the technique. For example, some patients report perceptual changes immediately following ATT.

The next step is to elicit feedback concerning the ease with which the procedure could be performed, and any difficulties that were experienced. It is helpful at this stage for the therapist to point out that the procedure is difficult and demanding and requires practise. It is important to be aware of comments that indicate unhelpful assumptions about the performance of ATT. In particular, some patients assume that the procedure has been ineffective or that they were unable to perform it correctly because distracting thoughts were experienced during practice. The therapist should re-emphasise that the aim is not to remove all other material from consciousness during ATT, but to practise focusing attention in a particular way. Moreover, it is not disadvantageous to experience distracting thoughts, as these offer "background noise" which make the focusing of attention more difficult and hence the procedure potentially more effective (i.e. it is like introducing a further competing sound).

Homework practice

Individual practice of ATT for homework is a central component of training. Patients should be asked to practise the technique at least twice a day for a period of 10–15 minutes. The technique should be practised as in the training session and the basic sequence of instructions followed. It is often helpful for clients to review in detail with the therapist the types of auditory stimuli that they will introduce into their environment to practise.

FIRST SESSION OUTLINE

The first ATT session should consist of the following elements:

1. Review the nature of the patient's problem and elicit details of self-focus and key cognitions for rating purposes (e.g. belief, self-focus ratings).
2. Present the rationale for ATT using idiosyncratic material. Socialise by illustrating the role of attention with reference to the client's own experiences and/or use a self-attention experiment.
3. Check the credibility of the rationale. Take steps to enhance socialisation if necessary.
4. Administer therapist-guided practise of ATT.
5. Elicit patient ratings/feedback and correct faulty expectancies.
6. Set homework and review in detail how this will be implemented.

SITUATIONAL ATTENTION REFOCUSING (SAR)

Whilst ATT provides a means of retraining executive control processes and of reducing self-perseveration, it does not explicitly focus patients'

attention on information that can disconfirm the content of specific negative appraisals. Less intensive and situation-specific attention re-focusing
strategies provide a means of reducing maladaptive self-attention and
increase the flow of disconfirmatory information into processing. To this
end, situational attentional re-focusing (SAR) strategies have been developed. Rather than using periodic and systematic training in external
attentional control, this strategy attempts to over-ride biased attention
and/or facilitate the development of disconfirmatory processing routines
during stressful situations.

Wells and Papageorgiou (1998b) investigated the effect of a particular
SAR strategy used in conjunction with exposure in social phobia. When
entering anxiety-provoking social situations, individuals with social
phobia are insecure about creating a favourable impression, and tend to
shift attention inward onto processing of the self as a social object (Clark
& Wells, 1995). The social phobic processes interoceptive information and
forms an image or impression of how he/she thinks he/she appears to
others. This impression is often in the form of an image from an "observer
perspective", in which anxiety symptoms and signs of inadequate performance are exaggerated and conspicuous (Hackman, Suraway & Clark,
1998; Wells, Clark & Ahmad, 1998; Wells & Papageorgiou, 2000a). A
central problem with self-processing is that it interferes with processing
of external information, such as positive feedback from others, that is
capable of modifying negative self-appraisals. Shifting to external attention in social phobia should be advantageous in modifying negative beliefs and reducing anxiety. Moreover, external attention is likely to
interfere with in-situation coping behaviours that require high levels of
self-monitoring. Disrupting such responses may increase the propensity
for belief change, since the non-occurrence of social catastrophe can no
longer be attributed to the use of subtle self-control or coping behaviours.
Thus, the individual is more likely to revise his/her negative appraisals
and predictions.

Using a repeated measures cross-over design, Wells and Papageorgiou
(1998b) investigated the effects of attention strategies in social phobia by
comparing the effects of one session of brief exposure alone with one
session of exposure plus an external attention focus (SAR). Each condition
was accompanied by a specific and appropriate rationale and the duration of exposure was the same in each condition. It was predicted that
exposure plus external attention (SAR) would be more effective than
exposure alone in reducing negative beliefs, reducing anxiety and shifting
patients away from an observer perspective in post-exposure images of
the anxiety-provoking social situation. In this study, the exposure period

used was not intended to resemble the more extended exposures characteristic of behaviour therapy, but was intended to act as a control for
non-specifics, such as a credible rationale and in-situation variables.
Furthermore, brief exposure more closely resembles the nature of encounters experienced by people with social phobia in their daily life.
Mean change in anxiety, negative beliefs and perspective taking for the
exposure alone condition and the external attention (SAR) condition are
presented in Figure 9.0.

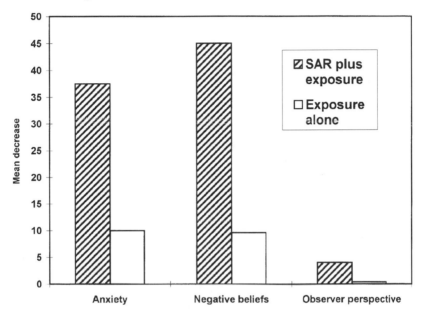

Figure 9.0 Effects of situational attentional refocusing plus exposure, versus
exposure alone, in social phobia

Patients rated the credibility of both interventions equally, and the external attention led to significantly greater decrements in anxiety and beliefs,
and a shift away from the observer perspective, compared to the exposure alone condition. Furthermore, a measure of focus of attention
confirmed that the attention condition had reduced self-focused processing as intended.

What mechanisms could account for the observed effects of external attention? In terms of our current theoretical approach, it is likely that
external focusing shifts attention onto social information that is capable of
disconfirming negative beliefs. In particular, if the patient believes that
he/she is the centre of everyone's attention, shifting to external focused

attention on other people offers a means of disconfirming this belief. Furthermore, external attention is likely to reduce awareness of anxiety symptoms and may also disrupt other unhelpful self-focused coping strategies that could deleteriously affect performance and prevent belief change. However, it could be argued that the effects observed are the result of distraction. That is, patients were merely distracted from their anxious experience. The study did not include a distraction condition and so the distraction possibility cannot be unambiguously tested in this instance. Nevertheless, any distraction interpretation requires an operationalisation of the distraction concept in the context of social phobia. As we saw earlier in this chapter, distraction usually refers to focusing attention on non-threat stimuli. In social phobia, the presence of other people may be considered to be a significant threat stimulus, therefore the external attention condition may be better defined as orientation towards threat.

In-situation attentional focusing strategies of a different kind have been used in the preliminary experimental treatment of social phobics with a fear of blushing (Bogels, Mulkens & DeJong, 1997). These authors have devised a technique of task concentration training (TCT), aimed at redirecting the attention of blushers away from the self and onto the social task during blushing. The TCT consists of three phases: (1) developing insight into attentional processes and the effects of heightened self-focus; (2) focusing attention outward in non-threatening situations; (3) focusing attention outward in threatening situations. This procedure differs from ATT and SAR outlined above in several respects. Most centrally, the rationale emphasises using outward attention to ". . . be able to break through the vicious circle and thereby cope with blushing" (p. 252). Thus, TCT is considered as a coping strategy, after which patients receive cognitive therapy. Neither ATT or SAR are presented as coping strategies but as a means of generally reducing self-focus (ATT), or as a means of refocusing attention to discover that fears are not true (SAR). A potential problem with using attentional manipulations as emotional control coping strategies, is that they remain closely tied to internal self-referent processing. The individual has to monitor on some level how well the strategy is impacting on emotional responses and there is a danger of continued time-sharing of internal and external (task-focused) attention. In addition, if the procedure is used to avert feared catastrophes, it may well prevent the individual from discovering that catastrophes do not occur.

Whilst the two patients treated by Bogels et al. showed a decrease in negative beliefs and blushing frequency following TCT alone, interpretation of the effects is difficult, since pre-treatment baselines were not established prior to the intervention. Nevertheless, these preliminary results suggest it may be worthwhile to examine TCT in a more controlled way.

THE DESIGN OF EFFECTIVE SAR STRATEGIES

In designing effective situational attention strategies, three factors should be taken into account:

1. The nature of existing unhelpful attentional strategies used by the patient in situation.
2. The goal of situational attentional modification.
3. Possible deleterious effects of the application of situational attention modification.

A challenge for therapists is the identification of in-situation attention strategies that contribute to stress and abnormal perceptions of threat. Freeing the individual from attention strategies that confirm dysfunctional appraisals and beliefs opens the way for restructuring maladaptive beliefs. I have referred to the use of metacognitive profiling in Chapter 7 to establish in detail the nature of an individual's in-situation processing routine. Specific aspects of maladaptive routines may be targeted. The nature of attentional treatment strategies used should be influenced by the goal of such procedures. If the goal is to increase the flow of disconfirmatory data into processing, then attentional strategies should focus attention on disconfirmatory data. If the aim is to enhance performance, attention should be directed to relevant task components. When the aim is to re-write metacognitive plans for processing, repeated practice of new in-situation attentional strategies will be required. Aside from the principle therapeutic goal, it is necessary to ensure that the patient's goals for practising SAR strategies are not inconsistent with the therapeutic aim of restructuring cognition. Some patients may use SAR maladaptively as a symptom avoidance strategy and under some circumstances this may impair cognitive restructuring.

Deleterious effects of the usage of SAR strategies may be encountered when such strategies excessively load attention so that insufficient resources are available for cognitive restructuring or efficient performance of tasks. Over-loading of attention is more likely in situations that are attentionally demanding. Problems are also likely to emerge if SAR strategies prevent the activation of dysfunctional self-knowledge, so that maladaptive knowledge cannot be directly challenged or plans re-written. Finally, as discussed previously, SAR should not become an avoidance strategy that could block habituation processes or higher-level restructuring. In some instances, SAR may be used to facilitate cognitive change. For instance, it is suggested that a shift to external attention plus abandonment of unhelpful coping behaviours should be used early in the treatment of social phobia (Clark & Wells, 1995; Wells, 1997). This is necessary to configure the patient's attention in a way that facilitates subsequent disconfirmatory processing. External attention is used with a rationale that emphasises focusing on disconfirmatory information. Care should be exercised to ensure that external attention does not become a coping behaviour in its own right that is directed at preventing potential social catastrophes. If this does occur, it may serve to maintain negative beliefs and predictions, since non-occurrence of catastrophes can be at-tributed to the use of attentional strategy rather than to the fact that such catastrophes are unlikely or not really catastrophic at all.

In general, the situational external attention manipulations that we have used have been presented with a detailed rationale that emphasises belief change or changes in cognitive processes that are likely to have beneficial therapeutic effects. In treating social phobics, Wells and Papageorgiou (1998b) used the following rationale for SAR:

> When you enter a feared social situation, you tend to focus your attention on yourself. For example, your anxiety symptoms become the centre of your attention, and because they feel bad you think that you must look bad. Focusing on yourself prevents you from getting a realistic sense of the social situation. In order to overcome your anxiety, you have to go into the situa-tion and allow yourself to discover that your fears are not true. To do this, you should observe other people closely in order to gain clues about their reaction to you. For example, when you are self-conscious and it feels as if everyone is looking at you, you should look around and check this out. By focusing attention on what is happening around you, you will become more confident and discover that your fears are not true (pp. 361–362).

In other experimental work in our clinic on PTSD, we have been using attention manipulations to modify patients' hypervigilance for threat and their general sense of vulnerability in situations. PTSD symptoms, such as hypervigilance for threat, can be viewed as unhelpful coping strategies that maintain a personal sense of vulnerability. In conjunction with ex-posure to situations, we have instructed patients to focus externally on safety signals in the environment and to use this information to update frozen images/memories of trauma.

INCLUSION OF SAR IN COGNITIVE THERAPY OF SOCIAL PHOBIA

In a recent attempt to abbreviate cognitive therapy for social phobia, Wells and Papageorgiou (2000b) used empirical data on the effects of attention manipulations, and the theoretical basis of the S-REF model to abbreviate treatment. The new form of brief treatment retains exposure experiments and video feedback techniques for correcting distorted and negative self-images, as used in the original Clark and Wells (1995) treatment. Greater emphasis is given to situational attention strategies during exposure, consisting of focusing attention on other people and aspects of the external environment. The treatment also emphasises the discontinuation of anticipatory worry and post-event worrying following exposure to difficult social situations. Decisions to terminate brief treatment in a single case experimental case series were based on weekly self-consciousness scores. When patients' self-attention scores were equal to or less than 1 on an 8-point rating scale, and this score could not be attributed to increased levels of avoidance, treatment was terminated. The treatment proved to be effective and treatment gains were maintained at three and six month follow-up periods. The use of self-attention as a clinical criterion for discontinuation of treatment appears to have been effective. Changes in emphasis in treatment that lead to a greater focus on cognitive processes of attention and worry provisionally appear to offer a basis for abbreviating cognitive therapy of social phobia when they are combined with exposure and strategies that specifically modify negative self-image.

CONCLUSIONS

Attentional retraining procedures offer a means of directly modifying cognitive processes with the aim of facilitating metacognitive control skills, disrupting perseverative negative processing, and enhancing the flow of corrective information into processing. The S-REF analysis places a dysfunctional cognitive-attentional syndrome as central to disorder maintenance. It follows that retraining of attention may be used to disrupt problematic elements of the syndrome, and to enhance processing operations that contribute to the acquisition of new beliefs.

The design of effective attention retraining procedures will depend on a detailed analysis of the interactions that exist between attention, self-regulation of cognition, beliefs and coping. We have seen how attentional strategies may be beneficial, and also how, under some circumstances, they may be unhelpful in restructuring self-knowledge.

Although procedures such as ATT and SAR are still a novelty, preliminary data signals that these procedures can have a powerful effect on negative emotions, dysfunctional beliefs and perseverative cognitions. It may be possible in the future to develop a hierarchical approach to treatment. General procedures, such as ATT, could be used to enhance executive control skills and break the cycle of negative self-focus. Specific SAR strategies could then be used in conjunction with exposure/activity strategies, to enhance disconfirmatory processing and facilitate the development of new plans for guiding attention under circumstances of idiosyncratic stress. It is evident that there is much to be learned from direct manipulations of attention and from studying the effects of such manipulations on other important dimensions of cognition.

Chapter 10

TREATING PATHOLOGICAL WORRY AND GENERALIZED ANXIETY DISORDER

Repetitive negative thinking is a feature of most types of psychological dysfunction. Depression is associated with rumination and anxiety is associated with worry. Both types of thinking share a number of similarities but these types of thought can also be distinguished (Papageorgiou & Wells, 1999a). Worry is a central defining characteristic of generalized anxiety disorder (GAD). In this chapter, a metacognitive-based model and treatment of GAD is presented. This will serve to illustrate a number of the salient conceptual and practical applications of a metacognitive approach. The GAD model (Wells, 1995) is a derivative of the general S-REF analysis. An application of this analysis to understanding and treating GAD is pertinent because GAD can be viewed as the most "normal" of the anxiety disorders, and it has been suggested that cognitive processes in GAD are similar to those in high trait anxiety (Eysenck, 1992, 1997). Therefore, an understanding of underlying cognitive processes and mechanisms in this disorder should contribute to our general understanding of anxiety vulnerability. In my opinion, GAD can be viewed as one of the most basic manifestations of general maladaptive metacognitions that comprise vulnerability to psychological disorder.

A DEFINITION OF WORRY

Much of the early pioneering work on worry was conducted by Borkovec and colleagues, who offered a tentative definition of worrying (Borkovec, Robinson, Pruzinsky and DePree (1983). They defined worry as:

> a chain of thoughts and images negatively affect-laden and relatively un-
> controllable; it represents an attempt to engage in mental problem-solving
> on a issue whose outcome is uncertain but contains the possibility of one
> or more negative outcomes: consequently, worry relates closely to fear
> processes (p.10).

Since the time of this definition, empirical research has supported several features of this definition but has also led to elaborations. An important characteristic of worry is that it involves a type of internal verbal linguistic activity. Worrying is experienced as predominantly verbal rather than imaginal. Moreover, worry can be distinguished from other types of anxious thought, such as obsessions (Wells & Morrison, 1994; Wells & Papageorgiou, 1998a), and it is distinct in several respects from depressive rumination (Papageorgiou & Wells, 1999a). Although worrying is normally equated with fear or anxiety, questionnaire studies suggest a connection between worry and depression. This overlap may be due to lack of specifity in self-report measures of these constructs, but it also raises the important implication that depressive and anxious processes may be contained within the experience of worry (Borkovec, 1994). According to the S-REF analysis, metacognitive beliefs concerning perseverative thinking processes should underlie both types of mental event.

Differences between worry and other types of intrusive mental experience characterised by obsessional thoughts have been explored. In a naturalistic study, Wells and Morrison (1994) demonstrated that normal worries were more verbal, less involuntary and more realistic than normal obsessions and were associated with a greater compulsion to act. Using retrospective ratings of normal worry and obsessions, Clark and Claybourn (1997) showed that worry was rated as focused more on the consequences of negative events, was rated as more distressing and caused more worry about feeling distressed. Worry was rated as more likely to lead to effective solutions, was more likely to be associated with checking and caused more interference with everyday life. In other work, it has been suggested that ego-dystonicity should be emphasised in differentiating obsessional thoughts and worry (e.g. Purdon & Clark, 1993). Ego-dystonicity refers to the personally abhorrent and apparently alien nature of obsessional thoughts. They are ego-dystonic rather than ego-syntonic; ego-syntonic thoughts are experienced as more characteristic of the self.

Wells (1994a, 1995) suggests that worry can be a form of coping, whilst Borkovec and Inz (1990) have emphasised that worry can serve as a cognitive avoidance function, in which individuals with GAD use worry to distract attention from more distressing images. Other functions have also been attributed to worrying. In particular, Borkovec et al. (1983) and Davey (1994) view worrying as involved in problem-solving under conditions of uncertainty. Wells and Matthews (1994) suggested that at least two varieties of worry should be distinguished, an adaptive and a maladaptive variety. The adaptive variety is oriented at problem-solving and leads to problem-focused behaviour. However, the maladaptive variety generates a repetitive range of negative outcomes, in which the individual attempts to generate coping solutions until some internal goal is achieved. As we will see later in this chapter, further distinctions between worry subtypes have been made in the context of understanding GAD. In view of the advances in the conceptual complexity surrounding the analysis of worry, a revised definition of this phenomenon has been presented by Wells (1999):

> Worry is a chain of catastrophising thoughts that are predominantly verbal. It consists of the contemplation of potentially dangerous situations and of personal coping strategies. It is intrusive and controllable, although it is often experienced as uncontrollable. Worrying is associated with a motivation to prevent or avoid potential danger. Worrying may itself be viewed as a coping strategy but can become the focus of an individual's concern (Wells, 1999: p.87).

GENERALIZED ANXIETY DISORDER

GAD is defined in DSM-IV (APA, 1994) in terms of excessive anxiety and subjectively uncontrollable worry in the presence of at least three somatic symptoms which have persisted for at least six months. The disorder has proved difficult to treat. Treatments have consisted of a range of methods, such as bio-feedback, relaxation therapies, anxiety management and cognitive therapy based on the methods of Beck, Emery and Greenberg (1985). Only approximately 50% of patients achieve high end-state functioning across studies of cognitive-behavioural therapies (Durham & Allan, 1993; Fisher & Durham, 1999). This disappointing outcome has been attributed to the lack of a specific model for the disorder that can account for uncontrollable and distressing worry (Wells, 1995).

A METACOGNITIVE MODEL OF GAD

A model of GAD should attempt to account for the maintenance of excessive generalized and uncontrollable worry as the central distressing characteristic of this disorder. In earlier work (Wells, 1995, 1997), I have developed a model accounting for pathological worry in GAD. In this model, metacognition in the form of beliefs, appraisals and control strategies are central factors in the development and maintenance of the disorder. The model differs from other cognitive conceptualisations of GAD by emphasising the role of metacognition rather than maladaptive beliefs about the world as a dangerous place. An implicit aspect of this model is that worry in GAD is not merely a symptomatic consequence of anxiety, but is an active and motivated style of appraisal and coping with threat that is driven by the individual's beliefs. It is proposed that the individual with GAD uses worry in order to cope with anticipated dangers and threats. This model is depicted diagrammatically in Figure 10.0. In this model, a distinction is made between two types of worrying, labelled Type 1 and Type 2. Type 1 worry is concerned with external events and non-cognitive internal events (e.g. physical symptoms), whilst Type 2 worry concerns negative appraisal of one's own thought processes. This is essentially worry about worry, which I have also termed "meta-worry", since it comprises metacognitive appraisals.

Worrying is often triggered by an intrusive thought that may occur as an image or in the form of a "what if" question (e.g. "What if my partner is involved in a traffic accident?"). External factors such as news items can act as triggers for initial intrusions. Once a trigger is encountered, positive metacognitive beliefs about the usefulness of worrying as a coping strategy are activated. Examples of positive beliefs include: "My worrying helps me cope"; "Worrying keeps me safe"; and "If I worry I'll be prepared". These types of belief are quite normal and are not specific to GAD. The individual with GAD executes worry sequences in which a range of "what if" danger-related questions are contemplated and potential strategies for dealing with these scenarios are generated. This process, called Type 1 worrying, is associated with emotional responses, as depicted by the bi-directional dotted line in Figure 10.0. The contemplation of dangerous scenarios leads to the activation of an inherent anxiety programme and thus to cognitive and somatic anxiety symptoms. However, the relationship between Type 1 worrying and emotional responses is such that Type 1 worrying can lead to a reduction in anxious emotions and accompanying symptoms. When the Type 1 worry process meets its goal of generating acceptable coping responses, anxiety

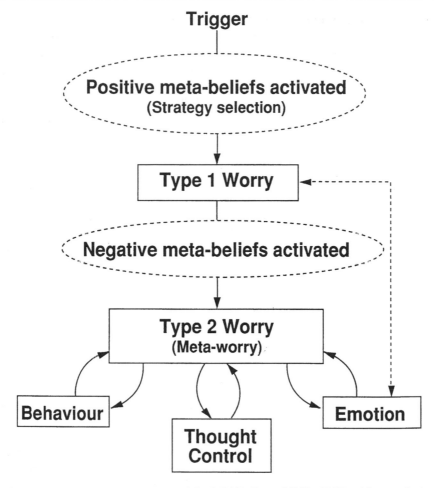

Figure 10.0   A metacognitive model of GAD. From Wells, 1997, with permission

diminishes. It follows that the duration of an anxiety response linked to Type 1 worry is associated with the length of time taken to meet goals for coping. The person with GAD continues to worry until he/she assesses that he/she will be able to effectively cope with anticipated threat. This assessment is often based on internal cues, such as a "felt sense" that one will be able to cope or the belief that all important outcomes have been considered in detail. Worrying stops when these internal goals are met. However, worrying may also stop when competing goals which have processing priority are activated and lead to a diversion of attention away from worrying.

Problems with worrying characteristic of GAD emerge as a consequence of negative metacognitive beliefs about the worry process and the consequences of worrying. Individuals with GAD hold negative beliefs as well as positive beliefs about worrying. Negative beliefs include: "Worrying could make me go crazy"; "I must control my worry or I will cease to function"; "Worrying is uncontrollable"; "Worrying could damage my health". During worry episodes, negative beliefs become activated and this leads to negative appraisals of the worry process. Such negative appraisals are known as Type 2 worry or "meta-worry" since they involve negative appraisal of the worry process, or "worry about worry". Type 2 worrying intensifies anxiety, as depicted by the cyclical arrows between Type 2 worry and emotion in Figure 10.0. If worrying and the symptoms associated with worrying are interpreted as a sign of imminent catastrophe, rapid escalations of anxiety in the form of panic attacks can occur. The relationship between Type 2 worry and emotion constitutes a vicious cycle in which cognitive and somatic symptoms associated with anxiety can be interpreted as evidence of loss of control and/or the negative effects of worrying. Once activated, Type 2 worry can intensify anxious and other emotional responses. Thus, it becomes increasingly difficult for the person with GAD to attain the goals (e.g. an internal felt sense) that signal that it is safe to stop worrying. These emotional symptoms contribute to a need for a continuation of Type 1 worrying when anxious responses are interpreted as a sign of a likely failure to cope with threat. Two further mechanisms contribute to problem maintenance. These are labelled "behaviour" and "thought control" in Figure 10.0.

Since positive and negative beliefs about worrying coexist and the individual is motivated to worry in response to initial "what if" threat appraisals or similar threat-related triggers, the person with GAD rarely attempts to actively interrupt a worry sequence once it is initiated. The interruption of such a worry sequence can be likened to asking the person with GAD not to cope with a particular threat, since worrying is a predominant mode of coping. Thought control rarely consists of an attempt to interrupt the worry process. Instead, the individual with GAD will attempt to avoid the need to worry in the first place. From a thought control perspective, this may involve attempts not to think about a particular worry topic, thereby avoiding triggering the need for a worry episode. For example, the individual currently concerned about relationships with a work colleague may attempt not to think about work when away from that situation. However, attempts not to think particular thoughts are rarely totally successful and there is some empirical evidence that suppression strategies may be counter-productive (Wegner, Schneider, Carter & White, 1987; Purdon, 1999). Thus, the individual is engaged in a control activity that generates information concerning a general inability to control thoughts in a desired fashion. This effect can reinforce negative appraisals concerning mental control and meta-worries. Moreover, a failure to interrupt worry sequences that are subject to personal control deprives the individual of control experiences that might otherwise modify negative beliefs and meta-worry.

In summary, few attempts are made to interrupt the worry process before the goal of worrying is achieved, although unsuccessful attempts may be made to remove the content of particular thoughts from consciousness. Therefore, the individual has few experiences of successfully controlling worry and negative appraisals of uncontrollability and danger remain unchallenged. Note that a distinction is made in this model between interrupting a worry process and suppressing a worry content. In interrupting the process, the content of a concern may remain in consciousness but the iterative and catastrophising process of worrying is suspended. This is different from suppression, in which the individual attempts to remove the content of a thought from consciousness.

The other relevant process in problem maintenance is behaviour. Whilst gross forms of avoidance are not a particular hallmark of GAD, more subtle forms of avoidance are relevant in some cases. For example, individuals seek reassurance in order to terminate worry sequences or in order to avoid the need to worry in the first instance. In addition, some patients avoid triggers for worry, such as situations, people or information. In order to resolve the dissonance that exists between positive and negative worry beliefs, it is better to avoid situations that trigger threat appraisals and thus the need to worry in the first instance. However, these behavioural strategies are problematic in several respects. The individual who avoids worry triggers is unable to practise alternative (non-worry) strategies for appraisal and coping. Avoidance or reassurance-seeking removes an opportunity to develop beliefs that worry is subject to cognitive self-control. In addition, avoidance, reassurance-seeking or similar behaviours, such as checking or information search, prevent the person with GAD from discovering that worrying is harmless. These behavioural strategies can prevent exposure to disconfirmatory evidence that proves that worrying is controllable, non-perpetual and harmless. Thus, Type 2 worries and negative beliefs are maintained as a consequence of these strategies.

Empirical status of the model

Research on patients with GAD and on worry-prone individuals has provided support for several central components of this model. Much of this experimental work was presented in Chapter 3, where the empirical support for metacognitions in emotional disorder was considered. However, a summary of this and related findings are as follows:

1. Positive and negative beliefs correlate positively with proneness to pathological worry (Cartwright-Hatton & Wells, 1997; Wells & Papageorgiou, 1998a).
2. Individuals meeting criteria for GAD give higher ratings for positive reasons for worrying involving superstition and problem-solving than non-anxious subjects (Borkovec & Roemer, 1995).
3. Patients with GAD report significantly greater negative beliefs about worrying than patients with panic disorder, social phobia or non-patient controls. However, they show equivalent levels of positive beliefs (Wells & Carter, 2000).
4. Type 2 worry is a better predictor than Type 1 worrying of pathological worry in non-patients (Wells & Carter, 1999).
5. Compared to patients with panic disorder, social phobia or non-patients, patients with GAD have significantly higher meta-worry scores (Wells & Carter, 2000).
6. Worrying appears to be associated with an increase in intrusive thoughts under some circumstances (Borkovec et al., 1983; York et al., 1987; Butler et al., 1995; Wells & Papageorgiou, 1995). These data support the idea that using worry as a processing strategy may well contribute to a proliferation of intrusive thoughts under some circumstances.
7. In a prospective study of predictors of GAD status and of pathological worry, meta-worry and negative beliefs emerged as significant predictors 12–15 weeks later in different equations (Nassif, 1999).

Wells and Carter (1999) tested the prediction, based on the GAD model, that Type 2 worry should be positively associated with pathological worry independently of Type 1 worries. They asked 140 non-patient subjects to complete a questionnaire battery consisting of the Anxious Thoughts Inventory (AnTI; a measure of Type 1 and Type 2 worries), the Penn State Worry Questionnaire (PSWQ; a measure of pathological worry like that found in GAD), the Speilberger Trait Anxiety Subscale, individual ratings of how much worry was a problem, and a rating of the controllability of worry. All three AnTI subscales (social worry, health worry and meta-worry) were significantly positively correlated with PSWQ and with problem level. The results of regression analyses controlling for the interdependency of trait anxiety, AnTI subscales and pathological worry measures showed that only trait anxiety and AnTI meta-worry significantly predicted pathological worry score when trait-anxiety and the other AnTI subscales were in the equation. Thus, Type 2 worry, but not Type 1 worry, was the best predictor of pathological worry measured by the PSWQ. A similar pattern emerged when problem level associated with worrying was treated as the dependent variable. Once again, Type 2 worry and trait-anxiety significantly predicted problem level but social and health worries did not. In subsequent analyses that additionally controlled for the uncontrollability of worrying, trait anxiety and Type 2 worry remained significant predictors of pathological worry. Type 2 worry also remained significantly positively associated with problem level, even when uncontrollability of worry and PSWQ were entered as predictors. These data suggest that Type 2 worry is a stronger and more reliable predictor of pathological worry than Type 1 worry, as predicted by the model.

In another test of the model, Wells and Carter (2000) examined Type 2 worry, Type 1 worry and metacognitive beliefs in patients with GAD, social phobia, panic disorder, and individuals with no history of disorder. Patients with GAD differed from other anxious groups in reporting higher levels of meta-worry and negative beliefs about worrying. There were no differences between groups in positive beliefs. Interestingly, in this study patients with depression showed some metacognitive similarity to GAD patients. These data are consistent with a central prediction of the present model that GAD patients should be characterised by meta-worry and negative beliefs. Furthermore, the dissonance between positive and negative beliefs can be inferred from the finding that GAD patients did not differ from non-patients or other patients in positive beliefs. Thus, they do not appear to compensate for their negative beliefs by a reduction in positive beliefs about worrying.

A prospective study by Nassif (1999) examined the meta-cognitive predictors of the development of GAD and pathological worry across a 12–14 week period. In this study, non-patients were tested at time 1 and again at time 2 and completed a battery of questionnaires consisting of the MCQ, AnTI, Trait anxiety, PSWQ and GAD-Q. The GAD-Q, developed by Borkovec and Roemer (1995), is a tool that allows for the identification of individuals meeting criteria for GAD as defined in DSM-III-R. The results of this study showed that meta-worry or negative beliefs were associated with GAD and pathological worry at time 2, when GAD status or pathological worry scores at time 1 were controlled. Moreover, partial correlations showed that relationships between metacognitive predictors and pathological worry were one-directional. Metacognitive factors appeared to cause pathological worry; however, pathological worry did not appear to be causally associated with metacognitions.

In summary, a growing body of evidence is supportive of the metacognitive model of GAD. A new form of metacognitive therapy based on the model has been developed (Wells, 1995, 1997). Treatment implications and an outline of this treatment approach are considered in the remainder of this chapter.

IMPLICATIONS FOR TREATMENT

The present model helps to explain the modest response rate in CBT interventions for GAD. Previous approaches have not been based on a specific model of the processes involved in the maintenance of uncontrollable worry. The use of general cognitive therapy methods based on schema theory leads to a therapeutic focus on challenging and restructuring Type 1 worries and corresponding non-metacognitive beliefs. It is likely that this approach will be of limited use, because it fails to substantially change patients negative appraisals and negative beliefs about worrying, and fails to provide alternative strategies for coping with threat. The effectiveness of cognitive therapy of GAD should be improved by formulating cases in terms of the metacognitions and maintenance processes outlined in the present model.

The present model shifts the focus of intervention onto modifying negative and positive beliefs about worrying, and onto the development of alternative non-worry-based strategies for appraising and dealing with threat. In implementing this treatment, clinical experience has suggested that a particular sequence to metacognitive modification is likely to produce optimum effects. First, negative appraisals and beliefs about the uncontrollability of worry should be elicited and modified. Second, meta-worries and negative beliefs about the dangers of worrying should be targeted for modification. Once these beliefs and meta-appraisals have been effectively modified, the therapist should then formulate and challenge positive beliefs about worry and finally introduce alternative strategies for appraising threat. The reason for this particular sequence is that when patients believe that worrying is uncontrollable, it is often too threatening for them to comply optimally with behavioural experiments consisting of attempts to "lose control" of the worry process. Experiments consisting of attempts to lose control of worry are useful for challenging negative beliefs about the dangers of worrying. The initial modification of uncontrollability beliefs increases compliance with subsequent experiments. Negative metacognitions should be targeted in therapy before positive beliefs, since these are most closely linked to acute anxiety. The practice of alternative strategies for processing threat should be introduced after metacognitive belief change, so that alternative strategies do not become behaviours that prevent the disconfirmation of dysfunctional beliefs about worrying. However, the clinician should remain flexible in deciding on this intervention sequence in individual cases.

ELICITING METACOGNITIONS

Treatment proceeds on the basis of an idiosyncratic case formulation, which in turn is based on the Cognitive Model of GAD (Figure 10.1). In order to construct an idiosyncratic case formulation, it is necessary to elicit the relevant metacognitions emphasised by the model. Two general categories of Type 2 worry and negative beliefs are relevant: (1) beliefs about uncontrollability, and loss of control of worry; and (2) beliefs and appraisals concerning the dangers of worrying. Positive beliefs about worrying may be less apparent at the outset of assessment. Relevant metacognitions can be elicited with self-report measures, such as those reviewed in Chapter 7, including the Anxious Thoughts Inventory (AnTI) and Metacognitions Questionnaire (MCQ).

However, a further instrument devised for clinical purposes, the Generalized Anxiety Disorder Scale (GADS; Wells, 1997; see Appendix VI) is particularly useful, since it measures a range of variables central to case conceptualisation. Furthermore, it facilitates monitoring of changes in key negative and positive beliefs and behaviours during the course of treatment. This instrument enables the therapist to keep track of changes in affective, cognitive and behavioural dimensions of generalized anxiety and to assess the impact of interventions on specific components in the case formulation.

Aside from self-report methods, interview strategies can be used to elicit metacognitions. One such technique is the advantages/disadvantages analysis. Here the therapist asks the patient to list the advantages of worrying and the disadvantages. The advantages correspond to positive metacognitive beliefs about worry, whilst the disadvantages correspond to negative beliefs. Another strategy consists of asking if, during a distressing worry episode, the patient has experienced negative thoughts about worry (meta-worry).

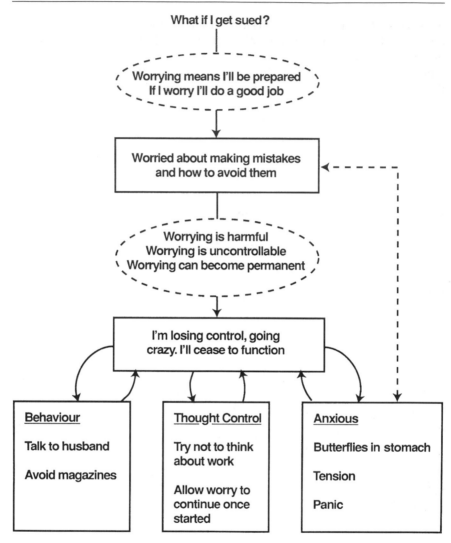

Figure 10.1   An idiosyncratic case conceptualisation based on the GAD model

GENERATING A CASE FORMULATION

Several interview methods are available for eliciting the components of a case formulation. One of the most useful strategies is to review with the client a recent episode of distressing worry. The episode should be traced out slowly and the different elements in the model elicited. Particular questions offer a useful means of exploring the nature of the worry episode. Metacognitions can be elicited by questioning the consequences of not controlling worry, and by questioning the worst consequences of worrying. Data collected by this means can be combined with data from the GADS to produce a more complete case conceptualisation.

Once an episode of worry has been identified, the therapist first determines the nature of the trigger for worrying. This can be accomplished by asking, "What was the initial event or thought that triggered your worrying?". The therapist should aim to identify an initial thought that acted as the trigger. These thoughts most often occur in the form of "what if" questions (e.g. "What if my partner has been involved in a car accident?"). Identification of the trigger is then followed by tracking the nature of the patient's response to the trigger. In particular, the patient may be asked, "What happened when you had that thought; what did you think or what did you do?". At this juncture the therapist can explore with the patient the nature of Type 1 worry and also the emotional response associated with worrying. Once the worrying response has been identified, the next step is to proceed to identify negative thoughts about worry itself (Type 2 worry) and associated negative beliefs. Questions asked at this point include: "When you noticed yourself worrying and feeling anxious, did you think anything bad could happen as a result of your worry and feelings?"; "What was the worst that could have happened if you had continued to worry?".

Behaviours linked to meta-worry should be elicited and included in the appropriate section of the model. Questions that have proved useful for eliciting behaviours are: "When you noticed yourself worrying, did you do anything to deal with it?"; "What did you do?"; "What would have happened if you had not done anything?". Questioning the purpose of behaviours or the anticipated effects of failure to engage in behaviours provides a means of accessing negative appraisals and beliefs concerning worry.

The extent to which patients with GAD articulate positive beliefs about worry during assessment varies. However, positive beliefs may be determined from questionnaire measures such as the GADS, and by asking about the advantages of worrying. Initially, the model may be constructed with the positive component missing and a link in the formulation is made directly between the trigger and Type 1 worry.

The following extract of a dialogue with a GAD client illustrates the use of the Socratic methods outlined above to determine the information used to construct the idiosyncratic case formulation in Figure 10.1.

T: I'd like to ask you about the last time you had a bad worry episode and felt particularly distressed. When was the last time?

P: I had a couple of bad days last week on Wednesday and Thursday.

T: Was that a fairly typical worry episode?

P: Yes, only it was worse than I've been for a while.

T: Thinking back to Wednesday when the worry started, what was it that triggered the worry? Was it a thought or a situation that started it off?

P: I was at work and I'd just been reading a paper on litigation and a case of someone who had been sued by a customer.

T: So you were reading a paper, and what was the initial thought that triggered your worrying?

P: I thought that this could happen to me. What if I got sued, what would I do?

T: So the initial thought was, "What if I get sued?". When you thought that, what happened next? Did you begin to worry?

P: Yes, I started worrying about it and I felt the anxiety rising in my stomach.

T: So you felt anxious, let me make a note of that. You felt anxious and the sensations were in your stomach. What were the sensations like?

P: Like butterflies in my stomach, and feeling tense in my body.

T: Did you have any other anxious sensations at that time?

P: I don't remember any, but I seemed to get panicky later on.

T: OK, so when you felt that way, were you already beginning to worry?

P: Yes, I started to worry about what would happen and what I would do if I were in that situation.

T: What were the things you were worrying about? Can you give me some examples?

P: I was worried that I could make a mistake at work and if I did I was thinking about how I could deal with that, and how I might avoid making mistakes in the first place. Then I began to worry that maybe I couldn't handle the stress, and my colleagues might think that I was incompetent.

T: So it sounds as though you had a number of worries. How long were you worrying for?

P: It was on my mind for the rest of the day, but my mind was partly occupied with work as well, so it wasn't until the evening that it really got to me. I couldn't sleep and I had to talk to my husband about it.

T: It sounds as if you were worrying for an extended period of time. During that time, what was happening to your anxiety?

P: I was feeling anxious for most of the day but I got really anxious in the evening when I couldn't seem to get it out of my mind.

T: It sounds as if in the evening you tried to get it out of your mind or control the worry somehow. Is that right?

P: Yes, well, I started to feel really panicky.

T: What thought went through your mind when you felt panicky?

P: I thought I was losing my grip and I was going to be ill or something.

T: In what way did you think you might be losing your grip?

P: I thought I was just going to remain anxious and not be able to get my head back together.

T: What do you mean by not getting your head back together? What would that be like?

P: Like I would go crazy. I wouldn't be able to function.

T: So the thought was that you were going to lose control, go crazy and cease to function. Is that right?

P: Yes. That's it, I was worried in case I would need to take time off work and not be able to handle the stress like everyone else.

T: That sounds like a negative thing to think about your worries—that you could lose control and that they could cause you to not function. Do you have any other negative beliefs about your worries?

P: Well, it can't be good for me. You hear of people developing stress-related illnesses.

T: Let me make a note of that. It sounds as if you believe that worrying is harmful and can lead to illness, and it also sounds as if you believe that worrying is uncontrollable and you can become trapped in worry. Is that right?

P: Yes.

T: How much do you believe that worrying can damage your health, 0–100%?

P: Oh, I'm convinced it can, 90%.

T: How much do you believe that worrying is uncontrollable?

P: 90%.

T: How much do you believe that you could become trapped in a state of perpetual worry/anxiety?

P: 90%.

T: What happened to your anxiety when you thought you were losing it?

P: I became very anxious and panicky.

T: When you thought you were losing it, did you do anything to try and remain in control and stop yourself from losing it?

P: There wasn't much I could do. I talked to my husband about it, hoping that he could help me think it through logically. He can normally calm me down and help me see that I am just getting things out of proportion.

T: Do you ever do anything else to try and prevent or control your worries?

P: Well, normally I would not read professional magazines because they would start me worrying about my own competence and I would try not to think about work when I am at home.

T: So you try not to think about work. How does that help?

P: Well, if I think about it, that will start me worrying.

T: Once you start worrying, have you ever tried to discontinue the worry process? In other words, rather than trying not to think about work at all, have you ever had the initial negative thought but decided not to worry about it?

P: No, I don't think so. It's like I need to worry about it.

T: What do you mean you need to worry about it? It sounds as if there may be some advantages to worrying.

P: Well, I suppose if I think it through and dwell on what might happen, it means I will be prepared to deal with it and it means that I'll do a good job.

T: So you have some positive beliefs about worry. It sounds as if you believe that worrying helps you do a good job, and you believe that worrying helps you to deal with problems. Is that right?

P: Yes, I think worrying helps me.

In this dialogue, the therapist elicits the material needed for constructing an idiosyncratic case formulation, as depicted in Figure 10.1. Apart from the initial elicitation of a trigger it is not necessary to follow a particular sequence in the elicitation of material. However, the components of the formulation are often more easily elicited by questioning the content of Type 1 worry, and once this is determined, to elicit the nature of anxious reactions associated with Type 1 worry. It is then possible to track back to the content of Type 2 worries that represent negative appraisals of the Type 1 worry and associated anxious response. In this particular dialogue, positive beliefs about worrying emerged towards the end of construction of the formulation. Such beliefs may be less amenable at the outset of assessment. The basic formulation of a recent worry episode should be embellished by subsequent questioning to elicit a full range of behaviours used to control or avoid worry, and other positive and negative beliefs and meta-worries.

Once the formulation has been constructed, treatment can then proceed based on the case formulation. Treatment consists sequentially of:

socialisation; modification of Type 2 worry and negative beliefs; modification of positive beliefs (plans); and relapse prevention work. Each of these will now be considered in turn.

SOCIALISATION

Socialisation consists of educating patients about the model and providing a mental framework for understanding the aims of cognitive-behavioural modification. Three methods of socialisation are typically used:

1. Sharing the idiosyncratic case formulation in verbal and diagrammatic form with the patient and eliciting feedback concerning the "goodness of fit" between the formulation and the nature of the problem.
2. Use of socialisation questions aimed at demonstrating the role of beliefs about worry in problem maintenance.
3. Socialisation experiments intended to illustrate components of the model.

The therapist should draw out an idiosyncratic case formulation like that depicted in Figure 10.1, and then proceed to describe the model to the patient. The goal is to introduce the concept that a central feature of the patient's problem is worry about worry and negative beliefs about worrying. The following dialogue illustrates this process:

T: I've drawn out the things you describe in your worry episode. Let's both take a look at this and I'll describe what seems to be going on, and what we need to do in treatment. How does that sound?
P: Fine.
T: Your worry was triggered by reading some material and having the initial thought, "What if I get sued". This was associated with feeling anxious, and you continued to worry in order to work things out. Is that right?
P: Yes.
T: As you worried and you had fewer distractions, you then began to have negative thoughts about your worry. In essence you began to worry about worry. What happened to your anxiety when you started to worry about worry?
P: It got worse.
T: That's right, and that is depicted by this loop in the model. If you had not worried about your worry, do you think your anxiety would have become so bad?

P: No, probably not.
T: So you can see that one part of your problem is that you have developed negative beliefs about your worry, and you have now begun to worry about worry. For example, you believe that your worries are uncontrollable and you could lose your mind or cease to function. If you no longer believed that, how much of a problem would you have?
P: Less of a problem, but I would still have difficulty controlling my worries.
T: It's important that you have raised that, because another part of your problem is your belief that worrying is uncontrollable. One of the problems is that you use unhelpful control strategies, like trying not to think worrying thoughts, but you have seldom tried to interrupt a worry once it has started. In a minute, we'll do an experiment to show you what happens when you try not to think a thought. Before that, what do you think of this explanation? Is there anything that doesn't seem to fit with your problem?

Socialisation questions are typically used to convey the central idea that worrying is problematic because the individual has now developed negative beliefs about worrying. For example, to introduce the idea that negative beliefs and appraisal of worrying is a central component of the problem, the therapist can ask the following questions:

● If you believed that your life depended on worrying, how much of a problem would worrying be?
● If you believed you had control over your worrying, how much of a problem would you have?
● Most people worry, it is normal to do so. What is it that makes your worry such a problem? If you no longer believed that, would you still have a problem?

The therapist should reflect on the patient's answers to these questions to emphasise that beliefs and appraisals of worry are a central issue linked to distress and problem maintenance. For example: "So the problem is that you believe that you have no control. If you no longer believe that, would there be a problem?" etc. Other verbal strategies, such as the advantages/disadvantages analysis of worry, can also be used as a socialisation tool. Here, the advantages are used to reflect positive beliefs about worrying, whilst the disadvantages are used to reflect the patient's negative beliefs. Having articulated these positive and negative metacognitions, the therapist should then highlight that the patient is "in two minds" about worrying (i.e. dissonance exists) and then explore with the patient the emotional and behavioural consequences of this dissonance. Once again, the problem is framed in terms of beliefs held about worrying. In particular, the patient may be asked if he/she would have a problem with worrying if only the positive beliefs were held.

Behavioural experiments provide a powerful means of socialisation. Thought suppression experiments offer a strategy to illustrate how some control attempts are ineffective and may be counter-productive. Patients can be asked to suppress a specific target thought, such as the thought of a "purple elephant". This type of experiment is normally presented without a rationale. The therapist merely states, "I'd like to try a brief experiment with you. For the next 60 seconds, I want you to avoid thinking about a purple elephant. Whatever you do, you must not have any thoughts related to a purple elephant. Off you go". At the end of the 60 second interval, the therapist then simply asks, "What happened?". Typically, patients report difficulty in suppressing the thought and report that the thought occurred. The therapist should then ask the patient what he/she concludes from this experience. The point of emphasis here is the idea that certain attempts to remove thoughts from consciousness are counter-productive or ineffective. This experience is used to illustrate the linkage between thought control and Type 2 worry, and that the failure of thought control attempts of this kind can reinforce negative appraisals and beliefs about loss of control or personal abnormality (i.e. Type 2 worry, negative beliefs).

MODIFYING TYPE 2 WORRY AND NEGATIVE BELIEFS

A range of verbal reattribution and behavioural experiments have been devised for modifying negative metacognitive appraisals and beliefs (Wells, 1997). Initially, uncontrollability beliefs and appraisals should be modified and then specific beliefs and appraisals concerning the dangers of worrying are the target of intervention.

Challenging uncontrollability beliefs

Verbal methods for challenging beliefs in the uncontrollability of worrying include reviewing in detail situations in which worrying was interrupted by the activation of competing goals. For example, the therapist can ask, "Was there a time recently when you were worrying, and then something happened to distract you from worrying?". Such events can be used as evidence that worrying can be displaced by alternative activities, and therefore that worrying is subject to control. A further possibility is to review occasions in which a trigger that would normally elicit worrying was encountered and yet worrying did not occur, perhaps because of alternative task demands. A further standard technique of verbal reattribution is questioning the evidence and counterevidence for uncontrollability of worries. Note that the model predicts that there is likely to be a high degree of ambivalence about fully interrupting worry, therefore it is important to ask the client if he/she has ever actually tried to give up worrying or interrupt worrying once it is initiated. Many patients report that they attempt to reason with their worry or feel that they must worry through a topic in order to feel better able to cope. Moreover, whilst attempts may have been made to suppress worry triggers (i.e. remove the content of worry from consciousness), this is distinct from interrupting the worry process, in which the content of the thought may actually remain in consciousness but the individual disengages repetitive processing of worry material. There is a high likelihood that the patient does not actually know whether worry can be postponed, since this has not been practised as a control strategy. Verbal methods, such as asking patients how it is that worry ever ceases if it is uncontrollable, can also be used.

Behavioural experiments

One of the most effective strategies in challenging uncontrollability appraisals and beliefs is the "worry postponement experiment". As a homework assignment, patients are asked to notice the onset of a worry and postpone the worry sequence until a specified time period later in the day. Once this specified time period arrives, the patient can either decide not to worry or to worry for a fixed time period to further test that worrying can be controlled. Often patients forget to worry or decide that worry is unnecessary. The postponed worry experiment should be repeated for homework across several sessions, as necessary. Ratings of belief in the controllability of worrying are tracked across the use of experiments and verbal reattribution methods to determine their effectiveness. Note that postponing a worry process is not the same as thought suppression. Patients are merely asked to interrupt the process of catastrophising and thinking through worries, although the content of a concern may still remain accessible to consciousness.

Modifying danger-related beliefs

Beliefs concerning the dangers of worrying can be challenged by similar verbal and behavioural reattribution methods. The belief that worrying can cause mental or physical catastrophe, such as a "mental breakdown", are amenable to modification through verbal methods that question the evidence and counter-evidence for worrying causing such calamities. Similarly, the pervasiveness and normal nature of worrying can be discussed in the context of the relative rarity of disorders characterised by a mental breakdown. Another method is to question the underlying mechanisms by which worrying could lead to mental or physical catastrophe. Where appropriate, education can be undertaken to correct faulty knowledge concerning proposed mechanisms. For example, a recent GAD client believed that worrying would lead to bodily damage in the form of cardiovascular disease. The patient believed that the mechanism was one of elevated heart rate and adrenaline production under conditions of worry. The therapist discussed with the patient the role of adrenaline in increasing heart-rate, but also emphasised that adrenaline is harmless and furthermore is used to re-start the heart following a heart attack. The patient was asked: "Would adrenaline be used under such circumstances if it was potentially damaging?". Discussions then centred on counter-evidence. In particular, it was apparent that the patient's mother was also a chronic worrier, had been a worrier as long as the client could remember, and yet her physical health had always been good.

Behavioural experiments provide one of the best means of challenging danger-related beliefs. The person with GAD can be asked to deliberately try to lose control or cause mental or physical harm by worrying intensely during the allotted postponed worry period previously introduced to challenge uncontrollability beliefs. Experiments of this kind can be followed by asking individuals to worry more and try to lose control next time a worry episode occurs, rather than postponing these paradoxical attempts.

MODIFYING POSITIVE BELIEFS

Positive meta-beliefs are challenged by reviewing the evidence and counter-evidence for them and by the use of "mismatch strategies". The "mismatch strategy" (Wells, 1997), consists of asking a patient to write out a detailed description of the events portrayed in a worry scenario. These events are then compared with the events that actually happened in a worried-about situation. This strategy can be practised for situations that are avoided and in combination with exposure as a behaviour experiment. For example, a patient may be asked to worry about, and predict the negative consequences of, entering an avoided situation. The worry narrative can be written out in detail and the patient then enters the avoided situation whilst comparing the content of the worry narrative with the actual events and features of the situation. This strategy is used to illustrate how worries distort reality and allow the therapist to pose the question: "If worries do not accurately depict reality, how helpful can they be?". Another experiment for challenging positive beliefs about worry consists of asking patients to engage in activities normally associated with worrying whilst deliberately increasing or decreasing worry. More specifically, if an individual predicts that worrying helps performance and coping, manipulations of the level of worrying on a day-to-day basis can be examined in the context of whether or not they improve performance or coping. If the client is correct in believing that worrying improves coping, then abandonment of worrying for 1 or 2 days should lead to evidence of poor coping, whilst increasing worrying for 1 or 2 days should lead to evidence of improved coping. To maximise the effects of experiments of this type, it is beneficial to operationalise, in observable and testable terms, precisely what is meant by "coping", and what would be a sign of lowered or increased levels of coping.

STRATEGY SHIFTS (DEVELOPING NEW PLANS)

In the last few sessions of treatment, therapist and patient should introduce alternative strategies for thinking about threat. Since many patients have been worriers for most of their lives, it is often helpful to discuss and practise alternative strategies for dealing with "what if" triggers for worrying. A factor that is stressed is that it is possible to think about distressing events in different ways. One strategy is to encourage patients to use positive endings for "what if" thoughts or potential worries. Thus, rather than contemplating a range of the worst consequences in response to these triggers, patients are asked to practise generating positive outcomes and consequences and to use evidence other than a "felt sense" to make predictions about coping. In particular, as worrying is seen as unrepresentative of real situations, it is helpful for patients to develop more positive thinking strategies that contain a positive inferential bias that counteracts catastrophising. Patients can be asked to practise positive endings for worries and also positive affirming self-talk whenever a worrying situation emerges. However, caution should be exercised, as these strategies should not become techniques that are used to avert the feared consequences of worrying. An important focus for the latter stages of treatment is on eliciting any residual negative beliefs about worrying, since these must be challenged to prevent the re-establishment of meta-worry.

RELAPSE PREVENTION AND CO-MORBIDITY

Relapse prevention consists of generating a summary of the patient's understanding of the nature of GAD and a description of effective strat-egies for dealing with worry. The patient's summary should constitute a "therapy blueprint", comprising an example of an idiosyncratic formula-tion, examples of key metacognitions, and summaries of data that discon-firm maladaptive metacognitive beliefs. Residual positive and negative beliefs should be assessed and challenged and avoidance of situations that might trigger worrying should be eliminated by continued exposure combined with worry abandonment or enhancement strategies tailored to modifying residual metacognitions. GAD may be one of a number of co-morbid presenting problems. In co-morbid cases, the therapist should use skilled judgement to determine the preliminary focus of intervention—whether this will be on GAD-related problems and/or other co-morbid disorders (e.g. social phobia). The generic S-REF model predicts that, in cases of chronic and on-going worry, it will be useful to modify worry-related metacognition as a prerequisite to formulating and dealing with co-morbid problems. Where co-morbid symptoms persist, appropriate cognitive models of specific disorders, such as social phobia (Clark & Wells, 1995; Wells, 1997), may be used to guide formulation and treat-ment of concurrent problems.

CONCLUSIONS

Pathological worry and GAD have been conceptualised from a metacog-nitive perspective in this chapter. A specific model of the maintenance of GAD grounded in S-REF theory has been described. The treatment based on this model provides a new emphasis on conceptualising and modify-ing metacognitive factors underlying the worry process. This approach differs markedly from traditional CBT for GAD, which typically focuses on the provision of anxiety management strategies and on cognitive tech-niques aimed at challenging the validity of Type 1 worries. A range of metacognitive-focused therapy strategies have been presented. Whilst these strategies have been used in GAD treatment, there is no reason to expect that these or similar strategies should not be useful for modifying metacognitions in other disorders. For a further description of metacognitive-focused cognitive therapy of GAD, the interested reader may wish to consult Wells (1997; Chapter 8). Preliminary systematic single case evaluations of the effectiveness of this treatment suggest that the approach is effective and can be implemented within a course of 12 1-hour weekly sessions.

Chapter 11

TREATING OBSESSIVE-COMPULSIVE DISORDER

Obsessive-compulsive disorder (OCD) is characterised by recurrent obsessions or compulsions that are time consuming (take more than 1 hour a day) or cause marked distress or impairment (DSM-IV; APA, 1994). Obsessions are persistent thoughts, impulses, or images that are experienced as intrusive and inappropriate. For example, a religious person may have persistent blasphemous thoughts, or a mother may have thoughts of harming her new-born child. The most common obsessions concern thoughts about contamination (e.g. becoming contaminated by touching money), doubting (e.g. wondering whether one has locked a door or whether one has unknowingly collided with someone whilst driving the car), aggressive or horrific impulses (e.g. the urge to shout out in church, or to hurt one's child), and sexual imagery (e.g. a recurrent pornographic image). Obsessions can be differentiated from other types of intrusive thoughts, such as worry (Wells, 1994a; Wells and Morrison, 1994). Unlike negative thoughts such as worrying or depressive rumination, obsessions are appraised as abhorrent or alien to the self, in other words they are ego-dystonic.

A compulsion is a repetitive behaviour that is overt or covert. Overt compulsions include hand washing, checking, ordering or alignment of objects. Covert compulsions are mental acts, such as praying, counting or repeating words. The goal of these acts is to prevent or reduce anxiety or distress. In some instances individuals perform stereotyped acts according to idiosyncratic rules, and are often unable to indicate why they are doing them.

PREVALENCE OF OBSESSIONS AND COMPULSIONS

Obsessions and compulsions occur as normal phenomena; however, in OCD they cause more distress or disruption. Normal obsessions occur in 80–88% of individuals, and the content of normal and abnormal obsessions are similar (Rachman & de Silva, 1978; Salkovskis & Harrison, 1984). Estimates of the prevalence rates of OCD vary. The Epidemiological Catchment Area survey indicated that the lifetime prevalence of OCD was 2.5%, and the 6-month prevalence rate was 1.6%, making it the fourth most common psychiatric disorder in the USA (Karno, Golding, Sorenson & Burnam, 1988).

A METACOGNITIVE PERSPECTIVE

Wells and Matthews (1994) presented a prototypical model of OCD grounded in the S-REF model, which was subsequently elaborated by Wells (1997). They suggest that obsessional thoughts activate metacognitive beliefs concerning the meaning of the thought. At the same time, individuals access instrumental beliefs about behavioural responses that can be used to minimise appraised danger associated with obsessional thoughts.

One of the features of OCD is a tendency to focus attention on thought processes. This heightened *cognitive self-consciousness* increases the detection of unwanted target thoughts, and may trigger intrusions. Wells and Matthews (1994) suggest that obsessionals have a tendency to assign priority to internally generated events rather than external events. Thus, even when sensory input confirms the execution of a behaviour, individuals focus excessive attention on fantasies concerning the consequences of not performing the action. This tendency to focus on doubts or internal fantasies reduces confidence in memory for actions/events and may contribute to checking behaviour (note, however, that checking is likely to also be stimulated by beliefs concerning the advantages of checking). Maladaptive self-processing tendencies are also manifested in the guide states that OCD patients use to signal the cessation or maintenance of overt and covert rituals. In particular, there is a tendency to rely on internal cognitive criteria, such as "perfect" uninterrupted memories of events, or "felt senses", such as "feelings of certainty" as stop signals for rituals. Unfortunately, such signals are difficult to accomplish and are prone to disruption by a range of factors.

A PROTOTYPICAL MODEL

A prototypical metacognitive model (Wells, 1997) of factors contributing to OCD maintenance is presented in Figure 11.0.

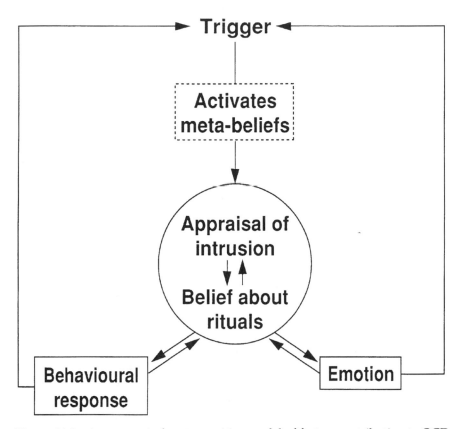

Figure 11.0 A prototypical metacognitive model of factors contributing to OCD maintenance. From Wells, 1997, with permission

In this model a trigger (most often an intrusive thought or doubt, although an intrusive feeling/emotion can also act as a trigger), activates metacognitive beliefs concerning the meaning of the trigger. The beliefs relevant at this level include beliefs about the dangers and meaning of thought. Typically in OCD, metacognitive beliefs blur the boundaries between thought and events, and thought and actions. For instance, patients believe that having a particular thought will make an event happen (e.g. "If I think of the Devil, the Devil will appear"), and believe that having a thought probably means that the event has happened (e.g. "If I think I've abused her, I probably have done so"). These types of belief have been labelled thought–event fusion (TEF; Wells, 1997), and Rachman and Shafran (1999) have extended the concept of thought–action fusion (TAF; Rachman, 1993) to describe the belief that specific intrusive thoughts can directly influence a relevant external event. However, TAF also encompasses the belief that having an intrusive thought is morally equivalent to carrying out a prohibited action. Further sub-categories of metacognitive belief also appear important. For instance, some patients believe that having a thought about an action will lead to commission of the action (e.g. "If I think about stabbing him, I probably will stab him"). A further category of belief important in OCD, emphasised by the meta-cognitive model (Wells & Matthews, 1994; Wells, 1997), is concerned with the meaning of impulses and "feelings". Many obsessional patients believe that negative impulses or feelings will become unbearable, dangerous or permanent unless restitutive actions are taken. Finally, recent clinical observation based on metacognitive profiling suggests that a subgroup of contamination obsessions are associated with beliefs that may be termed "thought–object fusion" (TOF). Here, individuals believe that thoughts or feelings can be transferred into objects, and these "contaminated" objects can then transfer thoughts and feelings to other people or objects by contagion.

Metacognitive beliefs influence the nature of appraisals of intrusions. A further influence on appraisals of intrusion results from beliefs that the individual holds concerning rituals and behavioural responses. Two types of belief are relevant here: positive beliefs (e.g. "If I wash without thinking a bad thought, bad things won't happen"; "I must perform my ritual or else the feeling will never end"), and negative beliefs (e.g. "My rituals are out of control"; "My mental rituals could damage my body"). Beliefs about the dangers and advantages of available responses influence the selection and implementation of behaviours, and influence the intensity of short-term emotional reactions. Individuals perform rituals or checking behaviours until an internal goal-state is satisfied. So the beliefs or knowledge guiding these behaviours contain a representation of a goal and involve monitoring and control operations; thus, they constitute a plan for processing in S-REF terms. The failure or success of the ritual can be interpreted in a way that increases or decreases anxiety and perceptions of threat.

Two feedback loops operate, as depicted in Figure 11.0. Anxiety and other negative emotional reactions resulting from the appraisal of intrusions may be subject to negative interpretation. For example, anxious symptoms may be misinterpreted as a sign of loss of control or a sign of other dangers associated with intrusions. In some cases, anxiety symptoms are misinterpreted as evidence supporting negative interpretations of intrusions. For example, a patient with sexual obsessions misinterpreted particular anxious symptoms as evidence that he was becoming sexually aroused by his repugnant thoughts, and this was further evidence that he must be a "pervert". Emotional responses increase the likelihood of further intrusions, as depicted by the feedback loop back to the trigger. Emotional responses are likely to lower thresholds for the detection of obsessional stimuli and can disrupt the attainment of internal states that act as stop signals for neutralising. The emotional state may act as a trigger in its own right, such that some individuals believe that they will be overwhelmed with negative feelings or that feelings will be unremitting unless a ritual is performed.

The behavioural responses implemented by the OCD patient maintain the problem through two feedback cycles, illustrated in Figure 11.0. Behavioural responses that meet the patient's internal goals prevent disconfirmation of belief in dysfunctional appraisals of intrusions. The non-occurrence of catastrophic actions or events resulting from intrusions is attributed to the ritual, and not to the fact that beliefs about the consequences of obsessional thoughts are not valid. However, failure to meet the goal of the ritual (e.g. failure to remember clearly the sound of the door locking) can be interpreted as evidence that a desired action has not been committed. Inverted reasoning can also be in evidence here, such that a patient believes that lapses in memory for actions means an unwanted act has been committed. The feedback cycle back to triggers represents how behavioural responses exacerbate intrusions. Three main mechanisms are implicated here. First, attempts to suppress thoughts may cause an enhanced awareness of unwanted thoughts. Second, attempts to ruminate on intrusions or mentally neutralise them can maintain preoccupation with mental events, making intrusion more likely. Third, activities such as repeated checking or cleaning set up associations between a range of stimuli and intrusions, such that a widening array of stimuli/actions can trigger intrusions. Different overt and covert behavioural responses can be identified, including overt checking, rituals, ordering, repeating, washing/cleaning, thought suppression, rumination, counting, focusing, controlling one's mind and distraction.

Domains of metacognitive beliefs

On the basis of the present working model and clinical experience, three domains of metacognitive belief about obsessional thoughts seem relevant to conceptualising cases. One or more domains may be present in individual cases. Examples of beliefs in each of these domains reported by patients are as follows:

1. Thought–event fusion (TEF):
   - Thinking about an event means it has happened or it will happen.
   - My thoughts become reality—if I think something it will come true.
   - Thinking something is contaminated means it is contaminated.
   - Thinking bad thoughts can make bad things happen.
2. Thought–action fusion (TAF):
   - If I think of harming someone, I probably will harm them.
   - If I have thoughts about harming myself, I will act on them.
   - If I have (unwanted) thoughts, it must mean I want to have them.
3. Thought–object fusion (TOF):
   - Objects can become contaminated with memories.
   - Objects can become contaminated with thoughts/feelings.
   - If things look old and used, they are contaminated with other people's experience (and I could catch it).

Aside from beliefs about thoughts and feelings, instrumental beliefs about the commission of rituals and neutralising responses are also relevant to the metacognitive formulation. The role of this category of beliefs has been largely ignored by previous cognitive approaches. However, appraisals of the success/failure or meaning of events linked to rituals is an important influence on distress and continued maladaptive coping efforts. Beliefs about these strategies fall into two broad categories:

1. Positive beliefs:
   - If I keep my mind in check, bad things won't happen.
   - Performing my rituals keeps me safe.
   - If I check my memory for actions, I can know I've done no harm.
   - If I can remember everything, I can know I've not committed unwanted acts.
   - I need to do this.
   - If I don't perform my rituals, my emotions will overwhelm me/ become permanent.
   - Ruminating/dwelling makes things turn out OK.
2. Negative beliefs:
   - I could lose control/go crazy.
   - My rituals could make me ill.
   - I have no control over my rituals.
   - My rituals will take me over.

EMPIRICAL SUPPORT FOR A METACOGNITIVE MODEL

Data from several sources provides support for a metacognitive conceptualisation of OCD. Briefly these studies show that:

1. Metacognitive beliefs characterised by inverse inference, a belief similar to TEF, and beliefs about the consequences of thoughts are predictive of obsessional rumination and impulses, even when depression is controlled (Emmelkamp & Aardema, 1999).
2. Inverse inference and TAF are significant independent predictors of compulsive checking (Emmelkamp & Aardema, 1999).
3. Experimental manipulation producing an increase in TAF leads to an increase in the frequency of intrusive thoughts and discomfort (Rassin, Merckelbach, Muris & Spaan, 1999).
4. Negative metacognitive beliefs concerning the uncontrollability and danger associated with thoughts are positively associated with obsessional symptoms, and this relationship is independent of general worry-proneness (Wells & Papageorgiou, 1998a).

GENERAL IMPLICATIONS FOR TREATMENT

The metacognitive approach to OCD, whilst only a prototype, suggests that treatment should include a significant focus on modifying underlying metacognitive beliefs, and maladaptive internal criteria (goals) that are used to regulate behaviour. A range of different metacognitive beliefs may be relevant across cases. These include the domains of TEF, TAF and TOF.

Patients with OCD are operating in object-processing mode, in which they unquestionably accept appraisals of the meaning of intrusions as valid. An initial step in treatment is to shift patients to metacognitive processing mode, so that they may become more aware of the role of metacognitive beliefs underlying distress and behaviour. This step is important in that it shifts the emphasis of treatment away from the goal of stopping obsessional thoughts, to the goal of learning that obsessional thoughts or other types of intrusion need not be acted upon. The goal is to challenge beliefs and appraisals about obsessional thoughts, rather than prevent obsessions. Most patients are unaware of the contribution of metacognitive beliefs to their presenting problems. To facilitate patient awareness the therapist should apply skilful use of guided discovery to elicit key metacognitions.

In modifying metacognitions, it is helpful to manipulate the individual's behaviour and rumination/worry strategies in a way that enhances the capacity for belief change. Early in treatment, strategies should be directed at reducing the frequency and duration of rumination/worry. Strategies that can be used for this purpose were discussed in Chapter 10, and consist of the advantages/disadvantages analysis, and worry postponement experiments. Training in "detached mindfulness" and attention training (ATT) procedures may be useful for interrupting perseverative processing and gaining distance from intrusive mental experience.

Specific verbal and behavioural reattribution techniques should be directed at challenging specific thought–fusion beliefs. Exposure to thoughts and response prevention can be configured with an appropriate rationale to act as a test of predictions based on maladaptive metacognitive beliefs. For this purpose, the P–E–T–S protocol can be applied (see p. 124). Since the S-REF-based metacognitive formulation of OCD implies that procedural knowledge or plans are relevant to understanding disorder maintenance, it is necessary to explore the activation of specific beliefs, behaviours and attentional biases during exposure to obsessive stimuli. Having patients perform rituals (neutralising responses) in-session, in conjunction with exposure to thoughts/contaminants, provides a means of eliciting the goals and internal criteria that are linked to the modulation of these behaviours.

A treatment strategy suggested by the present analysis is the modification of criteria that the patient uses to decide on the initiation, continuation and cessation of rituals. For example, a patient troubled by thoughts that he might have collided with a pedestrian whilst driving home would try to remember and mentally re-trace his entire journey. Any gaps in his memory were interpreted as evidence that he might have hit someone, and he therefore needed to repeat his journey. Here, the criterion that he used to decide that he might have hit someone was a memory gap. This is clearly a maladaptive self-regulatory strategy. A more appropriate strategy for deciding whether his negative thoughts were valid, and if he needed to repeat his journey, would be to rely on a memory of actually having hit someone, rather than on a gap in memory. Treatment should focus on modifying the strategies that patients use to (1) evaluate the validity of intrusions, and (2) decide on the need for further rituals/checking. According to this approach, it is also likely to be conceptually beneficial to explore beliefs about the "worst consequences" of not performing a neutralising response, so that these consequences can be subject to behavioural test. When neutralising or avoidance responses are extensive and highly practised, patients often have limited access to underlying beliefs concerning the consequences of not performing these actions. However, exposure and response prevention can offer a means of eliciting this material.

A general goal of treatment is for patients to adopt a detached acceptance of intrusive thoughts as irrelevant for further processing or action. Whilst this will depend on the modification of metacognitive beliefs that endow obsessional thought with special and negative significance, it is also likely to require extensive practice of disengaging from obsessional thoughts/ stimuli in order to over-ride more reflexive maladaptive coping responses. In this way, new metacognitive strategies (plans) for dealing with intrusions can be developed.

GENERATING A CASE FORMULATION

In order to translate the prototypical model depicted in Figure 11.0 into an individual case formulation, it is necessary to elicit information concerning: (1) the nature of the obsessional and compulsive symptoms; (2) triggering influences; (3) appraisals (beliefs) concerning the meaning and significance of obsessions *and* neutralising strategies.

Therapists should review with the patient a recent obsessive-compulsive episode and attempt to elicit triggers for overt and covert neutralising, checking behaviour, etc. Initially, patient insight may be poor. An initial aim of treatment is to increase the patient's level of metacognitive awareness so that he/she is able to identify intrusive thoughts, doubts or feelings prior to the commission of behavioural responses. This task can be initiated through a detailed review of several recent episodes, through behaviour tests involving exposure to problematic situations, and through detailed self-monitoring.

ELICITING DYSFUNCTIONAL BELIEFS AND APPRAISALS

Therapists should aim to explore different categories of appraisals of, and beliefs about, intrusions. In assessing appraisals/beliefs, questions should be directed at eliciting the meaning and dangers of intrusions. Aside from direct questions about intrusions, an indirect strategy is to question the consequences of not engaging in neutralising (coping) behaviour. Below are a series of examples of questions used to elicit metacognitive beliefs/appraisals and the nature of maladaptive criteria for the control of rituals:

Useful questions:

1. *Beliefs about obsessional thoughts*
   - When you had obsessive thought (OT), how did you feel (e.g. anxious, afraid, guilty)?
   - When you felt (e.g. anxious), what thoughts went through your mind?
   - What does having this OT mean to you?
   - Could anything bad happen as a result of having the OT?
   - What could happen?
   - Does the OT mean something bad has happened?
   - What is that?
   - What's the worst that could happen if you have an OT?
   - What would happen if you couldn't get rid of these OTs?
   - What's the worst that could happen if you had an OT and did nothing to deal with it?
2. *Beliefs about rituals/coping*
   Examples follow of questions that are useful for eliciting beliefs associated with ritual behaviours. Note that for clinical purposes it is often necessary to elicit material by questioning the worst consequences of not engaging in a ritual behaviour, rather than only questioning about the benefits of engaging in behaviour:
   - Do you do anything to prevent (catastrophe associated with intrusion) from happening? What do you do?
   - How does (checking, ruminating, neutralising) help?
   - How much control do you have over your (checking, neutralising, rumination)?
   - What's the worst that could happen if you don't stop it?
   - Does your (checking, ruminating, neutralising) keep you safe in some way? How does that work?
   - Have you tried to stop (specific ritual)?
   - Is there a reason for not trying to stop?
   - What happens to your feelings/thoughts when you are prevented from (neutralising, checking, ruminating)?
3. *Eliciting stop signals for rituals*
   - When you start (specific ritual), what it is that tells you it is safe to stop?
   - What is the goal of (specific ritual); what are you aiming to achieve?
   - How do you know your ritual is working?
   - What is another way of determining whether you need to act (what would your best friend do?)—useful for exploring replacement strategies in treatment.

- Are you acting on the absence of a memory or the presence of a memory (can an absence tell you that you have done something?)—useful for cognitive restructuring in treatment.

The following extract of a dialogue with a patient suffering from OCD illustrates the use of some of the questions outlined above to elicit information for building the idiosyncratic case conceptualisation in Figure 11.1.

T: When was the last time you were bothered by these thoughts?
P: Yesterday I became really scared. My daughter was getting on my nerves and I had an image of the Devil jumping on her.
T: It sounds as if that was frightening. What were you afraid of?
P: Wouldn't you be scared if you kept getting thoughts like that?
T: I suppose it isn't a nice thought, but I don't think it would scare me. Did you think anything bad could happen as a result of thinking that?
P: I don't know why I thought it. Do you see many people who have thoughts like that?
T: Yes. People troubled by obsessional thoughts are usually bothered by blasphemous thoughts, or thoughts of a sexual or violent nature. But that doesn't mean they are bad people. What's the worst that could happen if you think about the Devil jumping on your daughter?
P: It's too scary to think about (becomes tearful).
T: It sounds like something bad could happen.
P: It means I might want it to happen—but I know I don't.
T: Could it make anything bad happen?
P: Yes, it could make the Devil appear.
T: So the thought is distressing because of what it means, or what it might cause. You seem to be concerned that having the thought will make the Devil appear. Is that right?
P: Yes.
T: When you had that thought, did you do anything to prevent the Devil appearing?
P: I tried to imagine Jesus with his arms around us protecting us.
T: Did you do anything else for protection?
P: I said the Lord's Prayer.
T: Did you have to do that in any special way?
P: I had to say it without getting an image of the Devil.
T: How did you do that?
P: I concentrated on every word as if I really meant it.

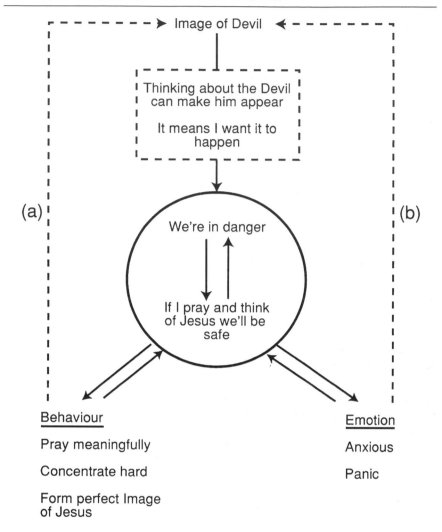

Figure 11.1   An idiosyncratic case conceptualisation based on the metacognitive model of OCD

T: How did you know when to stop your ritual?
P: I repeated it until I could say the prayer without getting any bad thoughts, and whilst having a perfect clear image of Jesus.
T: Is it easy to do that?
P: No. I can spend hours trying to get it right. If I can't get it right, I worry about it and get into a panic.

T: What would happen if you didn't engage in your ritual or get it right?

P: I couldn't do that. I'd be panicking all day.

T: What's the worst that could happen?

P: I'd be worried that something bad would happen. The Devil would harm us.

T: So it sounds as if you believe your rituals keep evil away. Is that right?

P: Yes. God will protect us.

T: It sounds as if you are trying hard to control your thoughts and prevent bad thoughts.

P: Yes.

T: Do you think there are any problems with trying to get perfect images and avoid all distractions when praying?

P: It doesn't work always, and now sometimes when I try to see Jesus he can have horns growing out of his head.

Note that this material can also be represented as an A–M–C (reformulated A–B–C) analysis (see Figure 11.2).

SOCIALISATION

Socialisation proceeds by sharing the conceptualisation with the patient. Socialisation begins in communicating the concept that negative beliefs about intrusions along with behavioural responses and worry about intrusions, are the main problem, rather than the occurrence of the intrusion alone.

Socialisation is facilitated by the use of questions like those in the therapy extract presented earlier. In particular, questions should be directed at determining the consequences in emotional terms of having intrusions if the individual no longer believed that they were harmful, indicative of negative events, or characterologically meaningful.

Thought control experiments can be used to demonstrate how behavioural responses are rarely fully effective and may exacerbate intrusions (feedback cycle "a" in Figure 11.0). For instance, patients can be asked to try and suppress a thought of a "white bear" for a period of 1 minute, and the effects of this strategy are then discussed in terms of the model. The impact of emotional reactions on intrusions (triggers) can be demonstrated by reviewing the effects of mood (feedback cycle "b" in Figure 11.0) on the frequency of intrusions and doubts.

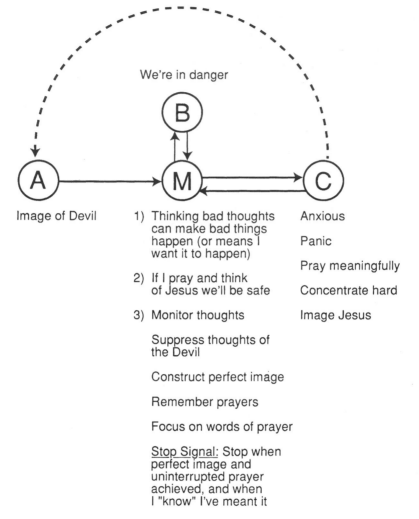

Figure 11.2   A formulation of the OCD case in Figure 11.1 in terms of the A–M–C analysis, for illustrative purposes

COGNITIVE DE-FUSION

Treatment strategies should be directed at challenging fusion beliefs. This can be done with verbal reattribution strategies and with behavioural experiments.

Initially, de-fusion aims to challenge beliefs about the validity of appraisals of intrusions and to teach patients alternative strategies for behaving in response to intrusions. The first step requires establishing the mental framework in which to build an alternative belief system. It is therefore necessary to socialise patients in the role of metacognitive beliefs. This is accomplished through guided discovery. Many patients are operating at the level of how catastrophic it would be, or how responsible they would feel, if their appraisal of an obsession were valid. However, this is operating in object mode and not in metacognitive mode. The therapist should shift the patient to working at the metacognitive level. That is, focus on challenging the validity of the appraisal of the intrusion, coupled with the abandonment of counter-productive ritual and coping strategies. Some useful questions for establishing the metacognitive mode include the following:

- What prompts you to engage in your (overt/covert) ritual behaviour?
- If you didn't believe your thought (appraisal of obsession) was realistic, would you need to engage in rituals?
- How would you feel if you knew your fears and beliefs about your thought were unrealistic?
- How does your checking behaviour/avoidance affect your confidence in your memory?
- How does your checking behaviour/avoidance affect your ability to discriminate between imagined and real events?

The last two questions should be modified to incorporate the patient's idiosyncratic behaviours (checking, ruminating, neutralising, rituals, avoidance, reassurance seeking, etc.). Through use of this form of questioning, the therapist should help the patient to acquire a metacognitive model of his/her problem. The unhelpful nature of behavioural strategies for the long-term resolution of the obsessional problem should be highlighted.

Once the basic framework is established, the next step consists of challenging metacognitive fusion beliefs. This can be accomplished by verbal strategies and behavioural experiments.

Verbal strategies include:

1. *Questioning the mechanism of fusion*: how does thinking a thought cause an event/action? What is the mechanism?
2. *Inducing dissonance*: the incompatibility of appraisals of obsessions with general self-beliefs should be highlighted and questioned. Example questions are:

- What sort of person is likely to worry about having thoughts of harming someone—is it the kind of person who is likely to act on the thought?
- What kind of person are you? The kind that always acts on his/her thoughts?
- Where's the evidence you will act on your obsessional thoughts?

3. *The historical review*: a review of occasions on which the patient experienced an obsessional thought but was unable to neutralise it or otherwise prevent feared outcomes should be undertaken. The identification of these episodes can be used as evidence that thoughts do not lead to action or catastrophe.

Rational responses that invalidate belief about intrusions should be formulated (e.g. "This is just a thought, not a reality"; "I don't need to reason with fantasy—let it go").

Behavioural experiments

Behavioural experiments should be used to test belief in fusion. Patients who believe that thoughts can influence events (TEF) can be asked to try and increase the frequency of positive and negative events by changing thinking patterns. For example, a patient may be asked to cause his/her car to break down by thinking about this, or asked to think about winning the lottery to see if this happens.

Beliefs in thought–action fusion (TAF) can be challenged by running experiments in which patients are exposed to feared situations whilst deliberately eliciting obsessional thoughts. For example, a patient was worried that if he had thoughts about stabbing someone when in the vicinity of sharp objects, he would carry out the action. Behavioural experiments consisted of holding a sharp pen and repeatedly thinking about stabbing the therapist during a session. As a homework task, the patient was asked to leave a knife on the kitchen work-top at home whilst having thoughts of stabbing his wife when they were at home together.

Belief in thought–object fusion (TOF) can be tested by asking patients to touch and examine particular objects, and guess the history of the objects and the characteristics of people that owned them. The therapist should write out a brief summary of these details before the experiment so that the patient's description can be compared against the predocumented facts.

Negative appraisals concerning the unremitting nature of discomfort or worry should rituals/checking be abandoned should be challenged, by questioning the evidence for this belief and by exposure and response prevention experiments designed to test this out. Detached mindfulness, in combination with tracking of discomfort over time, can also be used to disconfirm beliefs about perpetual discomfort.

Exposure and response prevention experiments

In the present framework, overt and covert rituals act as behaviours that prevent exposure to information that can correct dysfunctional beliefs. Mental rituals in particular prolong rumination episodes and maintain preoccupation with thinking, thus extending the conscious accessibility of intrusions. Moreover, some mental rituals and mental control strategies may increase obsessions, as in examples of the paradoxical effects of attempts to suppress thoughts (e.g. Wegner et al., 1987). The overall effect is failure to revise, in a favourable way, dysfunctional beliefs about intrusive thoughts and rituals. In addition, patients fail to acquire general metacognitive knowledge that supports more adaptive appraisal and control of cognition.

Overt rituals are easier to identify and manage than mental rituals, and thus blocking of them is more readily accomplished—an effect possibly accounting for differences in treatment efficacy between cases of obsessions with, or cases without, overt rituals. In addition, mental rituals are likely to resemble rumination, and this form of activity may deplete attention needed for executive metacognitive operations necessary for belief change, i.e. individuals are unable to maintain a detached objective awareness of their intrusions and challenge their negative appraisals of them.

Exposure plus prevention of neutralising rituals is an effective treatment of OCD. In a behavioural paradigm, this strategy is thought to facilitate habituation. The cognitive perspective alters the rationale for exposure and response prevention. The rationale should emphasise exposure to thoughts, contaminants or events as a means of *challenging metacognitive beliefs* concerning the catastrophic nature of contact with such stimuli. Response prevention then becomes a "disconfirmatory manoeuvre", that facilitates attribution of the non-occurrence of catastrophe to the falseness of the original belief. As with preparing for exposure and response prevention used in a behavioural context, detailed examination of the full range of overt and covert strategies is required. An example of a rationale for introducing exposure and response prevention *experiments* is as follows:

> One problem is that you believe that having bad thoughts will lead to bad things happening. It is understandable that you should want to prevent these things, and so in order to do so you have developed a range of coping strategies or things that you do to keep the situation safe. It is important for you to understand that it is quite normal for people to have thoughts like yours. However, you are unable to discover that your thoughts are harmless and meaningless in the real world, because you do things to prevent any harm. So long as you do these things, your anxiety will remain. It is necessary for you to discover that your thoughts are harmless, and in order to do this you must not take safety precautions. By allowing yourself to have thoughts and by not taking safety precautions you will discover that your thoughts are harmless and do not mean anything.

Detailed analysis of covert and overt behaviours is required, so that these may be abandoned during the exposure experiment. Such experiments should follow the P–E–T–S protocol presented in Chapter 8.

STOP SIGNALS AND CRITERIA FOR KNOWING

A novel implication of the S-REF-based metacognitive model presented here is the idea that patients with OCD use maladaptive internal criteria to guide rituals/checking, and they interpret the effects of rituals/ checking as evidence of safety or threat (negative outcomes). Rituals are performed until specific internal criteria are met. These target criteria are taken as evidence that the individual will be safe or that unwanted actions have not been committed. Conversely, failure to meet these criteria is interpreted as evidence of continuing threat or the possibility that unwanted behaviours have been committed. These latter attributions often represent a type of inverted reasoning, associated with memory performance in obsessional checkers. Here, failure to remember particular events is interpreted as evidence that negative events have probably happened. This is clearly an inversion of the norm—for non-patients, memory of negative events actually happening is the criterion used for knowing, not the absence of aspects of memory. An example presented earlier in this chapter was that of a patient troubled by checking rituals. He would return to work and repeat his drive home to check that he had not collided with anyone. When he first arrived home, he would frequently have the obsessional doubt: "What if I've knocked someone down?". In response to this obsession, he typically retraced his memory of the entire journey. The criteria for knowing he had not caused an accident was an ability to remember all of the journey clearly without any gaps in memory. If gaps or vagueness in memory were encountered, he interpreted these as evidence that he probably had caused an accident. As a result he would become increasingly concerned and drive back over his route to check for casualties.

Aside from dysfunctional memory-based criteria for guiding behaviour and "knowing" that one is safe or has performed behaviours appropriately, some patients use attentional strategies. These strategies consist of hypervigilance for threat stimuli in the environment, such as insects, signs of dirt or contamination, and also consist of heightened cognitive self-consciousness and monitoring for mental events. The metacognitive perspective suggests that it is necessary to modify attentional priorities in "risky" situations in order to revise processing plans and enhance the flow of disconfirmatory information into processing. As well as monitoring for threat, maladaptive attentional strategies in OCD can be linked to rituals and consist of expending too much effort in monitoring one's actions or preventative behaviours in an attempt to be "certain" that actions have been performed.

In these circumstances, patients can be provided with an alternative plan for attention and processing that should be repeatedly practised in "difficult" situations. The replacement plan should be a mutually agreed new set of strategies that can be practised in therapy in conjunction with exposure to situations, and practised for homework. The replacement plan often consists of executing particular appraisals, attentional strategies and behaviours that are opposite to the strategies normally executed in situations. For instance, a compulsive checker who repeatedly checked that he had turned off the power at work, which often meant returning to work to check even after a long journey home, agreed to develop and practise an alternative plan. In therapy, his original plan for reducing doubt and threat was elicited in detail, and a replacement plan devised. The content of these plans was as follows:

Original plan
- I focus hard on turning off each switch, and try to remember the feel of it.
- I question myself after performing the action (e.g. "Have I turned off all the power points?").
- I go over my behaviour to see if I can vividly remember turning each one off.
- If I don't have a clear recollection, I interpret this as meaning I may have not done it.

- I worry and dwell on it until I go back and check.

Replacement plan

- Switch off each power point and focus on what I see rather than what I feel.
  Focus only briefly on each switch.
  Do it automatically rather than trying hard.
- When I have switched them off, say to myself, "There is no question, I have done it".
- Do not go over my memory. Repeat to myself, "I know I have done it".
- Ban any worrying or dwelling. If I start to worry, interrupt this and avoid checking my memory or repeating my actions.
- Tolerate doubts. Tell myself that doubts are not facts.

Doubt reduction

The occurrence of compulsive checking has been linked to deficits in memory function in obsessive-compulsives (e.g. Sher, Mann & Frost, 1984; Sher et al., 1989). However, evidence of an actual memory deficit is inconclusive. It is more likely that checkers merely show metacognitive dysfunction of reduced confidence in their memory. In these circumstances, memory tests may be used in treatment to show patients that their memory performance falls within the normal range. It is important to examine the mental strategies that patients are using during the performance of, or after performing, critical behaviours. Typically, maladaptive metacognitive strategies, memory checks or unhelpful internal criteria are being used that contribute to doubt. Techniques that make behaviour "stand out" in memory may be useful for reducing the doubt that motivates checking. Tallis (1993) reports three cases of compulsive checking treated with a doubt reduction procedure that used distinctive stimuli. The procedure consisted of providing patients with a set of coloured cardboard shapes (star, square, triangle, circle, rectangle). Each particular shape was the same colour (e.g. all triangles were red, all squares were green, etc.) but each shape ranged in size, forming a graded continuum of size. Patients were instructed to associate target behaviours (e.g. closing a door) with large figures first, and then to work through to the smallest figures. When subjects doubted an action, this was reduced by forming a mental image of the figure employed at the time. The use of graded reduction in stimulus size was intended as a "fading" component to maintain treatment gains after the programme was completed. The procedure was effective at eliminating checking at 12 month follow-up.

DETACHED MINDFULNESS

Many of the treatment strategies described in this chapter can be viewed as a means of promoting detached mindfulness, in which OCD patients learn that obsessions or doubts are irrelevant for further appraisal or action. However, many patients have difficulty in disengaging from obsessions and associated compulsions. In these instances, exposure and response prevention, in which patients actively hold an intrusion in awareness without engaging in rituals, provides a means of practising detached mindfulness. The closed loop tape can also be used, in which patients record their obsessional thoughts on a personal stereo, and listen to this repeatedly whilst practising behavioural disengagement from the articulated thoughts. Procedures such as ATT may provide a further strategy for enhancing disengagement from obsessional ruminations and provide a means of allowing intrusions to enter consciousness without commanding full attention and maladaptive behavioural responses.

CONCLUSIONS

Obsessive-compulsive disorder consists of a heterogeneous presentation of behaviours and fears. Further research is necessary to isolate the specific contribution of metacognitive components to different manifestations of the disorder. A prototype model emphasising the role of a range of metacognitive belief domains has been presented in this chapter. OCD appears to be a disorder in which metacognitive dysfunction in beliefs and self-regulatory strategies are a primary psychological substate contributing to problem maintenance.

The metacognitive approach focuses conceptualisation and treatment on: (1) modifying a range of metacognitive beliefs concerning fusion; (2) modifying dysfunctional beliefs about rituals; (3) revising the use of inappropriate internal signals/criteria for making appraisals and guiding behaviour; (4) developing replacement strategies for guiding behaviour; (5) increasing skills of detached mindfulness. Repeated practice of alternative behaviours and strategies during exposure to problematic situations is likely to lead to the revision and strengthening of new plans for cognition and behaviours.

Chapter 12

CONCLUDING REMARKS

In Part I of this book, theoretical issues linking metacognition to emotional disorder were discussed, and the S-REF model for representing cognitive processing, metacognition and self-regulation was presented. In Part II, treatment innovations based on the S-REF analysis were described and specific strategies and conceptualisations of emotional disorder were offered.

The present model identifies a general core cognitive-attentional dysfunction in emotional disorders of anxiety, depression, obsessionality, and possibly other disorders as well. This dysfunction consists of excessive self-focused attention, activation of negative self-knowledge and dysfunctional metacognitions, threat monitoring, and cycles of maladaptive coping, especially cognitive perseveration (e.g. worry/rumination). Specific features of disorders are superimposed on this general dysfunction and are determined by the nature of self-knowledge activated, the content of S-REF appraisals, coping strategies and goals. All processing in emotion and emotional disorder is constrained by the operating characteristics of the S-REF. We have seen how two basic modes of processing can be identified, and how dynamic factors are associated with system changes that can lead to the revision of self-knowledge, or the maintenance of "vicious cycles" of processing that contribute to disorder. On-line operations of the S-REF are guided by metacognitive plans, and the outcome of S-REF processing operations and coping behaviours feed back to shape the individual's knowledge base.

The S-REF model differs from other cognitive approaches, such as schema theory, network theory and Interacting Cognitive Subsystems

(ICS) in system architecture, in explicitly linking disorder with metacognitions, and by identifying how knowledge (beliefs) interact with the control of cognitive-attentional processing. The S-REF model avoids over-reliance on low-level reflexive processing characteristic of network theory, and avoids the circularity and definitional problems of ICS. The present approach meshes most closely with schema theory, since both emphasise the role of the individual's knowledge (beliefs) in the development of emotional disorder. However, schema theory does not specify how knowledge influences or is influenced by on-line processing. The S-REF model advances beyond schema theory by conceptualising self-knowledge as a multi-component library of information and plans that have metacognitive and non-metacognitive components. This knowledge both controls processing and is revised by processing, depending on the nature of the metacognitive plan activated. Specific beliefs and appraisals can be viewed as outputs of running particular plans for processing. Thus, it is necessary in therapy to modify metacognition and plans for processing as well as non-metacognitive declarative beliefs.

It has been argued that metacognition has a central role in emotional vulnerability and in the maintenance of emotional disorder. An understanding of metacognitive processes within the S-REF model provides a basis for generating a range of new treatment implications. Consistent with schema theory, the model suggests that therapy should aim to modify dysfunctional beliefs. It goes considerably beyond this general specification, however, by pointing to a wider range of beliefs that need to be revised in treatment, and specifying in detail the conditions in on-line processing that are required for revision of the person's knowledge base.

The S-REF model is based on the principle that different emotional disorders have features in common: self-focus of attention, worry/rumination, and a tendency to monitor for threat. Disorders may be differentiated on the basis of the content of beliefs about the sources of threat. This commonality suggests that a core set of treatment strategies may be developed that can be effective in alleviating a wide range of emotional disorders. However, within the S-REF framework more specific models can be developed that provide a basis for conceptualising the information-processing mechanisms that may be unique to a particular disorder. We saw in earlier chapters how trauma reactions can be conceptualised, and specific models of GAD and OCD were presented in detail. Elsewhere, the S-REF model has shaped the development of a Cognitive Model of Social Phobia (Clark & Wells, 1995).

FUTURE DIRECTIONS

Depression and rumination

The S-REF model offers a perspective on conceptualising the onset and maintenance of depression. Depressed mood is associated with an appraised failure to meet important personal goals. The duration and severity of depression is modulated by metacognitions that influence attentional and ideational strategies. Individuals prone to depression activate self-focused processing, typified by monitoring for thoughts and bodily sensations. Metacognitive beliefs specify the implementation of ruminative thought as a mode of coping and self-regulation. Whilst this thinking style is not always voluntarily initiated, continued execution of rumination is subject to voluntary control, and is associated with positive beliefs about the usefulness of this strategy. Self-focus and rumination divert attention away from more adaptive forms of coping, such as problem-solving; moreover, they contribute to metacognitive inefficiency, as the individual loses flexibility over functional processing.

At the present time, little is known about the precise nature of metacognitions tied to ruminative styles of coping in depression, and future work is required in this area. Papageorgiou and Wells (2000a) have identified a range of positive and negative beliefs about rumination held by patients with recurrent major depression.

Positive beliefs include:

1. "I need to ruminate about my problems to find answers to my depression."
2. "Ruminating about my depression helps me to understand past mistakes and failures."
3. "Ruminating about my feelings helps me to recognise the triggers for my depression."

Negative beliefs include:

1. "I cannot stop myself from ruminating."
2. "Ruminating about my depression could make me kill myself."
3. "It is impossible not to ruminate about the bad things that have happened in the past."

In addition, Papageorgiou and Wells (2000b) have developed the Positive Beliefs about Rumination Scale (PBRS) to explore predicted associations between metacognitions and depression vulnerability. The identification of negative and positive beliefs links depressive metacognitions closely with those observed in anxiety disorders. For instance, patients with recurrent major depression and patients with generalized anxiety (GAD) worry about their own ideational style. The concept of worry, at least at the meta-worry level, may well be a unifying construct in explaining common depression and anxiety mechanisms. In particular, patients who suffer from recurrent depression are likely to worry about recurrences, and this process will serve to maintain unhelpful self-focus, monitoring of signs and symptoms of depression, and negative misinterpretation of internal states as a sign of re-occurrence. This type of threat monitoring is likely to amplify negative affect and lead to renewed rumination efforts, which then prolong depressed mood. Positive metacognitions about depressive rumination suggest that rumination is viewed as a coping strategy that promotes understanding of past mistakes, failures and negative feelings, and allows the individual to recognise triggers for worsening mood. Paradoxically, however, rumination activity requires retrieval of memories of failure, which may support the perpetuation of self-discrepancies and depression. This self-perpetuating cyclical process could contribute to appraisals of loss of control over depressive experience.

Varieties of thought

The S-REF framework offers a particular taxonomy for distinguishing different types of thought in emotional disorder. Thoughts may be non-metacognitive or metacognitive in content, a concept utilised in Wells' (1995) GAD model, in which a distinction is made between Type 1 and Type 2 worries. Further distinctions are indicated by considering the functional significance of different kinds of thinking. Whilst the S-REF model emphasises the role of perseverative styles of thinking as a form of coping, this does not mean that all thinking of this kind is voluntarily initiated. Plans that initiate perseverative mentation may be automatically primed when self-discrepancies and failures of self-regulation are detected. Moreover, perseveration may not only serve a coping function. In a happy mood, dwelling on thoughts of one's successes may not constitute a form of coping; however, it could still represent a self-regulatory strategy for the prolongation of desirable mood states. Further studies are required to examine the functional significance of varieties of thought.

Aside from criteria of metacognitive/non-metacognitive content and the functional significance of thoughts, differences appear to exist in the process dimensions of thought. Worry can be distinguished from obsessions on a number of parameters (Wells & Morrison, 1994; Clark & Claybourn, 1997). It appears that anxious and depressive thoughts are also distinguishable on several dimensions. Papageorgiou and Wells (1999) compared dimensions of naturally occurring anxious and depressive thoughts and showed that there was considerable overlap in the dimensions measured. However, anxious thought was significantly more verbal, associated with a greater compulsion to act, and rated as involving more effort to problem-solve and greater confidence in problem-solving. Depressed thoughts were significantly more past-oriented than anxious thoughts. When examining the dimensions of each type of thought that correlated with respective anxious and depressed affect whilst partialling out affective overlap, it was discovered that depression was positively associated with lower confidence in problem-solving ability, and greater past orientation of thought. In contrast, greater anxiety was associated with reduced dismissability of thoughts, greater distraction by thoughts, higher meta-worry, greater compulsion to act on the thought, and more attention to the thought. These studies show that distinctions other than content distinctions can be made between thoughts, and that metacognitive judgements and attentional dimensions are associated with emotional intensity.

Auditory hallucinations

Recent applications of the S-REF framework to understanding psychotic symptoms has examined the metacognitive predictions of auditory hallucinations. Baker and Morrison (1998) compared scores on the Meta-Cognitions Questionnaire (MCQ) of patients with a diagnosis of schizophrenia who were experiencing auditory hallucinations, non-hallucinating schizophrenics, and non-psychiatric control subjects. Patients experiencing hallucinations scored higher than the other two groups on metacognitive beliefs about the uncontrollability and danger of thoughts, and on positive beliefs about worry. In logistic regression analyses predicting hallucination–non-hallucination status, metacognitive beliefs about uncontrollability and danger emerged as the only significant predictor amongst anxiety, intensity ratings for source monitoring, and IQ.

In a further study examining relationships between predisposition to hallucinations, metacognitive beliefs and thought control strategies, Morrison, Wells and Nothard (2000) showed that individuals high in predisposition had higher scores on beliefs about uncontrollability and danger associated with thoughts, and greater cognitive self-consciousness, than subjects with low predisposition. High hallucinators also reported greater use of punishment and re-appraisal to control thoughts. Positive beliefs about unusual perceptual experiences emerged as the best predictor of predisposition to auditory hallucinations when trait anxiety, depression, paranoia, predisposition to visual hallucinations, and negative beliefs about unusual perceptual experiences were also entered as predictors.

Further applications of metacognitive concepts to understanding the development and maintenance of auditory hallucinations may provide useful insights. An implication of the S-REF model in exploring auditory hallucinations is that such experiences are activated and maintained by patients' attentional monitoring plans and metacognitions concerning hallucinatory experience. In particular, patients may be running cognitive and behavioural strategies of eliciting or enhancing certain auditory hallucinations, thereby building a hallucinatory skill base. However, this may be coupled with strategies of attempting to control or neutralise the appraised dangers associated with specific malevolent voices. An incompatibility between these responses will contribute to a diminished appraisal of control and to increasing distress linked with hallucinatory experience.

CLOSING COMMENT

In conclusion, this book has presented a case for the detailed consideration of metacognition in emotional disorder vulnerability and maintenance. The Self-Regulatory Executive Function (S-REF) model was the first to emphasise a central role for metacognition, self-focused attention and strategic processes in disorder maintenance. It provides an architectural and dynamic conceptualisation of information processing that is consistent with schema theory, but avoids its limitations and the limitations of other cognitive approaches to psychopathology. An exciting contribution of the present approach is the possibility that, for the first time, we can begin to understand the mechanisms that lead to the maintenance and modification of maladaptive beliefs. In this book I have attempted to provide answers to some crucial questions that are important for the future development of cognitive theory and therapy. These questions include: how should we model self-regulation mechanisms in emotional disorder?; how are beliefs modified as processing unfolds?; what are the mechanisms of interaction between beliefs and the pattern of functioning of an individuals cognitive system?

It is unusual amongst theories based on information processing to find wide-ranging clinical implications that have clear practical applications. However, in this work I have endeavoured to show how the S-REF model provides guidelines for conceptualisation in cognitive therapy, and have described how the metacognitive analysis informs the choice of assessment and treatment strategies. A unification of cognitive science with cognitive therapy provides one future for the advancement of theory and treatment. It is my hope that the ideas presented in this book will continue to shape our understanding.

APPENDICES

Appendix I

METACOGNITIONS QUESTIONNAIRE (MCQ)

Developed by Sam Cartwright and Adrian Wells

This questionnaire is concerned with beliefs people have about their thinking. Listed below are a number of beliefs that people have expressed. Please read each item and say how much you *generally* agree with it by *circling* the appropriate number. Please respond to all the items, there are no right or wrong answers.

Sex: _____ Age: _____

	Do not agree	Agree slightly	Agree moderately	Agree very much
1. Worrying helps me to avoid problems in the future	1	2	3	4
2. My worrying is dangerous for me	1	2	3	4
3. I have difficulty knowing if I have actually done something, or just imagined it	1	2	3	4
4. I think a lot about my thoughts	1	2	3	4
5. I could make myself sick with worrying	1	2	3	4
6. I am aware of the way my mind works when I am thinking through a problem	1	2	3	4
7. If I did not control a worrying thought, and then it happened, it would be my fault	1	2	3	4
8. If I let my worrying thoughts get out of control, they will end up controlling me	1	2	3	4
9. I need to worry in order to remain organised	1	2	3	4

	Do not agree	Agree slightly	Agree moderately	Agree very much
10. I have little confidence in my memory for words and names	1	2	3	4
11. My worrying thoughts persist, no matter how I try to stop them	1	2	3	4
12. Worrying helps me to get things sorted out in my mind	1	2	3	4
13. I cannot ignore my worrying thoughts	1	2	3	4
14. I monitor my thoughts	1	2	3	4
15. I should be in control of my thoughts all of the time	1	2	3	4
16. My memory can mislead me at times	1	2	3	4
17. I could be punished for not having certain thoughts	1	2	3	4
18. My worrying could make me go mad	1	2	3	4
19. If I do not stop worrying thoughts, they could come true	1	2	3	4
20. I rarely question my thoughts	1	2	3	4
21. Worrying puts my body under a lot of stress	1	2	3	4
22. Worrying helps me to avoid disastrous situations	1	2	3	4
23. I am constantly aware of my thinking	1	2	3	4
24. I have a poor memory	1	2	3	4
25. I pay close attention to the way my mind works	1	2	3	4
26. People who do not worry, have no depth	1	2	3	4
27. Worrying helps me cope	1	2	3	4
28. I imagine having not done things and then doubt my memory for doing them	1	2	3	4
29. Not being able to control my thoughts is a sign of weakness	1	2	3	4

	Do not agree	Agree slightly	Agree moderately	Agree very much
30. If I did not worry, I would make more mistakes	1	2	3	4
31. I find it difficult to control my thoughts	1	2	3	4
32. Worrying is a sign of a good person	1	2	3	4
33. Worrying thoughts enter my head against my will	1	2	3	4
34. If I could not control my thoughts I would go crazy	1	2	3	4
35. I will lose out in life if I do not worry	1	2	3	4
36. When I start worrying, I cannot stop	1	2	3	4
37. Some thoughts will always need to be controlled	1	2	3	4
38. I need to worry, in order to get things done	1	2	3	4
39. I will be punished for not controlling certain thoughts	1	2	3	4
40. My thoughts interfere with my concentration	1	2	3	4
41. It is alright to let my thoughts roam free	1	2	3	4
42. I worry about my thoughts	1	2	3	4
43. I am easily distracted	1	2	3	4
44. My worrying thoughts are not productive	1	2	3	4
45. Worry can stop me from seeing a situation clearly	1	2	3	4
46. Worrying helps me to solve problems	1	2	3	4
47. I have little confidence in my memory for places	1	2	3	4
48. My worrying thoughts are uncontrollable	1	2	3	4
49. It is bad to think certain thoughts	1	2	3	4

	Do not agree	Agree slightly	Agree moderately	Agree very much
50. If I do not control my thoughts, I may end up embarrassing myself	1	2	3	4
51. I do not trust my memory	1	2	3	4
52. I do my clearest thinking when I am worrying	1	2	3	4
53. My worrying thoughts appear automatically	1	2	3	4
54. I would be selfish if I never worried	1	2	3	4
55. If I could not control my thoughts, I would not be able to function	1	2	3	4
56. I need to worry, in order to work well	1	2	3	4
57. I have little confidence in my memory for actions	1	2	3	4
58. I have difficulty keeping my mind focused on one thing for a long time	1	2	3	4
59. If a bad thing happens which I have not worried about, I feel responsible	1	2	3	4
60. It would not be normal, if I did not worry	1	2	3	4
61. I constantly examine my thoughts	1	2	3	4
62. If I stopped worrying, I would become glib, arrogant and offensive	1	2	3	4
63. Worrying helps me to plan the future more effectively	1	2	3	4
64. I would be a stronger person if I could worry less	1	2	3	4
65. I would be stupid and complacent not to worry	1	2	3	4

Please ensure that you have responded to all items. Thank you.

From Wells, 1997, with permission.

Appendix II

SCORING KEY FOR THE METACOGNITIONS QUESTIONNAIRE

	Factor 1	Score	Factor 2	Score	Factor 3	Score	Factor 4	Score	Factor 5	Score
Item No.	1		2		3		7		4	
	9		5		10		15		6	
	12		8		16		17		14	
	22		11		24		19		20*	
	26		13		28		29		23	
	27		18		43		34		25	
	30		21		47		37		61	
	32		31		51		39			
	35		33		57		41*			
	38		36		58		49			
	44*		40				50			
	46		42				55			
	52		45				59			
	54		48							
	56		53							
	60		64							
	62									
	63									
	65									
	Total		Total		Total		Total		Total	

*Reverse-scored items

1 = Positive worry beliefs.
2 = Beliefs about uncontrollability and danger.
3 = Beliefs about congnitive competence.
4 = General negative beliefs (including responsibility, superstition and punishment).
5 = Cognitive self-consciousness.

From Wells, 1997, with permission.

Appendix III

ANXIOUS THOUGHTS INVENTORY (AnTI)

Developed by Adrian Wells

Instructions: A number of statements which people have used to describe their thoughts and worries are given below. Read each statement and put a circle around the most appropriate number to indicate how often you have these thoughts and worries.

Do not spend too much time on each statement. There are no right or wrong answers and the first response to each item is often the most accurate.

	Almost never	Sometimes	Often	Almost always
1. I worry about my appearance	1	2	3	4
2. I think I am a failure	1	2	3	4
3. When looking to my future I give more thought to the negative things than the positive things that might happen to me	1	2	3	4
4. If I experience unexpected physical symptoms I have a tendency to think the worst possible thing is wrong with me	1	2	3	4
5. I have thoughts about becoming seriously ill	1	2	3	4
6. I have difficulty clearing my mind of repetitive thoughts	1	2	3	4
7. I worry about having a heart attack or cancer	1	2	3	4
8. I worry about saying or doing the wrong thing when among strangers	1	2	3	4
9. I worry about my abilities not living up to other people's expectations	1	2	3	4

	Almost never	Sometimes	Often	Almost always
10. I worry about my physical health	1	2	3	4
11. I worry that I cannot control my thoughts as well as I would like to	1	2	3	4
12. I worry that people don't like me	1	2	3	4
13. I take disappointments so keenly that I can't put them out of my mind	1	2	3	4
14. I get embarrassed easily	1	2	3	4
15. When I suffer from minor illnesses such as a rash I think it is more serious than it really is	1	2	3	4
16. Unpleasant thoughts enter my head against my will	1	2	3	4
17. I worry about my failures and my weaknesses	1	2	3	4
18. I worry about not being able to cope in life as adequately as others seem to	1	2	3	4
19. I worry about death	1	2	3	4
20. I worry about making a fool of myself	1	2	3	4
21. I think I am missing out on things in life because I worry too much	1	2	3	4
22. I have repetitive thoughts such as counting or repeating phrases	1	2	3	4

Please check that you have responded to all of the items. Thank you.

Name:..   Date:...

Scores: S   H   M   Total

From Wells, 1997, with permission.

Appendix IV

SCORING KEY: ANXIOUS THOUGHTS INVENTORY (AnTI)

Subscale:	Social	Health	Meta
Item:	1	4	3
	2	5	6
	8	7	11
	9	10	13
	12	15	16
	14	19	21
	17		22
	18		
	20		

From Wells, 1997, with permission.

Appendix V

THOUGHT CONTROL QUESTIONNAIRE

Developed by Adrian Wells and Mark Davies

Age: Sex: M/F

Most people experience unpleasant and/or unwanted thoughts (in verbal and/or picture form) which can be difficult to control. We are interested in the techniques that you *generally* use to control such thoughts.

Below are a number of things that people do to control these thoughts. Please read each statement carefully, and indicate how often you use each technique by *circling* the appropriate number. There are no right or wrong answers. Do not spend too much time thinking about each one.

When I experience an unpleasant/unwanted thought:

	Never	Sometimes	Often	Almost always
1. I call to mind positive images instead	1	2	3	4
2. I tell myself not to be so stupid	1	2	3	4
3. I focus on the thought	1	2	3	4
4. I replace the thought with a more trivial bad thought	1	2	3	4
5. I don't talk about the thought to anyone	1	2	3	4
6. I punish myself for thinking the thought	1	2	3	4
7. I dwell on other worries	1	2	3	4
8. I keep the thought to myself	1	2	3	4
9. I occupy myself with work instead	1	2	3	4
10. I challenge the thought's validity	1	2	3	4
11. I get angry at myself for having the thought	1	2	3	4
12. I avoid discussing the thought	1	2	3	4
13. I shout at myself for having the thought	1	2	3	4
14. I analyse the thought rationally	1	2	3	4

	Never	Sometimes	Often	Almost always
15. I slap or pinch myself to stop the thought	1	2	3	4
16. I think pleasant thoughts instead	1	2	3	4
17. I find out how my friends deal with these thoughts	1	2	3	4
18. I worry about more minor things instead	1	2	3	4
19. I do something that I enjoy	1	2	3	4
20. I try to reinterpret the thought	1	2	3	4
21. I think about something else	1	2	3	4
22. I think more about the more minor problems I have	1	2	3	4
23. I try a different way of thinking about it	1	2	3	4
24. I think about past worries instead	1	2	3	4
25. I ask my friends if they have similar thoughts	1	2	3	4
26. I focus on different negative thoughts	1	2	3	4
27. I question the reasons for having the thought	1	2	3	4
28. I tell myself that something bad will happen if I think the thought	1	2	3	4
29. I talk to a friend about the thought	1	2	3	4
30. I keep myself busy	1	2	3	4

Please check that you have responded to all of the items. Thank you.

SCORING KEY

	D	P	R	W	S	
*Reverse scored	1. ☐	2. ☐	3. ☐	4. ☐	5. ☐	*
	9. ☐	6. ☐	10. ☐	7. ☐	8. ☐	*
	16. ☐	11. ☐	14. ☐	18. ☐	12. ☐	*
	19. ☐	13. ☐	20. ☐	22. ☐	17. ☐	
	21. ☐	15. ☐	23. ☐	24. ☐	25. ☐	
	30. ☐	28. ☐	27. ☐	26. ☐	29. ☐	
TOTAL	☐	☐	☐	☐	☐	
					☐	

Appendix VI

GENERALISED ANXIETY DISORDER SCALE (GADS)

1. How distressing/disabling have your worries been in the last week?

0	1	2	3	4	5	6	7	8
Not at all				*Moderately*				*Extremely—the worst they have ever been*

2. In the past week how much effort have you put into trying to control your worries?

0	1	2	3	4	5	6	7	8
None at all				*Moderate effort*				*Full effort—I could not try more*

3. Place a number from the scale below next to each item to show how often in the past week you have done the following in order to cope with your worry

0	1	2	3	4	5	6	7	8
Not at all				*Half of the time*				*All of the time*

(a) *Tried to distract myself* ___	(d) *Asked for reassurance* ___	(g) *Looked for evidence* ___
(b) *Tried to control my thinking* ___	(e) *Talked to myself* ___	(h) *Acted cautiously* ___
(c) *Tried to reason things out* ___	(f) *Tried not to think about things* ___	(i) *Planned how to cope if my worries were true* ___

4. How often in the past week have you avoided the following in order to prevent worrying? Place a number from the scale below next to each item

0	1	2	3	4	5	6	7	8
Not at all				*Half of the time*				*All of the time*

(a) *News items* ___	(c) *Uncertainty* ___	(e) *Thoughts of accident/loss* ___
(b) *Social situations* ___	(d) *Thoughts of illness* ___	(f) *Other (specify)*
		_____ ___
		_____ ___

5. Below are a number of thoughts that people have about their worries. Indicate how much you believe each one by placing a number from the scale below next to each one

0	10	20	30	40	50	60	70	80	90	100
Do not believe the thought at all										*Completely convinced the thought is true*

I could go crazy with worry ___		*Worrying helps me cope* ___
Worrying could harm me ___		*If I worry I'll be prepared* ___
Worrying puts my body under stress ___		*Worrying keeps me safe* ___
If I don't control my worry it will control me ___		*Worrying helps me get things done* ___
My worrying is uncontrollable ___		*Something bad would happen if I didn't worry* ___
If I worry too much I could lose control ___		*Worrying helps me solve problems* ___

From Wells, 1997, with permission.

REFERENCES

American Psychiatric Association (APA) (1994). *Diagnostic and Statistical Manual of Mental Disorders*, Revised, 4th edn. Washington, DC: APA.

Amir, N., Cashman, L. & Foa, E.B. (1997). Strategies of thought control in obsessive-compulsive disorder. *Behaviour Research and Therapy*, **35**, 775–777.

Anderson, J.R. (1982). Acquisition of cognitive skill. *Psychological Review*, **89**, 369–406.

Arntz, A., Rauner, M. & van den Hout, M.A. (1995). "If I feel anxious there must be danger": ex-consequentia reasoning in inferring danger in anxiety disorders *Behaviour Research and Therapy*, **33**, 917–925.

Baker, C.A. & Morrison, A.P. (1998). Cognitive processes in auditory hallucinations: attributional biases and metacognition. *Psychological Medicine*, **28**, 1199–1208.

Beck, A.T. (1967). *Depression: Causes and Treatment*. Philadelphia, PA: University of Pennsylvania Press.

Beck, A.T. (1976). *Cognitive Therapy and the Emotional Disorders*. New York: International Universities Press.

Beck, A.T., Emery, G. & Greenberg, R.L. (1985). *Anxiety Disorders and Phobias: A Cognitive Perspective*. New York: Basic Books.

Beck, A.T., Rush, A.J., Shaw, B.F. & Emery, G. (1979). *Cognitive Therapy of Depression*. New York: Guilford.

Beck, A.T., Ward, C.H., Mendelson, M., Mock, J. & Erbaugh, J. (1961). An inventory for measuring depression. *Archives of General Psychiatry*, **4**, 561–571.

Bogels, Mulkens & de Jong (1997). Task concentration training and fear of blushing. *Clinical Psychology and Psychotherapy*, **4**, 251–258.

Borkovec, T.D. (1994). The nature, functions and origins of worry. In: G.C.L. Davey & F. Tallis (Eds), *Worrying Perspectives in Theory, Assessment and Treatment* (pp. 5–34). New York: Wiley.

Borkovec, T.D. & Inz, J. (1990). The nature of worry in Generalised Anxiety Disorder: a predominance of thought activity. *Behaviour Research and Therapy*, **28**, 153–158.

Borkovec, T.D., Robinson, E., Pruzinsky, T. & DePree, J.A. (1983).   Preliminary exploration of worry: some characteristics and processes. *Behaviour Research and Therapy*, **21**, 9–16.

Borkovec, T.D. & Roemer, L. (1995).   Perceived functions of worry among generalised anxiety subjects: distraction from more emotionally distressing topics? *Behaviour Therapy and Experimental Psychiatry*, **26**, 25–30.

Bouman, T.K. & Meijer, K.J. (1999).   A preliminary study of worry and metacognitions in hypochondriasis. *Clinical Psychology and Psychotherapy*, **6**, 96–102 (Special Issue: Metacognition and Cognitive Behaviour Therapy).

Bower, G.H. (1981).   Mood and Memory. *American Psychologist*, **36**, 129–148.

Bower, G.H. (1992).   How might emotions affect learning? In: S.A. Christianson (Ed.), *The Handbook of Emotion and Memory: Research and Theory*. Hillsdale, NJ: Erlbaum.

Bower, G.H. & Cohen, P.R. (1982).   Emotional influences in memory and thinking: data and theory. In: S. Fiske & M. Clark (Eds), *Affect and Social Cognition*. Hillsdale, NJ: Erlbaum.

Broadbent, D.E., Broadbent, M.H.P. & Jones, J.L. (1986).   Performance correlates of self-reported cognitive failure and of obsessionality. *British Journal of Clinical Psychology*, **25**, 285–299.

Broadbent, D.E., Cooper, P.F., Fitzgerald, P. & Parkes, K.R. (1982).   The Cognitive Failures Questionnaire (CFQ) and its correlates. *British Journal of Clinical Psychology*, **21**, 1–16.

Brown, A.L., Bransford, J.D., Campione, J.C. & Ferrara, R.A. (1983).   Learning, remembering and understanding. In: J. Flavell & E. Markman (Eds), *Handbook of Child Psychology: Vol. 3, Cognitive Development*. New York: Wiley.

Butler, G., Wells, A. & Dewick, H. (1995).   Differential effects of worry and imagery after exposure to a stressful stimulus: a pilot study. *Behavioural and Cognitive Psychotherapy*, **23**, 45–56.

Cartwright-Hatton, S. & Wells, A. (1997).   Beliefs about worry and intrusions: the Metacognitions Questionnaire. *Journal of Anxiety Disorders*, **11**, 279–315.

Carver, C.S. & Blaney, P.M. (1977).   Perceived arousal, focus of attention and avoidance behaviour. *Journal of Abnormal Psychology*, **86**, 154–162.

Carver, C.S. & Scheier, M.F. (1981).   *Attention and Self-regulation: A Control Therapy Approach to Human Behaviour*. Berlin: Springer-Verlag.

Carver, C.S., Blaney, P.M. & Scheier, M.F. (1979).   Focus of attention, chronic expectancy and responses to a feared stimulus. *Journal of Personality and Social Psychology*, **37**, 1186–1195.

Clark, D.A. & Claybourn, M. (1997).   Process characteristics of worry and obsessive intrusive thoughts. *Behaviour Research and Therapy*, **35**, 1139–1141.

Clark, D.M. & Wells, A. (1995).   A cognitive model of social phobia. In: R. Heimberg, M. Liebowitz, D.A. Hope & F.R. Schneier (Eds), *Social Phobia: Diagnosis, Assessment and Treatment*. New York: Guilford.

Cloitre, M. & Liebowitz, M.R. (1991).   Memory bias in panic disorder: an investigation of the cognitive avoidance hypothesis. *Cognitive Therapy and Research*, **15**, 371–386.

Clore, G.L. & Parrott, W.G. (1994).   Cognitive feelings and metacognitive judgements. *European Journal of Social Psychology*, **24**, 101–115.

Craske, M.G., Street, L. & Barlow, D.H. (1989).   Instructions to focus upon or distract from internal cues during exposure treatment of agoraphobic avoidance. *Behaviour Research and Therapy*, **27**, 663–672.

Davey, G.C.L. (1994).   Pathological worry as exacerbated problem solving. In: G.C.L. Davey & F. Tallis (Eds), *Worrying: Perspectives on Theory, Assessment and Treatment* (pp. 35–60). Chichester: Wiley.

Davey, G.C.L., Tallis, F. & Capuzzo, N. (1996).   Beliefs about the consequences of worrying. *Cognitive Therapy and Research*, **20**, 499–520.

Davies, M.I. & Clark, D.M. (1998).   Thought suppression produces a rebound effect with analogue post-traumatic intrusions. *Behaviour Research and Therapy*, **36**, 571–582.

Davies, D.R., Matthews, G., Wells, A., Holley, P.J., Taylor, A., Blanco, M.J. & Westerman, S.J. (submitted).   The Attentional Experiences Questionnaire: some correlates of everyday attention.

Durham, R.C. & Allan, T. (1993).   Psychological treatment of generalized anxiety disorder: a review of the clinical significance of results in outcome studies since 1980. *British Journal of Psychiatry*, **163**, 19–26.

Emmelkamp, P.M.G. & Aardema, A. (1999).   Metacognitive, specific obsessive compulsive beliefs and obsessive compulsive behaviour. *Clinical Psychology and Psychotherapy*, **6**, 139–146 (Special Issue, Metacognition and Cognitive Behaviour Therapy).

Epstein, S., Rosenthal, S. & Szpiler, J. (1978).   The influence of attention upon anticipatory arousal, habituation and reactivity to noxious stimulation. *Journal of Research in Personality*, **12**, 30–40.

Eysenck, M.W. (1992).   *Anxiety: The Cognitive Perspective*. Hove: Erlbaum.

Eysenck, M.W. (1997).   *Anxiety and Cognition: A Unified Theory*. Hove: Erlbaum.

Fenigstein, A., Scheier, M.F. & Buss, A.H. (1975).   Public and private self-consciousness: Assessment and theory. *Journal of Consulting and Clinical Psychology*, **43**, 522–527.

Fennell, M.J.V. & Teasdale, J.D. (1984).   Effects of distraction on thinking and affect in depressed patients. *British Journal of Clinical Psychology*, **23**, 65–66.

Fennell, M.J.V., Teasdale, J.D., Jones, S. & Damle, A. (1987).   Distraction in neurotic and endogenous depression: an investigation of negative thinking in major depressive disorder. *Psychological Medicine*, **17**, 441–452.

Fisher, P.L. & Durham, R.C. (1999).   Recovery rates in generalized anxiety disorder following psychological therapy: an analysis of clinically significant change in the STAI-T across outcome studies since 1990. *Psychological Medicine*, **29**, 1425–1434.

Fitts, P.M. (1964).   Perceptual motor skill learning. In: A.W. Melton (Ed.), *Categories of Human Learning*. New York: Academic Press.

Flavell, J.H. (1979).   Metacognition and metacognitive monitoring: a new area of cognitive-developmental inquiry. *American Psychologist*, **34**, 906–911,

Foa, E.B. & Kozak, M.J. (1986).   Emotional processing and fear: exposure to corrective information. *Psychological Bulletin*, **99**, 20–35.

Grayson, J.B., Foa, E.B. & Steketee, G.S. (1982).   Habituation during exposure treatment: Distraction versus attention-focusing. *Behaviour Research and Therapy*, **20**, 323–328.

Grayson, J.B., Foa, E.B. & Steketee, G.S. (1986).   Exposure in *vivo* of obsessive-compulsives under distracting and attention-focusing conditions: replication and extension. *Behaviour Research and Therapy*, **24**, 475–479.

Gordon, P.K. (1985).   Allocation of attention in obsessional disorder. *British Journal of Clinical Psychology*, **24**, 101–107.

Hackmann, A., Suraway, C. & Clark, D.M. (1998).   Seeing yourself through others' eyes: a study of spontaneously occurring images in social phobia. *Behavioural and Cognitive Psychotherapy*, **26**, 3–12.

Hasher, L., Goldstein, D. & Topping, T. (1979).   Frequency and the conference of referential validity. *Journal of Verbal Learning and Verbal Behaviour*, **16**, 107–112.

Harvey, A.G. & Bryant, R.A. (1998a).   The effect of attempted thought suppression in acute stress disorder. *Behaviour Research and Therapy*, **36**, 583–590.

Harvey, A.G. & Bryant, R.A. (1998b).   The role of violence in attempted thought suppression. *Behaviour Research and Therapy*, **36**, 757–763.

Hazlett-Stephens, H. (1997).   The role of relaxation in the reduction of fear: An investigation of speech anxiety. Paper presented at the Annual Meeting of the Association for the Advancement of Behavior Therapy, Miami, FL.

Higgins, E.T. (1990).   Personality, social psychology, and person-situation relations: standards and knowledge activation as a common language. In: L.A. Pervin (Ed.), *Handbook of Personality Theory and Research* (pp. 301–338). New York: Guilford.

Horn, J.L. (1965).   A rationale and test for the number of factors in factor analysis. *Psychometrika*, **30**, 179–185.

Ingram, R.E. (1984).   Towards an information processing analysis of depression. *Cognitive Therapy and Research*, **8**, 443–478.

Ingram, R.E. (1990).   Self-focused attention in clinical disorders: review and conceptual model. *Psychological Bulletin*, **107**, 156–176.

Ingram, R.E., Kendall, P.C., Smith, T.W., Donnell, C. & Ronan, K. (1987).   Cognitive specificity in emotional distress. *Journal of Personality and Social Psychology*, **53**, 734–742.

Kabat-Zinn (1990).   *Full Catastrophe Living: The Program of the Stress Reduction Clinic at the University of Massachusetts Medical Center.* New York: Dell.

Karno, M., Golding, J.M., Sorenson, S.B. & Burnam, M.A. (1988).   The epidemiology of obsessive-compulsive disorder in U.S. communities. *Archives of General Psychiatry*, **45**, 1094–1099.

Lang, P.J. (1977).   Imagery in therapy: an information processing analysis of fear. *Behavior Therapy*, **8**, 862–886.

Leonesio, R.J. & Nelson, T.O. (1990).   Do different metamemory judgements tap the same underlying aspects of memory? *Journal of Experimental Psychology: Learning, Memory and Cognition*, **16**, 464–470.

Lyubomirsky, S. & Nolen-Hoeksema, S. (1993).   Self-perpetuating properties of dysphoric rumination. *Journal of Personality and Social Psychology*, **65**, 339–349.

Matthews, G. & Campbell, S.E. (1998).   Task-induced stress and individual differences in coping. *Proceedings of the 42nd Annual Meeting of the Human Factors and Ergonomics Society* (pp. 821–825). Santa Monica, CA: Human Factors and Ergonomics Society.

Matthews, G. & Harley, T.A. (1993).   Effects of extraversion and self-report arousal on semantic priming: a connectionist approach. *Journal of Personality and Social Psychology*, **54**, 735–756.

Matthews, G. & Harley, T.A. (1996).   Connectionist models of emotional distress and attentional bias. *Cognition and Emotion*, **10**, 561–600.

Matthews, G., Mohamed, A. & Lochrie, B. (1998).   Dispositional self-focus of attention and individual differences in appraisal and coping. In: J. Bermudez, A.M. Perez, A. Sanchez-Elvira & G.K. van Heck (Eds), *Personality Psychology in Europe*, Vol. 6, (pp. 278–285). Tilburg: Tilburg University Press.

Matthews, G. & Wells, A. (1988).   Relationships between anxiety, self-consciousness, and cognitive failure. *Cognition and Emotion*, **2**, 123–132.

Matthews, G., Hillyard, E.J. & Campbell, S.E. (1999).   Metacognition and maladaptive coping as components of test anxiety. *Clinical Psychology and Psychotherapy*, **6**, 111–126 (Special Issue, Metacognition and Cognitive Behaviour Therapy).

Maylor, E.A. (1990).   Age and prospective memory loss in old age.   *Quarterly Journal of Experimental Psychology*, **42A**, 471–493.

Mayo, P.R. (1989).   A further study of the personality-congruent recall effect. *Personality and Individual Differences*, **10**, 247–252.

Mellings, T.M.B. & Alden, L.E. (2000).   Cognitive processes in social anxiety: the effects of self-focus, rumination and anticipatory processing. *Behaviour Research and Therapy*, **38**, 243–257.

Merckelbach, H., Muris, P., van den Hout, M. & de Jong, P. (1991).   Rebound effects of thought suppression: instruction dependent? *Behavioural Psychotherapy*, **19**, 225–238.

Metcalfe, J. & Shimamura, A.P. (1994).   *Metacognition*. Cambridge, MA: MIT Press.

Mogg, K., Mathews, A. & Weinman, J. (1987).   Memory bias in clinical anxiety. *Journal of Abnormal Psychology*, **96**, 94–98.

Morrison, A.P., Wells, A. & Nothard, S. (2000).   Cognitive factors in predisposition to auditory and visual hallucinations. *British Journal of Clinical Psychology*, **39**, 67–78.

Morrow, J. & Nolen-Hoeksema, S. (1990).   Effects of responses to depression on the remediation of depressive affect. *Journal of Personality and Social Psychology*, **58**, 519–527.

Moses, L.J. & Baird, J.A. (in press).   Metacognition. In: R.A. Wilson and F.C. Keil (Eds), *The MIT Encyclopaedia of the Cognitive Sciences*. Cambridge, MA: MIT Press.

McNally, R.J. & Ricciardi, J.N. (1996).   Suppression of negative and neutral thoughts. *Behavioural and Cognitive Psychotherapy*, **24**, 17–25.

Nassif, Y. (1999). Predictors of pathological worry. Unpublished M.Phil. Thesis, University of Manchester.

Nelson, T.O., Kruglanski, A.W. & Jost, T.J. (1998).   Knowing thyself and others: progress in metacognitive social psychology. In: V.Y. Yzerbyt, G. Lories & B. Dardenne (Eds), *Metacognition: Cognitive and Social Dimensions* (pp. 69–89). London: Sage.

Nelson, T.O. & Narens, L. (1990).   Metamemory: a theoretical framework and some new findings. In: G.H. Bower (Ed.). *The Psychology of Learning and Motivation* (pp. 125–173). New York: Academic Press.

Nelson, O.T., Stuart, R.B., Howard, G. & Crawley, M. (1999).   Metacognition and clinical psychology: a preliminary framework for research and practice. *Clinical Psychology and Psychotherapy*, **6**, 73–80 (Special Issue, Metacognition and Cognitive Behaviour Therapy).

Nisbett, R.E. & Wilson, T.D. (1977).   Telling more than we can know: verbal reports on mental processes. *Psychological Review*, **84**, 231–259.

Nolen-Hoeksema, S. (1991).   Responses to depression and their effects on the duration of depressive episodes. *Journal of Abnormal Psychology*, **100**, 569–582.

Nolen-Hoeksema, S. & Morrow, J. (1993).   Effects of rumination and distraction on naturally occurring depressed mood. *Cognition and Emotion*, **7**, 561–570.

Nolen-Hoeksema, S., Morrow, J. & Fredrickson, B.L. (1993).   Response styles and the duration of episodes of depressed mood. *Journal of Abnormal Psychology*, **102**, 20–28.

Nolen-Hoeksema, S., Parker, L.E. & Larson, J. (1994).   Ruminative coping with depressed mood following loss. *Journal of Personality and Social Psychology*, **67**, 92–104.

Norman, D.A. & Shallice, T. (1985).   Attention to action: willed and automatic control of behaviour. In: R.J. Davidson, G.E. Schwartz & D. Shapiro (Eds),

Consciousness and Self-regulation : Advances in Research, Vol. 4. New York: Plenum.

Oatley, K. & Johnson-Laird, P. (1987).   Towards a cognitive theory of emotions. *Cognition and Emotion,* **1**, 29–50.

Obsessive Compulsive Cognitions Working Group (1997).   Cognition assessment of obsessive-compulsive disorder. *Behaviour Research and Therapy,* **35**, 667–681.

Papageorgiou, C. & Wells, A. (1997).   Social self-perception: effects of false heart rate feedback in socially anxious subjects. Paper presented at the annual conference of the British Association for Behavioural and Cognitive Psychotherapies, Canterbury, UK.

Papageorgiou, C. & Wells, A. (1998).   Effects of attention training on hypochondriasis: a brief case series. *Psychological Medicine,* **28**, 193–200.

Papageorgiou, C. & Wells, A. (1999a)   Process and meta-cognitive dimensions of depressive and anxious thoughts and relationships with emotional intensity. *Clinical Psychology and Psychotherapy,* **6**, 156–162 (Special Issue, Metacognition and Cognitive Behaviour Therapy).

Papageorgiou, C. & Wells, A. (in press)   Treatment of recurrent major depression with attention training. *Behavioral and Cognitive Practice.*

Papageorgiou, C. & Wells, A. (in press a).   Metacognitive beliefs about rumination in recurrent major depression. *Behavioural and Cognitive Practice.*

Papageorgiou, C. & Wells, A. (in press b).   Positive beliefs about depressive rumination: Development and validation of a self-report scale. *Behavior Therapy.*

Purdon, C. (1999).   Thought suppression and psychopathology. *Behaviour Research and Therapy,* **37**, 1029–1054.

Purdon, C. & Clark, D.A. (1993).   Obsessive intrusive thoughts in non-clinical subjects. I. Content and relation with depressive anxious and obsessional symptoms. *Behaviour Research and Therapy,* **31**, 713–720.

Purdon, C. & Clark, D.A. (1999).   Meta-cognition and obsessions. *Clinical Psychology and Psychotherapy,* **6**, 102–111 (Special Issue, Metacognition and Cognitive Behaviour Therapy).

Purdon, C. & Clark, D.A. (2000a).   Suppression of obsession-like thoughts in non-clinical individuals. Part I. Impact on thought frequency, appraisal and mood state (submitted for publication).

Purdon, C. & Clark, D.A. (2000b).   Suppression of obsession-like thoughts in non-clinical individuals: Part II. The role of beliefs in thought frequency and appraisal (in preparation).

Rachman, S.J. (1976).   Obsessional-compulsive checking. *Behaviour Research and Therapy,* **14**, 269–277.

Rachman, S. (1980).   Emotional processing. *Behaviour Research and Therapy,* **18**, 51–60.

Rachman, S. (1993).   Obsessions, responsibility and guilt. *Behaviour Research and Therapy,* **31**, 149–154.

Rachman, S.J. & de Silva, P. (1978).   Abnormal and normal obsessions. *Behaviour Research and Therapy,* **3**, 89–99.

Rachman, S.J. & Hodgson, R. (1980).   *Obsessions and Compulsions.* Englewood Cliffs, NJ: Prentice Hall.

Rachman, S., Thordarson, D.S., Shafran, R. & Woody, S.R. (1995).   Perceived responsibility: structure and significance. *Behaviour Research and Therapy,* **33**, 779–784.

Rachman, S.J. & Shafran, R. (1999).   Cognitive distortions: thought–action fusion. *Clinical Psychology and Psychotherapy,* **6**, 80–86 (Special Issue, Metacognition and Cognitive Behaviour Therapy).

Radomsky, A.S. & Rachman, S.J. (1999).   Memory bias in obsessive-compulsive disorder (OCD). *Behaviour Research and Therapy*, **37**, 605–618.

Rassin, E., Merckelbach, H. & Muris, P. (1997).   Effects of thought suppression on episodic memory. *Behaviour Research and Therapy*, **35**, 1035–1038.

Rassin, E., Merckelbach, H., Muris, P. & Spaan, V. (1999).   Thought–action fusion as arousal factor in the development of intrusions. *Behaviour Research and Therapy*, **37**, 231–237.

Reynolds, M. & Wells, A. (1999).   The Thought Control Questionnaire—psychometric properties in a clinical sample, and relationships with PTSD and depression. *Psychological Medicine*, **29**, 1089–1099.

Roger, D., Jarvis, G. & Najarian, B. (1993).   Detachment and coping: the construction and validation of a new scale for measuring coping strategies. *Personality and Individual Differences*, **15**, 619–626.

Salkovskis, P.M. (1985).   Obsessional-compulsive problems: a cognitive-behavioural analysis. *Behaviour Research and Therapy*, **23**, 571–583.

Salkovskis, P.M. (1989).   Cognitive-behavioural factors and the persistence of intrusive thoughts in obsessional problems. *Behaviour Research and Therapy*, **27**, 677–682.

Salkovskis, P.M. & Campbell, P. (1994).   Thought suppression induces intrusions in naturally occurring negative intrusive thoughts. *Behaviour Research and Therapy*, **32**, 1–8.

Salkovskis, P.M. & Harrison, J. (1984).   Abnormal and normal obsessions: a replication. *Behaviour Research and Therapy*, **27**, 549–552.

Sanavio, E. (1988).   Obsessions and compulsions: the Padua Inventory. *Behaviour Research and Therapy*, **26**, 169–177.

Sarason, I.G. (1984).   Test anxiety, stress, and cognitive interference: reactions to tests. *Journal of Personality and Social Psychology*, **46**, 929–938.

Sartory, G., Rachman, S. & Grey, S.J. (1982).   Return of fear: The role of rehearsal. *Behaviour Research and Therapy*, **20**, 123–134.

Scheier, M.F., Carver, C.S. & Gibbons, F.X. (1981).   Self-focused attention and reactions to fear. *Journal of Research in Personality*, **15**, 1–15.

Schwarz, N. & Clore, G.L. (1983).   Mood, misattribution and judgements of well-being: informative and directive functions of affective states. *Journal of Personality and Social Psychology*, **45**, 513–523.

Schwarz, N. & Clore. G.L. (1988).   How do I feel about it? Informational function of affective states. In: K. Fiedler & J.P. Forgas (Eds), *Affect, Cognition and Social Behaviour* (pp. 44–62). Toronto: Hogrefe International.

Segal, Z.V. (1988).   Appraisal of the self-schema construct in cognitive models of depression. *Psychological Bulletin*, **103**, 147–162.

Shafran, R., Thordarson, D.S. & Rachman, S.J. (1996).   Thought–action fusion in obsessive-compulsive disorder. *Journal of Anxiety Disorders*, **10**, 379–391.

Sher, K.J., Frost, R.O., Kushner, M., Crews, T.M. & Alexander, J.E. (1989).   Memory deficits in compulsive checkers: replication and extension in a clinical sample. *Behaviour Research and Therapy*, **27**, 65–69.

Sher, K., Frost, R. & Otto, R. (1983).   Cognitive deficits in compulsive checkers: an exploratory study. *Behaviour Research and Therapy*, **21**, 337–363.

Sher, K.J., Mann, B. & Frost, R.O. (1984).   Cognitive dysfunction in compulsive checkers: further explorations. *Behaviour Research and Therapy*, **22**, 493–502.

Simon, H.A. (1967).   Motivational and emotional controls of cognition. *Psychological Review*, **74**, 29–39.

Slife, B.D. & Weaver, C.A. III (1992).   Depression, cognitive skill, and metacognitive skill in problem solving. *Cognition and Emotion*, **6**, 1–22.

Speilberger, C.D., Gorsuch, R.L., Lushene, R., Vagg, P.R. & Jacobs, G.A. (1983). *Manual for the Stait-Trait Anxiety Inventory*. Palo Alto, CA: Consulting Psychology Press.

Tallis, F. (1993). Doubt reduction using distinctive stimuli as a treatment for compulsive checkings: an exploratory investigation. *Clinical Psychology and Psychotherapy*, **1**, 45–52.

Teasdale, J.D. (1999). Metacognition, mindfulness and the modification of mood disorders. *Clinical Psychology and Psychotherapy*, **6**, 146–156 (Special Issue, Metacognition and Cognitive Behaviour Therapy).

Teasdale, J.D. & Barnard, P.J. (1993). *Affect, Cognition and Change: Remodelling Depressive Thought*. Hove: Erlbaum.

Teasdale, J.D., Segal, Z.V. & Williams, J.M.G. (1995). How does cognitive therapy prevent depressive relapse and why should attentional control (mindfulness) training help? *Behaviour Research and Therapy*, **33**, 25–40.

Thyer, B.A., Papsdorf, J.D., Himle, D.P., McCann, B.S., Caldwell, S. & Wichert, M. (1981). In vivo distraction-coping in the treatment of test anxiety. *Journal of Clinical Psychology*, **37**, 754–764.

Trinder, H. & Salkovskis, P.M. (1994). Personally relevant intrusion outside the laboratory: long-term suppression increases intrusion. *Behaviour Research and Therapy*, **32**, 833–842.

Warda, G. & Bryant, R.A. (1998). Cognitive bias in acute stress disorder. *Behaviour Research and Therapy*, **36**, 1177–1183.

Wegner, D.M., Schneider, D.J., Carter, S.R. III. & White, T.L. (1987). Paradoxical effects of thought suppression. *Journal of Personality and Social Psychology*, **53**, 5–13.

Wegner, D.M., Shortt, J.W., Blake, A.W. & Page, M.S. (1990). The suppression of exciting thoughts. *Journal of Personality and Social Psychology*, **58**, 409–418.

Wells, A. (1990). Panic disorder in association with relaxation-induced-anxiety: an attentional training approach to treatment. *Behavior Therapy*, **21**, 273–280.

Wells, A. (1994a). A multidimensional measure of worry: development and preliminary validation of the Anxious Thoughts Inventory. *Anxiety Stress and Coping*, **6**, 289–299.

Wells, A. (1994b). Attention and the control of worry. In: G.C.L. Davey & F. Tallis (Eds), *Worrying: Perspectives on Theory, Assessment and Treatment*. Chichester: Wiley.

Wells, A. (1995). Meta-cognition and worry: a cognitive model of generalised anxiety disorder. *Behavioural and Cognitive Psychotherapy*, **23**, 301–320.

Wells, A. (1997). *Cognitive Therapy of Anxiety Disorders: A Practice Manual and Conceptual Guide*. Chichester: Wiley.

Wells, A. (1999). A metacognitive model and therapy for Generalised Anxiety Disorder. *Clinical Psychology and Psychotherapy*, **6**, 86–96 (Special Issue, Metacognition and Cognitive Behaviour Therapy).

Wells, A. (in preparation). Metacognitive therapy for GAD: a preliminary test of treatment effectiveness.

Wells, A. & Carter, K. (1999). Preliminary tests of a cognitive model of GAD. *Behaviour Research and Therapy*, **37**, 585–594.

Wells, A. & Carter, K. (2000). Further tests of a cognitive model of GAD: worry and metacognitions in patients with GAD, panic disorder, social phobia, and depression. *Behavior Therapy* (in press).

Wells, A., Clark, D.M. & Ahmad, S. (1998). How do I look with my mind's eye?: perspective taking in social phobic imagery. *Behaviour Research and Therapy*, **36**, 631–634.

Wells, A. & Davies, M. (1994).   The Thought Control Questionnaire: a measure of individual differences in the control of unwanted thoughts. *Behaviour Research and Therapy*, **32**, 871–878.

Wells, A. & Matthews, G. (1994).   *Attention and Emotion. A Clinical Perspective.* Hove: Erlbaum.

Wells, A. & Matthews, G. (1996).   Modelling cognition in emotional disorder: The S-REF model. *Behaviour Research and Therapy*, **32**, 867–870.

Wells, A. & Morrison, T. (1994).   Qualitative dimensions of normal worry and normal intrusive thoughts: a comparative study. *Behaviour Research and Therapy*, **32**, 867–870.

Wells, A. & Papageorgiou, C. (1995).   Worry and the incubation of intrusive images following stress. *Behaviour Research and Therapy*, **33**, 579–583.

Wells, A. & Papageorgiou, C. (1998a).   Relationships between worry and obsessive-compulsive symptoms and meta-cognitive beliefs. *Behaviour Research and Therapy*, **36**, 899–913.

Wells, A. & Papageorgiou, C. (1998b).   Social phobia: effects of external attention on anxiety, negative beliefs, and perspective taking. *Behavior Therapy*, **29**, 357–370.

Wells, A. & Papageorgiou, C. (1999). The observer perspective: biased imagery in social phobia. Agoraphobia, and blood-injury phobia. *Behaviour Research and Therapy*, **37**, 653–658.

Wells, A. & Papageorgiou, C. (2000a).   Social phobic interoception: effects of bodily information on anxiety, beliefs, and self-processing. *Behaviour Research and Therapy*. (in press).

Wells, A. & Papageorgiou, C. (2000b).   Brief cognitive therapy for social phobia: a case series. *Behaviour Research and Therapy* (in press).

Wells, A., White, J. & Carter, K. (1997).   Attention training: effects on anxiety and beliefs in panic and social phobia. *Clinical Psychology and Psychotherapy*, **4**, 226–232.

Wenzlaff, R.M., Wegner, D.M. & Roper, D.W. (1988).   Depression and mental control: the resurgence of unwanted negative thoughts. *Journal of Personality and Social Psychology*, **55**, 882–892.

Williams, J.M.G., Watts, F.N., MacLeod, C. & Mathews, A. (1988).   *Cognitive Psychology and Emotional Disorders*. Chichester: Wiley.

Wise, E.H. & Hayes, S.N. (1983).   Cognitive treatment of test anxiety: rational restructuring versus attentional training. *Cognitive Therapy and Research*, **7**, 69–78.

York, D., Borkovec, T.D., Vasey, M. & Stern, R. (1987).   Effects of worry and somatic anxiety induction on thoughts, emotion and physiological activity. *Behaviour Research and Therapy*, **25**, 523–526.

AUTHOR INDEX

Index compiled by Liz Granger

SUBJECT INDEX

Wiley Books
of related interest...

Treating Anxiety and Stress
A Group Psycho-educational Approach Using Brief CBT

Jim White

Written for clinical psychologists, therapists, nurses and counsellors with a basic knowledge of CBT, this book focuses on the use of the Jim White's own method to treat stress and anxiety in both small and large group settings.

0471 49306 6   272pp   July 2000   Paperback

Understanding and Treating Panic Disorder
Cognitive-Behavioural Approaches

Steven Taylor

A comprehensive text and clinician's guide from this respected author which integrates theory, empirical findings, and treatment guidelines, to provide a framework for understanding and treating both routine and complex cases of panic disorder.

From the Wiley Series in Clinical Psychology
0471 98704 2   528pp   August 2000   Hardback
0471 49067 9   528pp   August 2000   Paperback

NOW IN PAPERBACK...

Treating Complex Cases
The Cognitive Behavioural Therapy Approach

Edited by Nicholas Tarrier, Adrian Wells and Gillian Haddock

This book brings together some of the most experienced and expert cognitive and behavioural therapists to share their specialist experience of formulation and treatment of complex cases, such as patients with co-morbidity, psychotic conditions, enduring vulnerabilities, and much more.

From the Wiley Series in Clinical Psychology
0471 97839 6   456pp   December 1999   Paperback

1772